THE FAMILY TREE
POLISH,
CZECH & SLOVAK
GENEALOGY GUIDE

Stolpe
Neustadt
Hela
G. of Dan zc.
Koenigsberg
Labiau
Tilsit
Ragnit
Menel or M.
Wic
Butow
Danzig
Pillau
Wehlau
Tapiau
Ostwethen
Stalhuponen
Szaki
Neustadt
Rummelsb9
Dirschau
G. Braun
Friedland
Tilster.
Darkhmen
Gumbinnen
Kalwary
Goldapp
Wilko
Baldenb9
Stargard
Elbing
Eylau
Rastenb9
Angersb9
Oletzko
Suwalki
Conitz
Marienburg
Guttstadt
Heilsberg
Rosset
Rhein
Raczki
Augusto
Serv
Sevny
Jastrow
Pr. Marck
Sensb9
Lyck
Arys
wo
Vistula &
Niemen
Crone
R. Veichsel or Vistula
Marienwerder
Allenstein
Johanisb9
Szczuczyn
Kusnia
Bobr
Lipsk
Graudenz
Drewg
Hohenstein
Ostelsb9
Kotbr
Myszyniec
Gonionde
Krysta
Sokolka
Bromberg
Strasburg
Soldau
Neidenb9
Narew
Stawszki
Volko
Wongrowitz
Netz
Thorn
Golub
Biezun
Mlawa
Chorzele
Praszmic
Jomza
Tylweczyn
Grodek
Radziejewo
Sluzewo
Wroclavek
Kikol
Szrensk
Ciechanow
Ostroleka
Surasz
Bialystok
R.Narew
Gnesen
Birsc
Sierps
Racionz
Bielsk
Plonsk
Rozan
Ostrow
Bransk
Bielsk
Posen
Slupce
Dbice
Dobrzyn
Wkra
Pultusk
Wyszkow
Brok
Nur
Ciechanowiec
Bochka
Novoidvo
R.Warta
Kowal
Flock
Modlin
Sierock
Wegrow
Prujin
Kalisz
Kolo
Klodawa
Gombin
WARSAW
Praga
Stanislavow
Drohiczyn
Litowsk
Charki
Krotoschin
Korin
Kutno
Lenczy
Lowiez
Bochaczew
Grochow
Wisola
Bockin
Zgier
Nadarzyn
Sokolowo
Siedlec
BrestLito
Warta
Sieradz
Rawa
Groje
Gora
Kaluszyn
Zbuczyn
Biala
Wieruszow
Widawa
Tuszyn
Nowemiasto
stenica
zelechow
Magnuszow
Midzyrzyc
Slawatica
Rudnia
Kemp
Petrikau
R. Pilica
Drzewica
Koszenice
Stezyca
Kock
Radzyn
Mokrani
Krzepice
Czenstochau
Dzialoszyn
Opoczno
Krzysucha
Radom
Pulawy
Ostrow
Wlodawa
Ratno
Oppeln
Przedborz
Konskie
Svdlowiec
Ostrowie
Belzyce
Urzulin
Szak
Da
Radomsk
Malogosz
Kielce
Opatow
Lublin
Biala
Ratibor
Sicwierz
Koniekpol
Rachow
Urzedow
Krasnostaw
Chelm
Swierze
Dubiekas
Turisk
Koritma
Gleiwitz
Wodzislaw
Staszow
Opatow
Wysokie
Horodlo
Wladim
Trappau
Zarnowiec
Pinczow
Sandomir
Zawichost
Josefow
Samosz
Krylow
Pless
Slomoikv
Skalmierz
R. Vistila
Bilgoray
Tomaszaw
Sokol
Teschen
Krakow
N. Brzesko
Noweminsto
Tarnogrod
Zolkiew
Biala
Myslenice
Bochnia
Tarnow
Rzeszow
Jaroslaw
Jaworow
R. Bug
Nanesto
Neumark
Neu Sandes
Przemysl
Lemberg
Rosenberg
S. Miklos
Poprad
Tatra
Duklo
Sanok
Sambor
Zloczow
Bobrka
Neu Sohl
Carpathia
Swidnik
WEST PRUSSIA
POLAND
RUSSIA
POSEN
POLAND
GALICIA

THE FAMILY TREE
POLISH,
CZECH & SLOVAK
GENEALOGY GUIDE

How to Trace Your Family Tree in Eastern Europe

LISA A. ALZO

**FAMILY
TREE
BOOKS**

CINCINNATI, OHIO
shopfamilytree.com

Contents

PART 1: LINKING YOUR FAMILY TREE TO POLISH, CZECH, AND SLOVAK LOCALITIES

CHAPTER 1

Take pride in your Eastern European heritage. This chapter briefs you on why you should research your Polish, Czech, and Slovak ancestors.

CHAPTER 2

Maximize your research time by planning ahead. This chapter outlines how to identify your goals, build a family tree, and apply key genealogical principles.

CHAPTER 3

Unlock the two keys to European research: the name of your immigrant ancestor and his hometown. This chapter offers strategies for finding these crucial pieces of info that will guide the rest of your research.

CHAPTER 4

Dive into the turbulent history of Poland with this crash course guide to Polish history through the Commonwealth era, the partitions, the world wars, and beyond.

CHAPTER 5

Catch a glimpse of these countries' histories, from their time in the Austro-Hungarian Empire to the formation of Czechoslovakia and eventual independence.

PART 2: GETTING TO KNOW THE OLD COUNTRY

CHAPTER 6

Learn how geography shaped your ancestors' lives by using maps, atlases, and gazetteers.

CHAPTER 7

Master the mother tongue with these resources for learning the basics of the Polish, Czech, and Slovak languages and naming conventions.

PART 3: TRACING YOUR FAMILY IN POLAND, THE CZECH REPUBLIC, AND SLOVAKIA

CHAPTER 8

Discover the most basic "wheres" and "whens" of your ancestor's life with this guide to birth, marriage, and death records.

Introduction

When I began researching my Slovak ancestors in 1990, librarians, clerks, and even fellow genealogists were often puzzled by the surnames or ancestral locations I mentioned and would ask me, "How do you spell that?" or "Where is that?"

At one time, uncovering information about an ancestor who hailed from a tiny town located in the Czech Republic, Poland, or Slovakia, proved to be a challenging and often impossible task.

As a novice researcher, I found the border changes, exotic-sounding surnames, language differences, and political turmoil associated with navigating the former, massive Austro-Hungarian Empire tried my patience. Despite my dedication, many myths and misconceptions hindered my progress. Since then, I have meticulously tracked down and have even had the life-changing experience of visiting the birthplaces of all four of my grandparents in the modern-day Slovak Republic. It is my hope that this book will help other Czech, Polish, and Slovak researchers do the same.

In the past twenty-five years, I have had the good fortune of working with many skilled research colleagues who were instrumental in helping me navigate the complexities of Eastern European genealogy. My journey back to find my ancestors would not have been possible without the guidance of these mentors whose names are included later in this book. One of the biggest lessons I learned early on as a genealogist is the importance of collaboration and networking with those researching similar surnames or geographical areas. While researching our individual families, we might have a tendency to hold on tightly to knowledge gleaned from our efforts, but there is a lot to be said for sharing what we learn. Thanks to collaborative efforts with other East European genealogists, I have been able to break down many of my own research brick walls.

In the same collaborative spirit, this guide is designed to teach and inspire others who have an interest in exploring their Polish, Czech, or Slovak heritage.

Lisa A. Alzo
September 2015

PART 1

LINKING YOUR FAMILY TREE TO POLISH, CZECH, AND SLOVAK LOCALITIES

1

Your Polish, Czech, or Slovak Heritage

W e all learn about our ethnic heritage in different ways. Perhaps you grew up hearing your Polish grandparents talking in a language you could not understand. Maybe you remember spending weekends at the local Czech *Sokol* or breathing in the delicious aroma of *páska* bread baking in your Slovak *baba*'s kitchen at Easter. Or perhaps you know little about your ancestors' ethnic identity because your family assimilated into American culture over time, but something triggered your interest in genealogy—a celebrity-roots TV show, an Ancestry.com commercial, the discovery of a mystery photo, or the passing of a relative.

However you became inspired to learn more about your Polish, Czech, or Slovak ancestry, you likely have many unanswered questions as you embark on your genealogical journey. You are also part of a growing number of family history enthusiasts who are discovering that Eastern European research is not the nearly impossible task it was a few decades ago. Foreign archives and repositories (many of which are being made available digitally on the Internet) contain many useful and well-preserved documents, dispelling the myth that all the records "over there" were destroyed. Geographic and language tools can help you over the hurdles of pinpointing your ancestral town or village and understand the funny-looking script on your grandmother's baptismal record. This guide will teach you about the tools and techniques that will help you discover new information about your Polish, Czech, and Slovak ancestors.

Before we get started, it's important to set the scope of this book. You may have heard Poles, Czechs, and Slovaks grouped together as "Slavs." Indeed, if you look up *Slavic* on Wikipedia <en.wikipedia.org/wiki/Slavs>, you will read that present-day Poles, Czechs, and Slovaks are classified as "West Slavic" peoples. Likewise, Russians, Belarussians, and Ukrainians are often referred to as "East Slavic," and Serbs, Bulgarians, Croats, Bosniaks, Macedonians, Slovenes, and Montenegrins are "South Slavic." Despite some of the similarities you may see in food, dress, music, dance, or certain holiday customs or traditions, these groups of Slavs have plenty of differences to help you distinguish between them.

You will also find many similarities in key strategies for tracking down essential records, but this book will cover the knowledge unique to these three countries. For example, this book will cover how and where to access records for ancestors in Poland, the Czech Republic, and Slovakia, the languages you will need to understand to interpret them, and the research challenges unique to crossing the ocean back to these three countries.

While not an exhaustive reference, this book will show you how and where to begin your search and how to overcome the most common pitfalls and obstacles in genealogical research. Think of this book as the roadmap for your journey.

This chapter will provide an overview of how Polish, Czech, and Slovak immigrants made their mark on American society and help you lay a foundation for your own Polish, Czech, or Slovak genealogy research.

POLISH IMMIGRANTS TO THE UNITED STATES

Tracing Polish ancestry can be challenging—especially since Poland did not officially exist as a country for 123 years. Yet millions of Americans can trace their roots to Polish ancestors, many of whom arrived less than one hundred years ago. Polish-Americans are one of the largest ethnic groups in the United States, numbering more than ten million.

Prior to 1880, most immigrants from Poland were political refugees, aristocrats, and adventurers. But between 1880 and 1914, most immigrants were peasant farmers unable to make a viable living due to a number of factors: a system that kept large lands in the nobles' hands, a surplus of rural labor, and a lack of industrialization. This, coupled with oppressive military service and cultural and religious persecution, forced many to abandon the homes their families had occupied for centuries. Despite restrictive immigration laws after World War I, small bursts of immigrants arrived throughout the twentieth century. Thousands of displaced persons fled to the United States, Canada, and Brazil from war-torn Europe during the late 1940s and early 1950s. Opponents of the Communist government (many part of the Solidarity movement) arrived in the early 1950s.

TIMELINE Poles in America

1608 Five Polish immigrants arrive in Jamestown, Virginia.

1619 Polish settlers in Jamestown organize what becomes the first labor strike in American history after the Legislative Assembly determines that only colonists of English descent are given the right to vote.

1777 Renowned Polish officer Casimir Pulaski arrives in Philadelphia and meets George Washington. Washington later places Pulaski in command, earning Pulaski the moniker "Father of the American Cavalry."

1852 The Democratic Society of Poles in America is the first Polish-American ethnic organization founded in America.

1854 The first Polish settlement is established in Panna Maria, Texas.

1861 As the American Civil War begins, approximately four thousand Polish-American fighters join the Union Army.

1865 The first wave of Polish immigration to America begins.

1880 The Polish National Alliance fraternal organization forms.

1898 The Polish Women's Alliance is established.

1900 The Polish Falcons of America, one of the largest Polish-American fraternal organizations, is founded.

1917 During World War I, approximately forty thousand Polish-Americans serve in the United States Armed Forces.

1919 The Polish embassy in Washington, D.C., opens.

1922 The Polish American Association is founded.

1939 A second wave of Polish immigration to America begins. On the eve of World War II, 20 percent of US forces were of Polish descent.

1944 The Polish American Congress is founded.

1950-1953 Polish-Americans participate in the Korean War.

1979 Polish-born Pope John Paul II makes his first papal visit to the United States.

1980 Polish-Americans support the Solidarity movement in Poland.

2010 Ten million Americans report Polish ancestry in the US census.

Polish immigrants almost always came to established Polish settlements in the United States. The Prussian Poles who came to America in the mid-1800s, for example, became part of the existing German or Czech communities or established separate Polish colonies in farming areas. Many other Polish immigrants put down roots in large cities such as Chicago, New York, Pittsburgh, Buffalo, Milwaukee, Detroit, Cleveland, and Philadelphia.

CZECH AND SLOVAK IMMIGRANTS TO THE UNITED STATES

The term Czech refers to the Czech-speaking inhabitants of what's now the Czech Republic (*Česká Republika*). The modern nation has its roots in the ancient kingdoms of Bohemia (the western part) and Moravia (the eastern part), collectively known as the "Czech lands." Northern Moravia also encompasses Silesia (*Slezsko*), a historical region that lies mostly in southwestern Poland. In the 1800s, the ethnic composition of the Czech lands was predominantly Czech and German. The Silesians (*Slezané*) mostly maintain their ethnic identity but are often considered a subset within the Czech culture.

Today's Slovak Republic, the Czech Republic's eastern neighbor, corresponds to the centuries-old region of Slovakia (or *Slovensko*, as it is referred to locally). The word *Slovak* derives from an old term for Slav (*Slovan*), and Slovaks share a common culture despite regional (eastern, central, and western) and local differences in dialect, customs, and religion.

The majority of Czech and Slovak immigrants arrived prior to World War I—Czechs and Moravians beginning in the 1850s, and Slovaks and other ethnic groups from Upper Hungary beginning in the 1880s. All told, about four hundred thousand Czechs and some six hundred thousand Slovaks came to America's shores between 1850 and 1914. Some sought better economic and social conditions; others wanted to avoid political persecution or conscription into the Austrian army.

Pre-Civil War Czech immigrants were farmers who settled in Iowa, Illinois, Texas, Wisconsin, Nebraska, and the Dakotas. Those who arrived after the Civil War opted for larger industrial or mining areas.

Slovak immigrants began arriving en masse in the 1880s and sought employment in American factories, mines, and mills in cities such as Chicago, Cleveland, and Pittsburgh. Indeed, Pittsburgh had the largest population of people claiming Slovak descent in the country according to the 1990 census.

In the early nineteenth century, the Slovak economy grew slowly because of worldwide economic slumps and because the Industrial Revolution came later to Slovakia than it did to Western Europe and the Czech lands. So while the Czech lands were becoming industrialized, Slovakia's economy remained agriculture-based. Slovak immigration to the United States increased rapidly at the end of the nineteenth century as many Slovaks became more dissatisfied with local conditions. By 1900, Slovakia had lost more than three hundred thousand inhabitants to emigration.

Czechs and Slovaks often followed the pattern of "chain migration," in which immigrants set out for America to join relatives or old-country neighbors who had already relocated there. For example, a husband might come over and later send for his wife and

TIMELINE Czechs and Slovaks in America

1633 Augustine Herman, believed to be the first Czech immigrant to America, arrives in New York.

1695 The first known Slovak immigrant to the United States, Isaac Ferdinand Sarosi, arrives.

1776 More than two thousand Moravian Brethren live in the American colonies when independence is declared.

1847 The first Czech settlement in Texas is established.

1850 Three Czech families settle in Cleveland.

1856 The first school teaching Czech language and history opens in New York.

1860 Frantisek Korizek publishes the first Czech newspaper in America, *Slovan Amerikansky*, in Racine, Wisconsin.

1870 *Sokol* gymnastics begin in Cleveland with the founding of *Sokol Perun*; the Benevolent Sisterhood Union and the Union of Czech Women are organized.

1873 A cholera epidemic and subsequent crop failures initiate large-scale emigration from eastern Slovakia.

1886 Jan Slovensky publishes *Amerikánszko-szlovenszké noviny*, the first printed Slovak newspaper in America.

1890 The First Catholic Slovak Union of America, or "Jednota," is founded in Cleveland; the National Slovak Society is founded in Pittsburgh.

1896 The Slovak Gymnastic Union Sokol is founded in Chicago.

1905 Slovak immigration to the United States peaks.

1915 Representatives of Slovak and Czech ethnic organizations sign the Cleveland Agreement to address the establishment of a common federal state.

1918 Slovak and Czech emigrants sign the Pittsburgh Agreement. Tomáš Garrigue Masaryk proclaims the autonomous position of Slovakia within a democratic Czechoslovak republic.

1941 Slovak-American writer Thomas Bell publishes *Out of This Furnace*.

1958 The Czechoslovak Society of Arts & Sciences is founded in Washington, DC.

1962 Pop art icon Andy Warhol, born to Slovak immigrants, publishes his famous *Campbell's Soup Cans*.

1969 Joseph M. Gaydos becomes the first Slovak-American Congressman.

1972 Astronaut Eugene Cernan, son of a Slovak father and Czech mother, walks on the moon in the Apollo 17 lunar mission.

1997 Prague native Madeleine Albright becomes US Secretary of State.

children, or a family might "sponsor" the journeys of as many aunts, uncles, and cousins as they could afford.

However, not all Czech and Slovak immigrants intended to settle permanently in the United States. Some planned to stay only until they could earn enough money to purchase land back home. These "birds of passage" sometimes returned to Europe several times before finally settling in America. But the outbreak of World War I hindered many of these immigrants' plans and prompted many to stay on either side of the pond for years—or in some cases, for good.

POLISH, CZECH, AND SLOVAK CULTURE IN AMERICA

As the large waves of Polish, Czech, and Slovak immigrants came to America, they brought with them cultures filled with rich heritage and traditions.

Polish Heritage

According to the 2010 US census, roughly ten million Americans share Polish heritage, making it the eighth-largest ancestry in the United States. If you have Polish roots, you also share the legacy of *Polonia*, a diaspora that built new communities abroad while the Polish homeland suffered more than a century of foreign occupation.

In the United States, Chicago is hands down the Polish epicenter. The Polish American Association estimates one million people of Polish ancestry live in the metropolitan Chicago area, a figure that is second only to Warsaw. The metropolitan areas of New York City, Cleveland, Philadelphia, Milwaukee, Detroit, and Buffalo—even the state of Texas—also have significant Polish populations.

Polish heritage celebrations are easy to find throughout the year, held in the cities noted above as well as in smaller towns throughout the United States. For example, you might recall your Polish relatives observing Saint Joseph's Day (March 19), a Catholic feast day recognizing the death of the Virgin Mary's husband. Saint Joseph's Day festivals are a staple of many Polish communities throughout the country.

RESEARCH TIP

Explore Tasty Traditions

Food and traditions are an integral part of Slavic heritage, and Polish, Czech, and Slovak cuisine consists of dishes that can be difficult to pronounce (think *golubky*, *kolache*, and *pirohy*—in English, that's stuffed cabbage, sweet pastry, and pierogies). But boy, are these foods delicious to eat!

Polish-Americans also have other celebrations throughout the year. In May, the Polish American Cultural Center in Philadelphia celebrates Polish Constitution Day, and each June, Milwaukee hosts Polish Fest **<www.polishfest.org>**, which claims to be the country's largest Polish festival. October, which since 1986 has been celebrated nationally as Polish-American Heritage Month, is also a popular time for Polish festivals. For example, on the second Sunday in October, there's a reunion in Panna Maria, Texas, for the descendants of Poles who came to that area.

Czech and Slovak Heritage

Not to be outdone, Czechs and Slovaks take great pride in their respective customs and traditions, too. With nearly 2.5 million Americans claiming Czech or Slovak ancestry, you can find celebrations of Czech and Slovak heritage across the United States each year. Several cities hold annual Kolache Festival celebrations (named for *koláč*, a traditional fruit-filled pastry), including Prague, Oklahoma; Cedar Rapids, Iowa; Kewaunee, Wisconsin; and Caldwell and several other towns in Texas. Several cities battle for the title of "kolache capital of the world," including Montgomery, Minnesota, and Verdigre, Nebraska; each hold an annual festival known as Kolache Days. Prague, Nebraska, claims to be the home of the world's largest kolach. Still more US communities hold Czech-American festivals where kolache may be found.

Slovak festivals are held each year in cities across Pennsylvania, Ohio, New Jersey, and other states. Every November, the Department of Slavic Languages and Literatures at the University of Pittsburgh **<www.slavic.pitt.edu>** hosts a Slovak festival at the Cathedral of Learning on its main campus. There, visitors can attend free lectures, listen to Slovak music, watch Slovak folk dancers, enjoy traditional Slovak food, and browse a hall full of vendors selling books, pottery, jewelry, and other Slovak-themed items.

FAMOUS POLISH PEOPLE

If you have Polish roots, you're in good company. You will find scientists, musicians, labor leaders, and even a pope among the prominent people who have Polish ancestry **<en.wikipedia.org/wiki/List_of_Polish_people>**.

Indeed, Poles have made contributions to society that date back hundreds of years. In 1543, Nicolaus Copernicus (Mikołaj Kopernik) published *On the Revolutions of the Heavenly Spheres*, in which he proposed that the earth revolves around the sun. Copernicus is said to be the founder of modern astronomy. Another notable scientist of Polish descent, Marie Curie (Maria Skłodowska), discovered radium and paved the way for nuclear physics and cancer therapy. She was awarded the Nobel Prize in Chemistry in 1911, becoming the first female Nobel Prize winner. Some Poles have also made contributions to the arts.

Pianist Frédéric Chopin, considered one of the world's greatest composers, was born in 1810 near Warsaw. For those with less classical tastes, American pop singer Bobby Vinton (whose original name is Stanley Robert Vintula, Jr.) had multiple number-one hits in the 1960s and affectionately became known as "the Polish Prince." In 1974, his "My Melody of Love," partially sung in Polish, became a multimillion-dollar hit single.

Two larger-than-life Poles became well-known leaders in their respective circles. Lech Wałęsa, an electrician from Gdańsk who headed up the Solidarity movement that led Poland out of communism, was elected president of Poland in 1990. In 1920, Karol Józef Wojtyła was born in Poland and served as the Archbishop of Krakow and later as a cardinal before being elected pope of the Roman Catholic Church in 1978. He's perhaps better known by the name John Paul II, the first non-Italian pope in more than four hundred years. Beloved by millions of Catholics worldwide, John Paul II was officially canonized into sainthood on April 27, 2014.

FAMOUS CZECH- AND SLOVAK-AMERICANS

At one time or another, you have probably stopped at a McDonald's for lunch or dinner. But did you know that the popular fast food chain's founder, Ray Kroc, was Czech? Other notable US personalities of Czech descent include former Secretary of State Madeleine Albright and astronaut and "last man on the moon" Eugene Cernan. Even presidents Barack Obama and George W. Bush can trace their lineages back to the Kingdom of Bohemia. Some famous Americans with ties to Slovakia include actors Paul Newman and Jim Caviezel, Supreme Court Chief Justice John Roberts, former Minnesota governor (and World Wrestling star) Jesse Ventura, parachute inventor Štefan Banič, and pop artist Andy Warhol.

KEYS TO SUCCESS

✴ Dig into your ancestry. An increasing number of digitized records and language resources has made Eastern European genealogical research, once considered prohibitively difficult, possible.

✴ Give context to your own family's history by learning about Polish, Czech, or Slovak immigration and cultural traditions. You'll see the bigger picture your ancestors were part of, and the history you study can help you better understand yourself and your family as well as inform future research.

2

Jump-Starting Your Polish, Czech, and Slovak Research

Now that you have decided to research your Polish, Czech, or Slovak roots, perhaps you're feeling a bit overwhelmed as you prepare to plunge into the uncharted waters of your family history. Not sure where or how to begin? Do you feel intimidated by the research process? Even if you've been doing genealogy for a while, a refresher on genealogy basics will ensure you get your ethnic research off on the right foot. In this chapter, we'll walk through how to start your genealogical search and discuss some fundamental concepts and principles.

THE FIRST STEPS

Before you start digging into records, you'll first want to assess what you already know about you and your ancestors, what information you'd like to have, and what you can reasonably accomplish through your research. By doing this prep work, you'll make your later research more purposeful and efficient. In this section, I'll outline five easy steps that will help enrich your research.

1 Identify What You Already Know

The first rule of genealogy is always start with yourself. Your research will be most effective if you work back in time starting with you and your parents instead of trying to establish a connection with a potential distant ancestor. Start by documenting your name, your birth date and birthplace, and your parents' names (your biological parents if known, adoptive if not). Then continue to add information about other ancestors to build a family tree (more on that in a moment).

2 Check for Home and Family Sources

Scour your attic, basement, closets, boxes, and desk drawers for home sources—that is, family Bibles, documents, letters, photographs, yearbooks, and any other items that contain genealogical information. By collecting certificates, birth and wedding announcements, deeds, passports, funeral/memorial cards, and other items your parents or grandparents may have hidden away for safekeeping, you could uncover basic information that can lead you to your next source and help identify the appropriate archives or repositories. Think of it as a family history scavenger hunt. Once you've looked through your own house, move on to the homes of your parents and grandparents.

As you search for home sources, be on the lookout for anything that includes evidence of Polish, Czech, or Slovak heritage, such as

- documents written in Polish, Czech, or Slovak
- twentieth-century US census returns with mother tongue noted as Polish, Czech, or Slovak
- Polish, Czech, or Slovak customs or recipes
- family stories about Polish, Czech, or Slovak heritage
- letters and envelopes (image **A**) with return addresses of relatives in the homeland
- association with an ethnic church
- membership in a Polish, Czech, or Slovak fraternal or social organization.

3 Build a Family Tree

The main goal of genealogy research is to document as many generations as you can. The best way to begin is to list everything you already know (or think you know) about your family. You'll want to ascertain names; dates of birth, marriage, and death; and other biographical facts about each ancestor's life. Keep this information organized and easy to reference by using a pedigree chart, a family group chart, an *Ahnentafel* ancestor table, and a biographical outline, all standard genealogy forms. These will help you keep track

A

This home source—an envelope—provides valuable genealogical clues, including a relative's name and an ancestral hometown in Slovakia.

of what you already know about your ancestors and help you identify further areas of research. You can download these and other free forms at **<www.familytreemagazine.com/info/basicforms>**.

While you can compile these charts and sheets by hand, it's easier to use computer software and an online family tree site to manage all the genealogy information you collect. Virtually every genealogy software program on the market offers ways to print selected information from your database into a chart or sheet. And you can easily share information with fellow researchers even if you don't use the same program through a standard file format called GEDCOM (short for "GEnealogical Data COMmunications").

Many genealogists choose to upload their family tree online to Ancestry.com **<www.ancestry.com>**, FamilySearch.org **<www.familysearch.org>**, MyHeritage **<www.myheritage.com>**, and other sites. If you are unsure about which software program to choose or which online family trees will work best for you, you can read user-based reviews at GenSoftReviews **<www.gensoftreviews.com>**.

4 Talk to Your Relatives

Don't wait until another generation passes away—the time to start is now. You'll want to begin by interviewing your closest blood relatives—parents and grandparents if possible—but don't limit yourself. Mention that you are researching the family's history to all your aunts, uncles, and cousins, including distant cousins. While they may not be close by blood (or in any physical or emotional way to living relatives), artifacts from common ancestors such as family Bibles or papers from an immigrant may have made their way down a cousin's line, so don't rule these folks out. Interviewing them may open the door to sharing these photos or documents in some way. Even living friends of your parents, grandparents, or great-grandparents can help, so interview them, too.

While it is preferable to conduct your interviews in person, you can also do them over the phone, via e-mail, or even on Skype **<www.skype.com>** or FaceTime **<www.apple.com/mac/facetime>**. Whatever method you use, you'll want to record the interview in some way. You can use a basic tape recorder, a digital recording device, a video camera, or your smartphone. When you set up the interview, let the person know you want to record the conversation and ask him what method would make him most comfortable. Always ask the person's permission first before you hit record.

For in-person interviews, bring your pedigree chart and some family group sheets and ask the interviewee to help you fill them out. Then ask for details about each person you add to the chart, such as a description of the ancestor's personality, occupation, and place of residence.

Be sure to ask relatives if they have any photographs or documents and where events happened. Talk to all your relatives who may have personal knowledge about your family's name and/or an ancestor's journey to America. Ask specific questions such as: Where did their ship land? Do you remember the name of the ship? Did Grandma or Grandpa come over alone or with other family members? What was the name of the town or province where they lived in the old country? And so on. Even if your relatives' recollections aren't totally accurate, you're getting important clues to follow up on—as well as stories and memories you won't find in any record.

Transcribe the interviews as soon as possible, preferably while the conversation is fresh in your mind. It also helps if you print out the transcript so you have a backup copy in a version that is not technology-dependent. Find more interview tips online at **<www.familytreemagazine.com/article/Oral-History-Interview-Question-Lists>**.

⑤ Outline Your Research Goals

Before you dive headfirst into tracing Polish, Czech, or Slovak ancestors, set up some goals for what you hope to accomplish. Think of it like this: You likely would not attempt to change the oil in your car without reading the owner's manual or cook kolache without following a recipe. The same goes for genealogy—you shouldn't just randomly start hunting for your ancestors without a research plan. Your research plan should consist of five basic steps:

1. **Identify your objective.** Write down as specifically as possible what it is you want to accomplish. Perhaps you want to identify the name of your great-grandfather's

ancestral town or village. Your objective should include both long-term and short-term research goals that will help you reach your overall objective.

2. **List your known facts.** Record what you already know (no matter how little) about the ancestor from original documents and records. Include names and spelling variations; family relationships; dates of birth, death, and marriage; and places where events may have taken place.

3. **Formulate a hypothesis.** Based on what you know, make some educated guesses about the possible answers to your research question or problem.

4. **Identify resources with related records.** Become familiar with those records most likely to prove or disprove your hypothesis (e.g., your third-great-grandpa's Civil War pension file or great-grandma's death certificate).

5. **Define research steps for using the known resources.** Decide the order in which you'll seek the records, and how to get to them (for instance: naturalization indexes, then online immigration databases, then microfilm, then books).

Think of a research plan as your "genealogy GPS" and the known facts about your ancestor as the data points you'll plug in to guide your trip. For more help, see my "Step-by-Step Guide: Creating a Research Plan" **<www.shopfamilytree.com/step-by-step-guide-creating-a-research-plan>**. In addition, use the free research calendar from *Family Tree Magazine* **<www.familytreemagazine.com/info/researchforms>** to organize and keep track of materials you've searched so you don't duplicate efforts.

Now that you have learned some of the basics of getting started with your Polish, Czech, or Slovak genealogy, it's time to begin tracking down the missing pieces of your family history puzzle. Are you ready to begin your genealogical journey?

KEY GENEALOGY PRINCIPLES

Once you've established the perimeters of your research and start searching for your Polish, Czech, or Slovak roots, you'll want to adhere to tried-and-true methods and concepts that apply to all genealogy research. Following these guidelines helps you avert unnecessary brick walls and trace the right ancestors.

Understand Primary and Secondary Information

In evaluating information, genealogists make distinctions between primary and secondary. **Primary information** is generally defined as being created in close proximity to the event(s) described by someone in a position to know the truth of the asserted facts. This includes such documents as civil birth, marriage, and death certificates; church baptismal and

Starting Your Search for Immigrant Ancestors

Once you've taken stock of what you already know about your ancestors and decide on a course of action for your research, you're ready to begin searching through records. This diagram shows how a typical research session progresses, from establishing a date of arrival for your ancestor to writing to archives. While researching each individual ancestor will require a slightly different process, the following eight steps illustrate a template that you can use when looking for your Polish, Czech, and Slovak ancestors. Note that when looking for ancestors in the old country, you can skip steps 1 and 4. You can learn more about finding your immigrant ancestors in chapter 3.

Establish the date of arrival for your immigrant ancestor.

This date serves as a benchmark moment in a person's life. All records from before this date will be in the old country while all records from after will be in the United States or Canada. Note that some "birds of passage" ancestors may have traveled the Atlantic multiple times before settling down.

Identify the original name and hometown.

Scour home sources and name websites for possible spelling variations or nicknames that your ancestor might have used or that his town might have been known by. This will help you make sure you're searching for the right person and place.

Search websites and online databases.

Websites and genealogical societies and message boards have digitized a growing number of records that can be searched online. Check large sites such as Ancestry.com **<www.ancestry.com>**, as well as small, volunteer-generated databases.

Visit or request records from North American repositories.

If you find a stateside record that's not online, contact the appropriate archive to receive a photocopy via mail or set up a visit.

Determine where your ancestor's hometown is today.

As you'll learn in chapters 4, 5, and 6, Eastern European borders frequently changed. Find where your ancestor's hometown currently is and trace its history throughout the centuries to identify where you might find your ancestor's records.

Check for old-country records through FamilySearch.org and local websites.

Having completed step 5, you'll know what district or county your ancestor's records will be kept in. Browse collections at FamilySearch.org **<www.familysearch.org>** or at local websites and archives to find records from that country or region.

Network with fellow researchers.

Other genealogists may have valuable information that can help you with your own research. Visit social media websites such as Facebook **<www.facebook.com>** and Twitter **<www.twitter.com>** and search for genealogical communities researching similar areas.

Write to archives, churches, or registrars, or hire a professional researcher.

As you did in step 4, identify and reach out to repositories with records that you can't access online. If you want to bring in the "big guns," consider hiring a professional researcher who has expertise in the area to help you access records and make connections in the old country.

Is It Primary or Secondary?

Sources of Primary Information

- civil birth, marriage, and death certificates
- church baptismal and burial records
- deeds
- passenger arrival lists
- tombstones
- wills

Sources of Secondary Information

- county biographical histories
- family Bibles
- newspaper clippings (including ethnic newspapers)
- online indexes
- oral histories
- published genealogies

burial records; tombstones; wills; deeds; and US census schedules. **Secondary information** is essentially anything else—but more specifically, details recorded long after the fact and/or containing secondhand data. Compiled family genealogies and county biographical histories are often the most prominently used sources for secondary information.

Why does this matter? Primary information is generally more reliable than secondary information. You should be able to trace each piece of secondary information to a source with primary information or a conclusion based on one or more reliable sources; if you can't, you have to question its accuracy.

Likewise, sources are classified as **originals** (exact replicas, such as microfilms, scans, or photocopies of original documents) or **derivatives** (such as published abstracts of records or hand-copied versions of original wills and deeds). Hand-copied versions and abstractions often include errors, so it's best to seek out original sources whenever possible.

It's not uncommon for different sources to give conflicting information about a life event. In this case, give more credence to the source created more closely to the event. For example, if two sources for an ancestor's death date are an obituary and a tombstone, the obituary is more likely to have the accurate date than a memorial marker, which might have been carved months or years later. If your sources for a birth date are an obituary and a baptismal record, the baptismal record is likely more accurate because it was created closer to the person's birth.

It's important to note that information from oral histories is secondary. Memories (even the best ones) can be hazy. You'll want to find sources that confirm the dates and stories you hear. Keep an open mind concerning family stories, especially when these stories involve legends about family origins or contain "unbelievable" information. You'll want to attempt to prove those stories and legends with other sources.

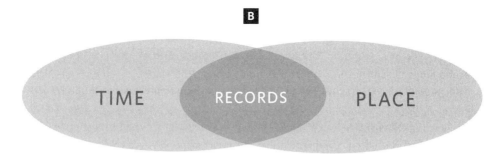

Available records for your ancestors depend upon the time and place they lived in.

Explore the Intersection of Time and Place

In genealogy, it is essential to consider time and place—where these two intersect serves as the base for your research (image **B**). With this concept, you use both the time when your particular ancestor lived and the place where he lived to determine what records may be available for that ancestor. You must put yourself in the time and place of your ancestor to accurately determine what documents might possibly exist. For example, it's useless to search for an official birth certificate for a Pennsylvania ancestor born in 1867 because Pennsylvania didn't start issuing official birth certificates until 1906. Likewise, a married woman's citizenship didn't become independent of her husband's until September, 22, 1922—which affects your search for naturalization records. Learning the laws and record-keeping practices of the places your ancestors lived (both in North America and Europe) will help you from chasing after records you are likely to never find.

Create Chronologies

It's a good habit to put together a chronology, or timeline, for each ancestor you research. A chronology lets you look at the events of the ancestor's life in time sequence, which will show you any gaps that exist in your ancestor's biography and help you identify the types of records to check for more information (image **C**). In short, a timeline serves to place your family in the appropriate historical context.

You can use a number of tools to create your timeline. Most genealogical software has built-in timeline features; other programs, including Aeon Timeline **<www.scribblecode. com>** and Genelines by Progeny Genealogy **<www.progenygenealogy.com/products/time-line-charts.aspx>**, exist just for this purpose. Or try a free online service such as Timetoast **<www.timetoast.com>**, Our Timelines **<www.ourtimelines.com>**, or HistoryLines **<www. historylines.com>**.

Record every life event you've found for your ancestor, from birth to death, on this timeline. Then look for blank spots: What facts and dates about this ancestor are still

Custom Timeline
For Elizabeth Fencsak Alzo
1897 to 1966

1837-1901:	Reign of Queen Victoria (Hanover) from before birth to age 4
1893-1897:	US Financial panic, depression from before birth to age 0
1897:	Erzsebet Fencsak born in Posa, Hungary in birth year
1897-1901:	William McKinley president of US from birthyear to age 4
1898:	Spanish American 1-year war at age 1
1899-1902:	Boer war from age 2 to age 5
1899-1923:	6th Cholera pandemic from age 2 to age 26
1900:	Hawaii organized as a territory at age 3
1900:	Boxer rebellion in China at age 3
1900:	Galveston Hurricane - 8,000 killed at age 3
1901:	Commonwealth of Australia founded at age 4
1901:	First British submarine launched at age 4
1901:	Oil discovered in Texas in significant amounts at age 4
1901:	US President William McKinley assassinated at age 4

A timeline shows what facts you've already learned about an ancestor and where you need to do more research.

missing? Do you have birth dates, marriage and death dates, and parents' names? List all the sources and places you've already checked and whether they yielded any clues. Where haven't you looked? The timeline will also help you see where your ancestor was at a particular point in time. You can then search for relatives, friends, neighbors, and colleagues who lived nearby.

Document Your Discoveries and Sources

It is essential to document where you've found information—otherwise, you (or someone else) won't be able to evaluate conflicting information and you'll likely end up duplicating your own work. Most genealogical software programs have fields for citing your sources or, at the very least, a notes section where you can enter documentation. To help streamline the process, you can use an external program such as EasyBib <www.easybib.com> to generate citations in widely accepted styles such as MLA (Modern Language Association) or *Chicago Manual of Style*. Consult *Evidence Explained: Citing History Sources from Artifacts to Cyberspace*, third edition by Elizabeth Shown Mills (Genealogical Publishing Co., 2015). You can also find Mills' research tips and learn about her publications at <www.historicpathways.com> and <www.evidenceexplained.com>. Learning to do correct citations now will save you time and effort down the road and will establish your credibility in the genealogy community and online family tree websites.

You also will want to learn how to document sources according to Board for Certification of Genealogists (BCG) standards. The organization developed the Genealogical Proof Standard (GPS) as a framework to promote genealogy through accurate research. Under the GPS, each conclusion you make about an ancestor must have sufficient credibility to be accepted as "proven." Learn more about the GPS at **<www.bcgcertification.org/resources/standard.html>**.

Keep a Research Log

During the research process, you might talk with your relatives, visit various websites, travel to repositories to scour books and microfilm, and yes, sometimes even request records via traditional mail. If you do your job correctly, you should collect plenty of data for each ancestor, but answers to research questions will likely lead to more questions. So how do you keep track of it all? How do you avoid revisiting the same sources because you forgot you already checked them? Since most people don't have photographic memories, the best way to record what you have done is to set up a simple document (like a spreadsheet or table) to log your research "to-dos."

This research log will be a comprehensive list of sources you already searched or plan to search, including the purpose of each search (what you want to find), a summary of what you have or have not found, notations and source citations, and comments about your search strategies, suggestions, questions, analysis, and discrepancies. You can use this important tool to help organize and track your work, analyze data, prepare for a research trip, or pick your work back up after leaving it for a while. In simple terms, a research log tells you where you've been in the research process, provides you with the ability for "instant recall," and reduces the need for do-overs.

Every genealogist researches differently, so no two genealogists' research logs will look exactly the same. The point is to set up a system that works for you and customize it to your needs so you can avoid randomly stumbling into your discoveries and cut down on unnecessary repetition.

As a general guideline, any research log should include

- date
- record name
- repository
- record type
- result (positive or negative)
- analysis

- source citation

- link (website URL)

- transcript or abstract

Of course, you can organize these items in whatever fashion makes sense to you. You might want to further customize your log with details such as

- record number

- result (positive, negative, or pending)

- file name/location

- evidence evaluation

- source type (original, derivative, primary, secondary, etc.)

- clarity of the record (good, bad, hard-to-read, "spot on the microfilm," etc.)

- information type

- evidence type (direct, indirect)

Most popular software programs have some sort of research log feature already built in. For example, RootsMagic **<www.rootsmagic.com>** has a Research Log report that asks, "What were you trying to find?"; "What source did you check?"; and "What were the results of your search?" Legacy Family Tree **<www.legacyfamilytree.com>** has a Source Quality feature that lets you record the quality (original vs. derivative, primary vs. secondary, direct vs. indirect, etc.) of each source as you attempt to prove your conclusions.

Other third-party software is ideal for creating research logs. Microsoft Excel **<products.office.com/en-us/excel>** is designed specifically for spreadsheets, which are a good format for research logs because of the program's ability to sort and analyze data. Have a Gmail account? You can create a research log spreadsheet in your Google Drive, **<drive.google.com>**, which you can access anywhere with an Internet connection (see image **D**). Another program, Zotero **<www.zotero.com>**, helps you collect, organize, cite, and share your research sources. Zotero has web browser integration and generates source citations. Evernote **<www.evernote.com>** allows you to create notebooks to capture ("clip") web content and take photos of documents at libraries and repositories. You can also create checklists for your research projects and sync notes across all your devices so you can use your log wherever your research takes you. To learn more about creating research logs in Evernote, see *How to Use Evernote for Genealogy* by Kerry Scott (Family Tree Books, 2015). If you're a Windows user, you'll find a similar note-taking application in Microsoft's OneNote **<www.onenote.com>**.

The free Google Sheets program allows you to create spreadsheets (including research logs) online.

Once you have created your research log, you will need to use it and maintain it. Print out a copy to take with you on research trips to the courthouse or library and keep it open as you search online databases and websites. Maintaining a research log takes discipline—but it's well worth the effort. Consider setting up an easy-to-use template with the most common source citations you use for your research. Taking a little time to set this up with the correct formatting is ultimately a real timesaver.

Trace the Whole Family with Collateral and Cluster Research

The primary (if not the sole) goal of most family historians is to find information about their direct-line ancestors. But expanding your search to include your ancestors' siblings, a practice called "whole-family genealogy," gives you a more accurate picture of your Polish, Czech, or Slovak family and provides for a more fulfilling research experience. Records for an ancestor's siblings may include information about your ancestors in the preceding generation. For example, you may be unable to find the names of your grandfather's parents, but you've found death certificates for a both a younger sibling and an older sibling of your grandfather. The same people are listed as parents on the death certificates, so you can reasonably conclude that these people are also your grandfather's parents.

A common principle of genealogy research is that people live and migrate in packs. The core "pack" is a family group, but the core group changes over time. Parents, spouses, children, and other relatives such as widowed in-laws, adult siblings, favorite cousins, and orphaned nieces or nephews can join or leave the pack. Close family friends, members of the same church congregation, neighbors, in-laws, and other connections may turn up, too. In genealogy, two overlapping approaches help you sort out the pack:

- **Collateral research** involves focusing research attention on relatives other than ancestors: for example, not just your great-grandparents, but also their siblings.

- **Cluster research** looks at all folks who live near each other and migrate together, whether they are blood kin or not.

This sideways approach is particularly valuable if your brick-wall ancestors were on the move—across America or the Atlantic. In our ancestors' day, families weren't as far-flung as they are today; it was common for them to pack up and travel in groups.

Chapter 3 will provide more details on the "Friends, Associates, and Neighbors (FAN) Club principle" for finding your Polish, Czech, or Slovak immigrant ancestor. Use the Cluster Research Worksheet at the end of this chapter while conducting your searches.

Keep in mind that genealogy is a journey. While your starting point and destinations may be unique, you will still need to plan how to get there, document, analyze, and evaluate your finds, and log where you've been. Reviewing and understanding the basic genealogy principles outlined in this chapter will position you for the research road ahead, especially when you make that long-anticipated jump across the ocean.

KEYS TO SUCCESS

✳ Begin by writing down everything you already know about your family tree. This will help you keep different generations and relatives straight and show you missing family details to pursue.

✳ Formulate a research plan before further investigating your Polish, Czech, or Slovak family tree. Setting concrete objectives will help you focus on answering the family history questions you're most curious about.

✳ Refer to the eight basic steps listed in the Starting Your Search for Immigrant Ancestors sidebar as you research each Polish, Czech, or Slovak immigrant ancestor.

✳ Master important genealogy concepts such as original and derivative sources, source citation, and the benefits of ancestor chronologies, research logs, and "whole-family genealogy" before you delve into the complexities of overseas research.

CLUSTER RESEARCH WORKSHEET

Person of Interest

Name	
Birth	
Marriage	
Death	
Other details	

Person of Interest's Cluster

Name				
Relationship to person of interest, if known				
Birth				
Marriage(s)				
Death				
Other events/ details				

3

Identifying Your Immigrant Ancestor

To successfully make the jump across the pond to explore your ancestral origins, you will need two key pieces of information: the immigrant's **original name** and **hometown**. Sounds simple enough, right? In reality, pinpointing these basic pieces of your family puzzle can be one of the most challenging aspects of the research process. In this chapter, we'll explore strategies and sources on this side of the ocean to obtain those critical clues.

DETERMINING NAMES

Chances are good that your immigrant ancestor went by a different name after coming to America than he did in the old country. Especially during that transition time between the Old and New Worlds, changes were bound to happen—be they variant spellings, translations, or just phonetic garbles. You may encounter a number of spellings. In order to correctly identify the immigrant, gather records made by or for the ancestor for the span of his life (from birth to marriage to death).

Name changes generally occurred after immigrants arrived in the United States or Canada, so expect your ancestors to appear in earlier records—including their passenger arrival lists—with their Polish, Czech, or Slovak moniker. This is where it helps to understand Polish, Czech, and Slovak naming practices, which we will review in chapter 7.

Unraveling Name Changes

The "Americanizing" of immigrants' names could take several forms. These are the most common scenarios to watch for—any or all of them could apply to your immigrant ancestor.

Polish, Czech, or Slovak immigrants sometimes "translated" their given names to the English equivalents. For example, *Jan* became *John*, or *Katarzyna* became *Katherine*. An immigrant with the surname *Krejči* might opt for *Taylor* in America. Use Behind the Name **<www.behindthename.com>** to research name translations; the Polish Genealogical Society of America also has a handy guide with Polish, Latin, and German versions of English given names at **<pgsa.org/wp-content/uploads/2015/09/FirstNameTrans.pdf>**. Some common changes to names are caused by

- **an Americanized spelling:** Because Polish orthography is so different from English, immigrants wanted to make their names look and sound less foreign. Czechs and Slovaks also experienced this issue due to nuances with their respective languages. As a result, the spelling or pronunciation of surnames often was altered. This might have involved dropping accent marks or adopting an English phonetic spelling, such as changing *Szymanski* to *Shemanski*. Sometimes, foreign-sounding endings would be dropped, as in *Andrzejewski* to *Andrews*.

- **a similar-sounding name:** An immigrant might choose an American surname that wasn't linguistically related to his native name, but sounded loosely like it: *Corrister* for *Kořista*.

- **a total name change:** Sometimes, immigrants simply picked completely different names for no other reason than their personal whims—and you end up with a Peter Fox who was originally *Branislav Jankovic*. Unless you have family stories or documents, tracking these changes requires good old-fashioned sleuthing, as they happened informally (without the legal paperwork required today).

To further your understanding of the complexity of Eastern European surnames, download and read "Mutilation: the Fate of Eastern European Names in America" by William F. Hoffman **<pgsa.org/wp-content/uploads/2015/09/Mutilation.pdf>**.

Tracking Name Variations

The number of name variations you'll encounter for a single ancestor can be mind-boggling. That's why it's helpful to create a list of all potential variants for each surname you are researching. Refer to the list when searching online databases and printed indexes to ensure you don't miss your ancestor.

RESEARCH TIP

Bust the Ellis Island Myth

It's a common misconception that officials at Ellis Island changed immigrants' names. In reality, immigration officials didn't record arriving passengers' names—they just checked lists filled out at the port of departure. Read immigration historian Marian L. Smith's article "American Names: Declaring Independence" **<www.ilw.com/articles/2005,0808-smith.shtm>** for more on immigrants' names.

Here's an example: For one of my Slovak ancestors, Verona Straka, I found the following variations:

- **first name:** Verona, Veronica, Veron, Vera
- **last name:** Straka, Sztraka, Stracha, Strakova, Strake

I created this chart to help me keep track of all the surname variations in just one glance. As I find additional variations, it's easy to go back to the list and record them.

Surname	Straka
Phonetic variants	Sztraka
Possible "translations" into English	Strake
Other spellings or variations	Stracha
Suffixes for women	Strakova, Sztrakova (Slovak name add -*ova*)

Making a chart of first name variants is useful, too. Be sure to include nicknames (such as Lizzie, Liz, Betty, Betsy, or Beth for Elizabeth, or Johnny, Johnnie, Jon, Jack, or Jackie for John). Use the Name Variants Worksheet at the end of this chapter to record your own list of name variations.

DETERMINING THE PLACE OF ORIGIN

To find records from the old country, you will need to know where your family lived. Knowing just the name of a province or nearby large city (Warsaw, Kraków, Prague, Prešov, etc.) isn't enough because repositories file records by locality. Many American researchers proceed under the illusion that an archivist in Poland, the Czech Republic, or Slovakia can tell them where their ancestor was born. It's pretty simple: If you don't have the exact birthplace of your ancestor, you can't successfully research records from Poland, the Czech Republic, or Slovakia.

	PLACE OF ABODE			NAME	RELATION	HOME DATA				PERSONAL DESCRIPTION					EDUCATION		PLACE OF BIRTH	
				of each person whose *place of abode* on April 1, 1930, was in this family. Enter surname first, then the given name and middle initial, if any. Include every person living on April 1, 1930. Omit children born since April 1, 1930	Relationship of this person to the head of the family							Age at last birthday	Marital condition	Age at first marriage			Place of birth of each person enumerated and of his or her parents. If born in the United States, give State or Territory. If of foreign birth, give country in which birthplace is now situated. (See Instructions.) Distinguish Canada-French from Canada-English, and Irish Free State from Northern Ireland	
	Street, avenue, road, etc.	House number (in cities and towns)	Number of dwelling house in order of visitation	Number of family in order of visitation			Home owned or rented	Value of home, if owned, or monthly rental, if rented	Radio set	Does this family live on a farm?	Sex	Color or race				Attended school or college since Sept. 1, 1929	Whether able to read and write	PERSON	FATHER
1	2	3	4	5	6	7	8	9	10	11	12	13	14	15	16	17	18	19
	32	144	144	Rose, John	son				no	m	W	11	S		yes	yes	Connecticut	Tennessee
			8	—, Kedina	daughter				v	f	W	9	S		yes		Connecticut	Tennessee
				—, Thomas V.	son				v	m	W	8	S		yes		Connecticut	Tennessee
				—, Robert	son				v	m	W	5½	S		no		Connecticut	Tennessee
				—, Charles	son				v	m	W	3¾	S		no		Connecticut	Tennessee
				—, George	son				v	m	W	1½	S		no		Connecticut	Tennessee
	34	55	145	Figlar, John	head	O	3500	A	no	m	W	44	m	25	no	yes	Czechoslovakia	Czechoslovakia
				—, Caroline	wife—n				v	f	W	43	m	24	no	yes	Czechoslovakia	Czechoslovakia
				—, Joseph	son				v	m	W	21	S		no	yes	Connecticut	Czechoslovakia
				—, John	son				v	m	W	20	S		no	yes	Connecticut	Czechoslovakia

The 1930 census gives John Figlar's birthplace as Czechoslovakia. Census records provide a country of birth, but generally not a town.

How do you get it? You'll be looking for this information in a variety of records. Just remember: When it comes to pinpointing an ancestor's birthplace, not all records are created equal. See the Sources for Town of Origin sidebar. Note that some of your ancestors may have listed their town of origin as a big city for convenience. Just as someone might list his hometown as Pittsburgh rather than his actual hometown of McKeesport since more people know where Pittsburgh is, your ancestor may have used a larger, more recognizable city as a point of reference.

TRACKING IMMIGRANTS IN US SOURCES

Before attempting to trace Polish, Czech, or Slovak ancestry abroad, exhaust all US sources first. This will help you find the right people overseas. Here, we'll review the most important records and the immigration clues they contain. The *Family Tree Magazine* Records Checklist, downloadable from **<www.familytreemagazine.com/upload/images/PDF/recordschecklist.pdf>**, provides a handy roster to ensure you've checked all available sources.

Censuses

You'll find many clues to help you identify immigrants in US census records, taken every ten years by the federal government. Censuses from 1790 to 1940 are publicly available (except 1890, of which only fragments survive) on websites including Ancestry.com, FamilySearch.org, and Mocavo **<www.mocavo.com>**. Enumerations through 1840 list only heads of household by name; from 1850 on, they name every member of a household. For Polish, Czech, or Slovak immigrants, the best data come from 1900 onward (see the Immigration Clues in US Censuses sidebar).

Sources for Town of Origin

This chart outlines US sources that might name your ancestor's town of origin, grouped from highest probability of giving a specific town name to least. While you should seek out all these records for your immigrant ancestor, use this table to prioritize your search and set expectations.

Best Bets

Source	Examples	Tips
Family members (especially older generations)	parents, aunts, uncles, cousins, grandparents	Ask about family lore and documents, as well as interviews recorded with other relatives.
Family documents	Bibles, photos, correspondence	Look particularly for foreign-language documents, which are more likely to have accurate place-name spellings than are American records.
Newspapers	obituaries, articles about achievements and celebrations	Ethnic newspapers in immigrants' native tongue are most likely to contain accurate place of origin names.
Church records	baptism, marriage, and burial documents	Vital records are most likely to name towns of origin.
Fraternal organizations	Czech-Slovak Protective Society, First Catholic Slovak Union of America (Jednota), Polish National Alliance	Consult the Balch Institute <www2.hsp.org/collections/Balch manuscript_guide/html/contents.html> and the Immigration History Research Center <www.ihrc.umn.edu>.
Naturalization records	declarations of intention, petitions for naturalization	Citizenship papers may be in different towns, and in any court of record (probate, common pleas, etc.). Naturalizations from 1906 on are most likely to contain ancestral town information.

In general, census records provide only a country of origin. During the 1800s and until after World War I, this would be Austria for Czechs and either Austria or Hungary for Slovaks. For Polish researchers, the country in the census tells you whether the family came from German, Russian, or Austrian Poland (see chapter 4 for more on the partitions of Poland).

For example, the 1930 census record of the John Figlar family shows John's birthplace as Czechoslovakia and his immigration year as 1921, giving a time frame to search for his passenger arrival list (image **A**).

Hit or Miss

Source	Examples	Tips
Civil vital records	birth, marriage, and death certificates	Here, you might find another jurisdiction that will help you.
Cemetery records	headstone inscriptions, plot cards	Many tombstones list a town of origin and/or have a picture of the deceased, plus inscriptions.
Social Security records	application, or SS-5 form	An SS-5 nearly always lists the applicant's birthplace.
Probate files	wills, estate papers	Read between the lines to get a sense for family dynamics.
Land records	deeds, property transfers, tax records, land patents	Many Polish and Czech immigrants sought to own land, so check for federal homestead records.
Local histories	commemorative county history books	Early volumes often give lists of settlers, sometimes including the place of origin.
Passenger lists	customs lists and passenger arrival lists for various US ports	Lists after 1900 show town of origin, next of kin in Europe, and destination.
Military records	Civil War pensions, WWI and WWII draft registrations	Draft cards typically give birthplace, while pensions give just birth (and marriage) date.

Long Shots

Source	Examples	Tips
US censuses	decennial schedules ten years from 1790 to 1940 (except 1890)	For Czechs and Slovaks, country of origin is often Austria or Austria-Hungary; for Poles, often Austria, Prussia, or Russia.
Directories	city directories, business directories	Search each year for the relevant period. Check ads as well as listings.

Sometimes you'll get a more specific location—for example, Ruthenia instead of Austria or Hungary (indicating possible Carpatho-Rusyn ancestry). Rarely will the census list an ancestral village.

When using censuses, keep in mind that your Polish, Czech, or Slovak ancestors likely spoke limited English and, in general, were suspicious or fearful of government officials—in Europe, a visit from a government representative might involve collecting more money for taxes or conscripting young men into the army for up to twenty-five years. If the person lied or made up the information, the census taker had no way of knowing. If a family was not home when the enumerator arrived, it was not unusual for a neighbor to

Immigration Clues in US Censuses

Here's a brief summary by census year of the columns that can clue you in to immigrant origins.

Census	Clues
1840	country of birth
1850	country of birth
1860	country of birth
1870	checkmarks for foreign-born parents, men ineligible to vote (potential clue to a non-naturalized immigrant, as only male citizens 21 or older could vote)
1880	birthplace, parents' birthplaces
1900	birthplace, parents' birthplaces, citizenship status (if over 21), immigration year, years in the United States
1910	immigration year, parents' birthplaces, naturalization status
1920	immigration year, year naturalized, person's and parents' mother tongues; parents' birthplaces
1930	immigration year, language spoken in home, parents' birthplaces
1940	birthplace, citizenship of foreign-born, residence in 1935; mother tongue and parents' birthplaces on supplemental schedule answered by random 5 percent of population

provide information. Therefore, mistakes and misinformation were not uncommon. Use the census to establish a sense of place for your family and focus your search for other sources, such as immigration and naturalization records.

Naturalization Records

If your ancestor became a US citizen, the resulting records are a place to glean clues about his origins. Most Polish, Czech, and Slovak immigrants would have followed a two-step process: filing a declaration of intention to become a citizen (first papers), then once residency requirements had been met, filing a petition for naturalization. Your ancestor could go to any courthouse—municipal, county, state, or federal—to file and could even start the process in one court and finish it in another. So you'll want to check records from all courts near where your immigrant arrived or settled.

Starting in 1906, the federal government standardized naturalization paperwork. Declarations of intention (image **B**) contain these critical immigration details:

- port of departure
- vessel

A declaration of intention contains information about an ancestor's origins, including hometown.

- date and port of arrival
- last foreign residence
- citizenship

Petitions for naturalization (image **C**) contain similar immigration information. They lack the last foreign residence, but add these helpful tidbits:

- date of emigration
- name changes
- spouse's and children's birthplaces

Ancestry.com, FamilySearch.org, and Fold3 <**www.fold3.com**> offer some digitized and searchable naturalization records. The easiest way to locate online records from

A petition of naturalization, issued once your ancestor had met certain requirements, also contains valuable information.

your ancestor's locality is via Online Searchable Naturalization Indexes and Records <www.germanroots.com/naturalization.html>, which has links organized by state. Many more naturalization records have been microfilmed; you can access those via local FamilySearch Centers and (for federal courts) the U.S. National Archives and Records Administration (NARA) regional facilities. Failing that, try city, county, regional, and state archives. Naturalizations made in municipal courts might be in the town halls or city archives of major cities such as Baltimore, Chicago, and St. Louis. You can request post-

Coming to America

When your ancestor decided to leave the old country, he usually bought his passage from a local transportation agent or received a ticket from a contact in America. Most immigrants sold their personal effects and livestock or borrowed from the local moneylender to raise the necessary funds. After 1880, steamship travel was the common mode of transportation, and most Polish, Czech, and Slovak immigrants sailed from a German port—usually Hamburg or Bremen—on the most popular lines: the North German Line and Hamburg-American Line.

It's worth looking for a record of your ancestor's departure as well as his arrival. You can access Hamburg's passenger departure lists from 1850 to 1934 on Ancestry.com and FamilySearch microfilm. Unfortunately, Bremen's passenger lists were destroyed, except for 1920 to 1939 (search those **<www.passengerlists.de>**).

The voyage might have included a stopover at another port, such as Liverpool or Southampton. If that's the case, you'll need to look for your ancestor on "indirect" departure lists. You also might find your ancestor in Findmypast's subscription database of twenty-four million outbound passenger lists from British ports covering 1890 to 1960 **<search.findmypast.com/search-world-records/passenger-lists-leaving-uk-1890-1960>**.

1906 naturalization documents from U.S. Citizenship and Immigration Services (USCIS) **<www.uscis.gov/genealogy>** for a fee, but expect a long wait time.

Immigration Records

Polish, Czech, and Slovak immigrants entered America through various ports, especially New York (at Castle Garden starting in 1855 and Ellis Island from 1892), Baltimore, Boston, and Philadelphia. Beginning in 1820, the federal government supplied preprinted manifests to document passengers on US-bound ships. These were called customs lists until 1891, then passenger-arrival lists after (image **D**). The volume of information collected on passenger lists increased over time, meaning records for late nineteenth- and early twentieth-century Polish, Czech, and Slovak immigrants will be the most detailed.

NARA has microfilmed passenger lists from all US ports in its custody, including these common Eastern European entry points:

- New York: 1820–1957
- Baltimore: 1820–1952
- Boston: 1820–1943
- Philadelphia: 1800–1945
- New Orleans: 1820–1945
- Galveston: 1846–1948

U.S. DEPARTMENT OF LABOR
IMMIGRATION SERVICE

List **14**

LIST OR MANIFEST OF ALIEN PASSENGERS FOR THE UNITED

ALL ALIENS arriving at a port of continental United States from a foreign port or a port of the insular possessions of the United States, and all aliens arriving at a port of said insular possession from a foreign port, a port of continental United
This (white) sheet is for the listing of

S.S. **"FRANCE"** Passengers sailing from **LE HAVRE** , **JUN 1 2 1920** , 191_

HEAD-TAX STATUS	Family name	Given name	Age Yrs. Mos.	Sex	Married or single	Calling or occupation	Able to— Read / what language / Write	Nationality (Country of which citizen or subject.)	Race or people.	Last permanent residence Country / City or town.	The name and complete address of nearest relative or friend in country whence alien came.	Final destination State / City or town.
ADMITTED	MARKOVIC	Apolina	20	F	S	—	yes	Slovakia	Slovak	Slovakia / SEKULE	mother Mrs Markovic Katarina at SEKULE	Ohio / BELLAIRE
	SENKO	Andrejova	30	F	M	housewife				/ WELKOVAC	mother Mrs Erza Terko at WELKOVAC	/ YOUNGSTOWN
	FRUSAK	Alberta	22	F	S	—				/ HRUBAR	relative Mr Frusak Janos at HRUBAR	Pa. / BAGOLEY
	SCHLESINGER	Rudolph	40	M	S	workman				/ VLOKOVICA	father Mr Schlesinger Ferdinand at VLOKOVICA	Mich. / MICHIGAN
	ILLUBUCEK	Theodor	19	M	S	employe				/ ZAMBERK	mother Mrs Illubucek Marie at ZAMBERK	Iowa / CEDARS RAPIDS
	MENNERD	Anna	17	F	S	maid				/ BARCI	relative Mr Istvan Mennerd at BARCI	Pa. / TRAFFORD
ADMITTED	BUTALA	Elisabeth	11	F	S	none				/ HRUBOVCE	aunt Mrs Butala Anda at HRUBOVCE	
ADMITTED	—	Anna	20	F	S	maid	yes	Slovak	yes			
	BERKA	Rosalie	22	F	S	—				/ HOLU	relative Mrs Berka Sefana at HOLU	N.J. / BINGHAMTON
	—	Berko	19	M	S	workman						
	—	John	16	M	S	—					relative Mr Vavra Stefan at	

Passenger lists, though filled out at ports of departure, sometimes contain an ancestor's place of origin.

All of the NARA-held passenger lists are available on microfilm via FamilySearch, as well as searchable and digitized on Ancestry.com. For the port of New York, also try <www.libertyellisfoundation.org> and <www.castlegarden.org>. Steve Morse's One-Step Webpages site <www.stevemorse.org> offers additional flexibility for tapping those online passenger list databases, allowing you to search phonetically, by town, and more. It's a good tool to try when you struggle on the hosting sites (note that you still need a subscription to view results on pay sites). When names are misspelled or mistranscribed, searching by village might be the only way to locate your immigrant ancestor.

Vital Records

Vital records, of course, are the building blocks of all genealogical research. When identifying and researching a Polish, Czech, or Slovak immigrant, these are the key details to look for in government-issued vital records:

- **death records:** These focus on birthplace, maiden name, parents' names, informant's name, and burial location. Some death records tell the parents' birthplaces. A good starting point to locate death records is Joe Beine's Online Searchable Death Indexes <www.deathindexes.com>.

- **marriage records:** Pay attention to the place of birth. Marriage records sometimes give the names of the bride's and groom's parents, providing clues for further

Probe for Passport Applications

If your Polish, Czech, or Slovak ancestor traveled back to the old country during one of the periods in which passports were required, you may find his application. Ancestry.com has a searchable online database of US Passport Applications, 1795–1925 **<search.ancestry.com/search/ db.aspx?dbid=1174>**.

research. Again, Joe Beine's Online Birth & Marriage Records Indexes for the USA site **<www.germanroots.com/vitalrecords.html>** is a useful place to begin.

- **birth records:** Look for information about a child's parents—these records sometimes state where the parents were born. Because these records were created by Americans who may have been unfamiliar with an immigrant's homeland, be aware that misspellings and other errors are common.

In addition to government vital records, look for church baptismal, marriage, and burial records. These often have more details than their civil counterparts because the priest, minister, or secretary knew the family. And because immigrant communities often had their own churches, knowing the church your ancestors attended might hint at where your family came from. Many US Polish, Czech, and Slovak parishes scrupulously recorded their parishioners' exact places of origins in marriage records and on the American-born children's baptismal certificates. The US parish is usually one of the best places to secure a geographical link to your European place of origin.

Polish immigrants were predominantly Roman Catholic, and their US parishes often recorded baptisms and other documents in Latin. For marriages, the Catholic Church might have granted a dispensation for an underage or mixed-religion relationship. Dispensations are kept in diocese archives. Remember that godparents usually were relatives and might come from the same village as your ancestors.

You'll need to contact a church or diocese directly to inquire about its records. Search Google by parish name and locality or use an online directory such as USA Churches **<www.usachurches.org>**. If you're unsure of your ancestors' place of worship, look in city directories for possible parishes. When approaching a parish for records, remember that sacramental records aren't necessarily public—it's at the priest's discretion to allow access. Be prepared to make a donation to the church in honor of your ancestors, but do not offer to pay the priest—a subtle but important distinction.

Newspapers

Obituaries, especially those published in the first half of the twentieth century, often give an immigrant's place of birth—though beware misspellings from survivors who report the information. Numerous websites offer online access to obituaries, including Genealogy-Bank <www.genealogybank.com> (subscription required), Legacy.com <www.legacy.com>, Obituary Central <www.obitcentral.com>, Obituary Daily Times <obits.rootsweb.ancestry.com>, USGenWeb Archives Obituary Project <www.usgwarchives.net/obits>, and USGenWeb Archives <searches.rootsweb.ancestry.com/htdig/search.html>. The Polish Genealogical Society of America <www.pgsa.org> has the death notice indexes from *Dziennik Chicagoski*, Chicago's Polish daily newspaper, and Baltimore's *Jedność-Polonia*. The First Catholic Slovak Union publishes obituaries in its Jednota newspaper. Use Chronicling America <chroniclingamerica.loc.gov/newspapers> to identify other newspapers published in your ancestors' area that you can access on microfilm.

Join the FAN Club

If you feel you've exhausted all the potential records and are still having trouble finding your immigrant ancestor, try the collateral and cluster approach introduced in chapter 2. This is also called the "FAN club principle" because it involves researching the "Friends, Associates, and Neighbors" of your immigrant ancestor. Pay special attention to the FANs listed here.

Friends

- executors in wills
- guardians of a decedent's children
- people who sponsor each other's children in baptism
- witnesses to an ancestor's naturalization

Associates

- people arriving on the same immigrant ship
- buyers named in estate sales
- people found together on membership rosters of churches or fraternal organizations
- people who worked closely with your ancestors
- witnesses to wills and deeds

Neighbors

- people found next to each other in censuses
- people listed in reverse city directories at adjoining addresses
- people next to each other on nonalphabetized tax lists

Your ancestor's application to an ethnic fraternal organization in the United States can provide information about where your ancestors hail from.

While it's tempting to focus on obituaries for immigration information, don't stop there. You may find mention of a village in articles about your ancestors or their businesses, articles about family reunions recounting history back to the boat, and genealogy columns. Again, use Chronicling America to identify target papers, then see if you can access them on GenealogyBank, Newspapers.com <www.newspapers.com>, Google News Archive <news.google.com/newspapers>, or Elephind <www.elephind.com> before seeking out microfilms.

Also, don't forget about foreign-language and ethnic-focused newspapers, which can help with tracing an immigrant's origins. Two excellent repositories for these are the Balch Institute, located at the Historical Society of Pennsylvania in Philadelphia <www.hsp.org>, and the Immigration History Research Center, located at the University of Minnesota in Minneapolis <www.umn.edu/ihrc>.

Fraternal Organization Records

Many Polish, Czech, and Slovak immigrants started their own fraternal benefit societies and social clubs to help preserve their heritage and to provide insurance in the event of the family breadwinner's death or serious injury. Perhaps your ancestor belonged to the Polish National Alliance, the Polish Falcons of America, the First Catholic Slovak Union of America, the Czech Catholic Union, the National Slovak Society, Sokol, or another organization. You can find a complete list of fraternal organizations at <www.exonumia.com/art/society.htm>. Organizations' records might include membership applications (image **E**), death benefit claim forms, and meeting minutes. Many fraternal organizations published member updates in newsletters, and some even established their own printing presses for publishing newspapers. If the group still exists, contact the local chapter or the national office to ask about historical records. Some organizations have turned over records to research repositories. See appendix H for a list of some of these societies.

WHAT IF YOU STILL CAN'T FIND THE VILLAGE?

Despite all these research possibilities, not every ancestor left an adequate breadcrumb trail to a village of origin. In some cases, you'll have information on a county or district name, but no village within that area. Depending on the size of that jurisdiction and the time you can put into the project, you might be able to sift through all of the church records for the particular locality. While that might require a lot of work, the payoff is big; with your immigrant ancestor's original name and hometown, you're able to travel back in time to the old country to look for his records in Europe.

KEYS TO SUCCESS

* Identify your Polish, Czech or Slovak immigrant's original name (the way it was spelled in the old country) and hometown (usually not a big city). These are the two most critical pieces of information you will need to successfully trace your family in Eastern Europe.

* Forget modern spelling conventions. The way your family's name is spelled today is likely not how your Polish, Czech, or Slovak immigrant ancestor spelled it in the old country. Make a list of all potential alternate spellings and variations for first names and surnames to plug into online databases and indexes.

* Check all US ports (not just Ellis Island) for your immigrant ancestor's arrival record, and see if you can find a departure record as well.

* Exhaust all US sources about your immigrant ancestor before trying to cross the Atlantic in your research. Building a complete picture of his life after immigration will help you trace the right people in foreign records.

POLISH, CZECH, AND SLOVAK NAME VARIANTS WORKSHEET

List at least two and as many as four Polish, Czech, or Slovak names you're researching. For each name, come up with as many spelling variants as possible, taking into account phonetics, "translation" into English, and possible transcription errors.

Surname	
Phonetic variants	
Possible "translations" into English	
Other spellings or variations	
Suffixes for women*	

Surname	
Phonetic variants	
Possible "translations" into English	
Other spellings or variations	
Suffixes for women*	

Surname	
Phonetic variants	
Possible "translations" into English	
Other spellings or variations	
Suffixes for women*	

Surname	
Phonetic variants	
Possible "translations" into English	
Other spellings or variations	
Suffixes for women*	

* Czech/Slovak: *–ova*
  Polish: *–ówna* or *–'anka* (unmarried women), *–owa* (married) or *–'ina/–'yna* (widowed)

4

The History of Poland

Poland is an Eastern European nation with a complex and troubled history, stretching back more than a thousand years. With no natural borders from which to protect its lands, Poland has long been plagued by political upheavals, wars, and a changing state of independence.

As a result, tracing Polish ancestry can be challenging—especially since Poland did not officially exist as a country for 123 years. The fact that Poland's external and internal borders changed frequently complicates the research process. In this chapter, we'll discuss the geographic and political changes Poland has experienced and how this affected your ancestors.

GETTING TO KNOW POLAND

The country's name derives from an agricultural Slavic tribe called the Polanie who settled in what's now Poland. According to legend, Mieszko I founded Poland in 966 A.D. The territory flourished in the fifteenth and sixteenth centuries as the Polish-Lithuanian Union, a political entity resulting from Queen Jadwiga's marriage to Władysław II Jagiełło of Lithuania in 1386. Poland and Lithuania formally united in 1569, forming the *Rzeczpospolita* or Commonwealth (known to history as the Polish-Lithuanian Commonwealth, shown at its height in image **A**). The state soon encompassed various ethnic

At its height of power, the Polish-Lithuanian Commonwealth encompassed territories now in Ukraine, Belarus, Russia, and the Baltic States.

groups, including Jews, Tartars, Armenians, Germans, Ukrainians, Lithuanians, White Ruthenians (Belarusians), and Czechs.

In the 1700s, however, Poland's three powerful neighbors—Austria, Prussia and Russia—carved up the *Rzeczpospolita* into the three Partitions of Poland between 1772 and 1795. From this time, the region was subjected to the rules of its governing powers, so learning about the record-keeping conventions of the Austrian, Prussian, and Russian empires during this period will aid your research. You'll learn more about the Partitions of Poland later in this chapter.

Foreign occupation of Polish lands affected both the legal and ethnic identities of Poles. While rising nation-states such as France had time to assimilate non-French ethnic groups into their population and develop a strong sense of nationalism, Poland was dismantled before this could occur. Instead, people more strongly identified with their individual ethnic groups than they did with a larger Polish identity. This ethnic identification even carried over to the New World. When Polish immigrants arrived in the United States in the

POLAND Fast Facts

OFFICIAL NAME: Rzeczpospolita Polska (Republic of Poland)

SHORT NAME: Polska

CAPITAL CITY: Warszawa (Warsaw)

AREA: 120,728 square miles

BORDERING COUNTRIES: Germany, Czech Republic, Slovak Republic, Ukraine, Belarus, Lithuania, Russia

OFFICIAL LANGUAGE: Polish

POPULATION: 38.5 million

MAJOR ETHNIC GROUPS: Polish, German, Ukrainian, Lithuanian

MAJOR RELIGIONS: Roman Catholicism, Orthodoxy, Lutheranism, Judaism

Poland today is a fraction of the size of its predecessor at its height in the fourteenth century.

late 1800s and early 1900s, they usually settled and associated with fellow Jews, Orthodox Russians, or ethnic Germans. Immigrants who *did* identify as Poles in the United States were typically Roman Catholic ethnic Poles who spoke Polish.

Poland as it is today is smaller and lies much farther west than its fourteenth-century predecessor (see the Poland Fast Facts sidebar). This is the result of the two world wars. After World War I, treaties set Poland's borders to encompass areas with Polish ethnic majorities within the territory of the fourteenth-century *Rzeczpospolita*. Poland re-emerged as a large, independent nation with territory extending from the Poznan area in the west to the Wilno (Vilnius) area in the east. In the interwar period, Poland included significant parts of what are today Lithuania, Belarus, and western Ukraine.

Poland was invaded by Germany in 1939, beginning World War II. During the conflict, Russian and German offenses ravaged southern Poland and resulted in nearly six million Polish deaths, and the Holocaust decimated Poland's Jewish population. Roughly 90 percent of Polish Jews were deported to concentration camps and killed between 1939 and 1945.

Following the Nazis' defeat, Poland came under the jurisdiction of the Soviet Union as the communist People's Republic of Poland. Its borders were shifted westward so that Poland gained territory from Germany in the west and lost territory to Lithuania, Belarus, and Ukraine in the east. Germans fled west to the new Germany, and the Poles of Ukraine and Belarus fled west to the new Poland.

This chapter's timeline of Polish history and the website "A Brief History of Poland in the Last 200 Years" <www.donhoward.net/genpoland/polhistory.htm> provide a snapshot of key time periods and events. For genealogists, it's critical to understand history as it relates to the creation, storage, and availability of records, so this chapter will focus on those aspects. If you desire a more in-depth understanding of Poland's changing external and internal borders and the resulting administrative complexities, you will want to read books such as *God's Playground: A History of Poland, Volume II: 1795 to the Present*, second edition by Norman Davies (Columbia University Press, 2005), the Polish History Helps sidebar, and appendix I.

POLAND'S THREE PARTITIONS

As discussed earlier, Poland ceased to exist as an independent country for 123 years. Once an expansive and prosperous commonwealth, Poland entered a period of chaos and decline in the early 1700s, marked by conflicts over the monarchy, the nobility's resistance to relinquishing its privileges, an inefficient bureaucratic structure, and Russian inter-ference in Polish affairs. This set the stage for the bleak period of partition executed by Poland's powerful neighbors—Prussia, Russia, and Austria. The partitions lasted for more than a century and in essence wiped Poland from the map of Europe (see image **B**), and

TIMELINE Polish History

966 The Polish nation is born.

1569 The Polish Parliament (*Sejm*) unifies Poland and Lithuania into the Polish-Lithuanian Commonwealth.

1655-1660 Sweden invades Poland, resulting in the death of 40 percent of Poles.

1772 Russia, Prussia, and Austria seize 30 percent of Poland's territory in the First Partition of Poland.

1792 Russia and Prussia take more than half of Poland's remaining territory in the Second Partition of Poland.

1795 Russia, Prussia, and Austria carve up the remaining Polish territory in the Third Partition of Poland.

1803-1815 The Napoleonic Wars engulf Europe, leading to territorial bartering of partitioned, formerly Polish lands. Napoleon forms the Duchy of Warsaw out of Prussian Poland.

1806 Serfdom in Prussian Poland is abolished.

1848 Serfdom is abolished in the Austro-Hungarian Empire.

1854 A cholera epidemic ravages Galicia.

1861 Serfdom is abolished in Russia.

1868 Russian officials ban the Polish language for record-keeping purposes.

1870s Russia and Germany each attempt to eradicate Polish culture; Galician Poles in the Austrian partition retain some autonomy.

1874 Separate civil registration is introduced in Prussian Poland.

1880 Poles emigrate in massive numbers.

1914-1918 Poland becomes a major fighting ground in World War I. After the war, Poland gains independence.

1919-1921 Polish forces hold off the Red Army in the Polish-Soviet War.

1918-1939 The Second Polish Republic governs Poland; Józef Piłsudski makes himself dictator after a 1926 coup.

1939-1945 Germany invades Poland, triggering World War II. Many Poles, including 90 percent of the country's Jewish population, are deported to labor camps.

1945 The Soviet Union sweeps in from the east, driving out the Nazis and establishing the Polish People's Republic.

1946 Poland establishes universal civil registration.

1989 Communist rule in Poland ends.

1999 Poland joins NATO.

2004 Poland becomes a member of the European Union.

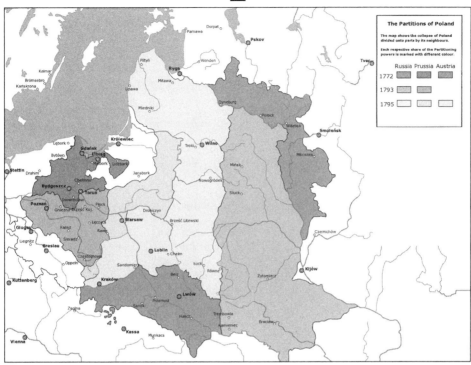

Russia, Prussia, and Austria carved up Poland's territory between themselves in the three Partitions of Poland (1772, 1793, and 1795). See **<upload.wikimedia.org/wikipedia/commons/3/30/Rzeczpospolita_Rozbiory_3.png>** for the original, zoomable image.

(even more confusingly) some areas in partitioned Poland changed hands between the occupying powers. Understanding the partitions will provide context for your genealogical search; you can learn more about each area's administrative divisions in chapter 6.

Prussian Partition (German Poland)

The Prussian partition (sometimes called Prussian Poland) refers to the former territories of the Polish-Lithuanian Commonwealth acquired by the Kingdom of Prussia, including

- East Prussia, known in German as *Ostpreußen* (the *ß* or "esset" might be replaced with a double *s*) and called *Prusy Wschodnie* in Polish

- West Prussia, referred to as *Westpreußen* in German and *Prusy Zachodnie* in Polish

- Posen, called *Provinz Posen* in German and *Prowincja Poznańska* in Polish

- Silesia, referred to as *Provinz Schlesien* in German and *Prowincja Śląsk* in Polish

In addition, part of the province of Pomerania (German: *Provinz Pommern*) became Poland's *Województwo Pomorskie* after World War II.

The Lands of Partitioned Poland

Polish researchers will quickly find that navigating the shifting borders within Eastern Europe is one of the most difficult aspects of ancestry research. More than one hundred years of Polish history were defined by the Three Partitions. Below is a table roughly showing what each occupying power received in each of the three partitions, as well as (for Austria and Prussia) how they were administered. See the Divisions of Partitioned Poland, 1772–1918 sidebar in chapter 6 for more.

	1772	1793	1795
Prussia	• Royal Prussia minus Gdańsk/Danzig and Toruń (*becoming West Prussia*) • northern Great Poland north of the Noteć River (*becoming the Netze District*)	• the cities of Gdańsk/Danzig and Toruń • the rest of Greater Poland (*becoming South Prussia*) • part of Mazovia (*becoming South Prussia*)	• the rest of Mazovia, including Warsaw (*becoming South Prussia and New Silesia*) • Lithuania west of the Neman River (*becoming New East Prussia*)
Russia	• all areas east of the Dvina and Dneiper rivers	• Lithuanian Belorussia • western Ukraine	• Courland • Lithuania east of the Neman River • the rest of Ukraine
Austria *(all land incorporated as New Galicia or the Kingdom of Galicia and Lodomeria)*	• Little Poland south of the Vistula River • Podolia west of the Zbruch River • Galicia	• n/a	• the rest of Little Poland

Russian Partition

When it acquired Polish territory during the Partitions, Russia organized its Polish lands by expanding or creating *guberniyas* (provinces). After the Congress of Vienna in 1815, Russian Poland was organized into the Kingdom of Poland, or Congress Poland. This territory was under Russian imperial rule from 1814 to 1915, with a population of 6.1 million in 1870 and 10 million in 1900. Ancestors might cite their place of birth as one of the larger cities in Russian Poland, such as Płock, Łomża, Białystok, Warszawa, or Lublin. But they are more likely to have come from villages or shtetls (small towns with a large Jewish population) such as Kuczbork-Osada, Posadow, or Iłża (*Driltsh* in Yiddish).

Austrian Partition (Galicia)

The historical region of Galicia was part of the Austro-Hungarian Empire, covering territory currently divided between southern Poland and Ukraine. The name changes slightly with the regional languages: *Galicja* in Polish, *Galician* in German, and *Galitzia* in Yiddish. Ethnic Polish ancestors coming from this region may be listed as Austrian, but the region was actually ethnically diverse, containing Poles, Ruthenians (Ukrainians), Germans, Armenians, Jews, Hungarians, and Romanians within its borders. If your ancestors came from this region, they might have listed their birthplace as a major city such as Lviv (Polish: *Lwów*, German: *Lemberg*), Kraków (German: *Krakau*, Yiddish: *Kruke*), or Przemyśl (Ukrainian: *Peremyshl*, German: *Promsel*). In most cases, immigrants were from outlying villages. Do not confuse this Galicia with a region of the same name located on the Iberian peninsula in Spain.

LOCAL HISTORIES

In addition to the history of the wider Polish region, you'll also want to delve into the details of your ancestral locality. Local histories are some of the most valuable—and most often overlooked—sources for this purpose. In them, you usually will find details about the area's settlement and the founding of churches, schools, and businesses. They often include lists of citizens, soldiers, and civil officials. Even if your ancestor is not listed, you could come across clues about your ancestor or information about additional records to research. Local histories can also help you understand your family's lifestyle, environment, and relationship to the community your ancestors lived in.

While published local histories for Polish towns and regions are relatively rare, it's worth conducting a careful search for any available resources. Try these tactics:

- Perform a search of the FamilySearch Catalog **<www.familysearch.org>** for published national, provincial, and local histories for Poland. Search for the locality in the Place field, and look for a History catalog heading (as in *Poland, Warszawa–History*).

- Perform a Google Search for the town or village. Don't forget the Polish version of Google **<www.google.pl>**; you can use the Chrome browser **<google.com/chrome>** to automatically translate websites when no English versions are available.

- Search Google Books **<books.google.com>**, the Internet Archive **<www.archive.org>**, and JSTOR **<www.jstor.org>**.

- Check libraries and repositories with Polish ethnic collections (see the Polish History Helps sidebar).

- Contact the village mayor (use e-mail whenever possible, but don't rule out postal mail for rural areas) to see if histories are available for your town.

- Search Facebook <www.facebook.com> for town and village pages and YouTube <www.youtube.com> for video histories.

See chapter 11 for more on miscellaneous printed records such as local histories.

AT-A-GLANCE: KEY EVENTS INFLUENCING POLISH HISTORY

Poland's tumultuous history will color every aspect of your genealogical research, beginning with your family's arrival in America. The majority of Poles journeyed to the New World during the time Austria, Prussia, or Russia ruled their homeland. Immigrants began coming from Prussian-occupied areas in 1848, and by the 1880s, the Austrian-governed province of Galicia and the Russian Empire were supplying a steady stream of Polish emigrants.

The influx peaked between 1880 and 1910, during America's "great wave" of immigration: An estimated three million Poles arrived in the United States by 1910. If your ancestors were among those immigrants, they didn't officially come from Poland but from one of those other three nations—a fact to keep in mind as you research in immigration records. Because Poland's territory shrank over time, it's also possible your Polish forebears came from an area that's outside the modern nation's borders.

Keeping track of all that border shifting can be confusing, especially if you are just starting out with your Polish family tree. In addition to the three partitions of Poland

Ethnic Polish Collections in the United States

Because of the numerous Polish settlements that blossomed in the United States, you should check for resources relating to Polish-American histories, traditions, and communities at libraries and other repositories with large Polish collections, including

- the Balch Institute for Ethnic Studies in Philadelphia <www.philadelphiahistory.org/node/112>
- Central Connecticut State University <www.ccsu.edu>
- the Immigrant History Research Center (IHRC) at the University of Minnesota <www.ihrc.umn.edu>
- the New York Public Library's Slavic and Baltic Division <www.nypl.org>
- the Polish Library in Washington <www.polishlibrary.org/links.htm>
- the Polonica Americana Research Institute <www.polishmission.com/genealogy/polonica-americana-research-institute>
- the University of Pittsburgh <www.pitt.edu>

Polish History Helps

Want to read up on details of Poland's complex history? Consult these helpful books. Use WorldCat **<www.worldcat.org>** to find a holding library so you can request them on interlibrary loan.

- *An Outline History of Poland* by Jerzy Topolski (Interpress Publishers, 1986)
- *History of Poland* by Aleksander Gieysztor (Polish Scientific Publishers, 1979)
- *The History of Poland Since 1863* edited by R.F. Leslie (Cambridge University Press, 1980)
- *The Lands of Partitioned Poland, 1795–1918* by Piotr S. Wandycz (University of Washington Press, 1975)

(1772, 1792, and 1795), the key changes you will need to understand to be successful with your genealogical research are

- **the Congress of Vienna (1815):** At the end of the Napoleonic Wars, the Congress of Vienna divided Napoleon's Duchy of Warsaw and established clear territorial boundaries that changed little until the end of World War I. The borders established at this time likely reflect the divisions of Europe during your ancestor's immigration from his homeland.

- **the end of World War I (1918):** Europe's borders were redrawn, and several of Eastern Europe's many ethnic groups gained independent nation status. Poland re-appeared as a republic.

- **World War II (1939–1945):** During the war, borders within the Axis area changed again. The borders of Eastern Europe were extensively redrawn at the war's end.

KEYS TO SUCCESS

✳ Study Polish history (and the history of Eastern Europe) to understand records from the old country and learn more about your ancestors' lives.

✳ Determine what country or state your ancestor's hometown would have belonged to during a particular time period (e.g., did your ancestor come from the Russian, Prussian, or Austrian partition?).

✳ Seek out Polish local histories and resources in ethnic collections stateside to gain a better understanding of the community your ancestors lived in.

POLISH PARTITION TRACKER WORKSHEET

List the town/village names you uncovered during your research in US sources. Note whether the town/village was within the Russian, Austrian, or Prussian partition. If you don't know or are unsure, note that and your plan to identify its location.

Ancestor's Name	Immigration Year	Town/Village Name	Partition	Notes/Next Steps

5

The History of the
Czech and Slovak Republics

The modern Czech and Slovak republics formed only recently; before their amicable "Velvet Divorce" in 1993, these neighboring states existed as a single country, Czechoslovakia.

But don't let that seventy-five-year union fool you into grouping Czechs and Slovaks into one, all-encompassing nationality. Though both groups have Slavic origins and similar languages, historical circumstances led them to develop distinct cultural identities.

The republics' location in the geographical center of Europe—bordered by present-day Germany to the west, Poland to the north, Ukraine and Romania to the east, and Austria and Hungary to the south—put them at the crossroads of expanding empires. For centuries, each country separately endured the turmoil of invasions, religious conflicts, and foreign rulers' attempts to erase their cultures. Today's Slovak Republic corresponds to the centuries-old region of Slovakia, while the Czech Republic has its roots in the ancient kingdoms of Bohemia and Moravia. Those three areas were united as Great Moravia in the ninth century, but evolved into separate regions after that empire collapsed.

The complete saga of the Czechs and Slovaks is quite complicated and detailed, but every family historian should know the key events in the region's history. In this chapter we will cover enough of that history for you to properly trace your Czech or Slovak ancestry.

GETTING TO KNOW THE CZECH REPUBLIC

Czech refers to the Czech-speaking inhabitants of the Czech Republic (*Česká republika*). The Czech Republic (see the Czech Republic Fast Facts sidebar) has its roots in the ancient kingdoms of Bohemia (the Western part) and Moravia (the Eastern part), collectively known as the "Czech lands." Northern Moravia also includes Silesia (*Slezsko*), a historical region that lies mostly in southwestern Poland. In the 1800s, the ethnic compo-

CZECH REPUBLIC Fast Facts

OFFICIAL NAME: Ceska Republika (Czech Republic)

CAPITAL CITY: Praha (Prague)

AREA: 49,005 square miles

BORDERING COUNTRIES: Austria, Germany, Poland, Slovakia

OFFICIAL LANGUAGE: Czech

POPULATION: 10 million

MAJOR ETHNIC GROUPS: Czech, Moravian, Slovak

MAJOR RELIGIONS: Catholicism

The historical provinces of Bohemia and Moravia became the present-day Czech Republic. The Czech lands were under Austrian control until the formation of Czechoslovakia.

sition of the Czech lands was predominantly Czech or German. The Silesians (*Slezané*) mostly maintain their ethnic identity but are often considered a subset within the Czech culture. For centuries, the country was known as Bohemia.

Historical Overview: Pre-World War I

Because of its position at the crossroads of central Europe, the present-day Czech Republic has been influenced by a number of different ethnic groups throughout its history. It's believed that a group of Celtic people first inhabited the area from circa 500 B.C. until the first century A.D. Their leader was named Boiohemus, and ancient historians called his land *Boiohaemum*—in English, Bohemia. Germanic and then Slavic tribes moved in over the next few centuries, intermingling.

Bohemia eventually became a part of the Holy Roman Empire. Later, Charles IV (Wenceslas), a member of the Luxembourg dynasty, came to power. He founded the first university in Eastern Europe, the University of Prague (Charles University). Charles' popularity earned him the moniker "father of the country." While King of Bohemia, he was also simultaneously made Holy Roman Emperor.

Following the Protestant Reformation, many kings and nobles in the Czech lands practiced Protestantism, but a Catholic family from Austria, the Habsburgs, began ruling in 1526. In 1618, Protestant Czech nobles rebelled against the Habsburgs and triggered the Thirty Years' War (1618–1648), a Europe-wide religious war between Catholics and Protestants. The Habsburgs forcibly put down the Protestants and brought them under Habsburg control, killing or exiling many, seizing their land, and destroying their records. Eventually, this counter-reformation, or re-Catholicization, saw the Czech lands turn back almost completely to Catholicism. (Catholicism would remain the dominant religion until World War II.)

Later, Empress Maria Theresa (1717–1780) launched a reform of the entire empire with a view to centralize the state as well as modernize the kingdom and bring it forward to western European monarchies. These reforms followed many of the Enlightenment ideas that were disseminated in Europe from France, including the Education Ratio, a scheme for organizing education that took place in 1777.

After Maria Theresa's death, the throne passed on to her son Joseph II, who followed his mother's guidance in the spirit of the Enlightenment. His most important reforms were the Patent of Toleration in 1781, which alleged civil equality for all members of the Christian faith, and the abolition of serfdom in 1785. Other reforms contributed to modern state administration, tax and transportation systems, and schools.

From 1804 to 1867, the lands of the Habsburg monarchy were formally unified as the Austrian Empire. A long period of unrest led Austria and Hungary to form a dual monarchy in 1867. Administratively, Bohemia, Moravia, and Silesia were provinces of Austria, while Slovakia remained under Hungarian control. This arrangement remained in place until the end of World War I, when Austria-Hungary was dissolved.

GETTING TO KNOW SLOVAKIA

The word *Slovak* derives from an old term for Slav: *Slovan*. Today's Slovak Republic (see the Slovakia Fast Facts sidebar) corresponds to the centuries-old region of Slovakia (or *Slovensko*, as it's referred to locally). Slovaks share a common culture despite regional (eastern, central, and western) and local differences in dialect, customs, and religion.

The Slovak territories were historically cut off from economic development by the Carpathian mountain range and by the political border between Austria and Hungary. This made it tough for the Slovak people because they were tied to the Czech lands by language and culture but were bound politically to the Hungarian government. Policies aimed at imposing or maintaining the dominance of Hungarian language and culture—commonly referred to as Magyarization—were established.

Historical Overview: Pre-World War I

Beginning with the rise of the Samo Empire through Great Moravia, the Turkish invasion, Magyarization, and communism—and even until its separation from the Czech Republic in 1993—Slovakia historically struggled to be recognized as a nation-state.

The earliest evidence of people living in Slovakia comes from a Neanderthal skull molding found in the village of Gánovce that dates back around two hundred thousand years. Other archaeological discoveries indicate that Celtic tribes came to Slovakia at the beginning of the Iron Age, and the Romans invaded the region in 6 A.D. Following the fall of the Roman Empire, the region that is now Slovakia was raided by various tribes, including the Huns, the Lombards, the Avars, and the Germanic Goths.

While it is anyone's guess when the Slavs (the true ancestors of the Slovaks) first came to Slovakia, it was clear they had become the dominant race by the seventh century. The Samo Empire (623–665) was the first organized community of Slavs in the region that is now Slovakia, but Magyar (Hungarian) tribes eventually made their way into Slovakia. In the year 1000, Slovakia became a part of the Hungarian state. Invasions by the Tartars in 1241 and the Turks in 1530 followed.

After a Turkish victory at the 1526 Battle of Mohács, the Kingdom of Hungary was soundly defeated and subsequently divided into three separate parts: the territory that is present-day Hungary (under Turkish rule), Transylvania (a Turkish protectorate controlled by the Ottoman Empire in modern Romania), and Slovakia. Slovakia itself managed to withstand the Turkish invasion, but found itself the center of the new Hungarian state,

TIMELINE Czech and Slovak History

833 Great Moravia is established.

907 Hungarians invade Great Moravia.

1000 Slovakia becomes part of Hungary.

1200 Mongols and Tartars conquer much of Eastern Europe.

1350 Prague is the capital of the Holy Roman Empire.

1515 The Reformation begins, setting the stage for tension between Protestants and Catholics over the next several centuries.

1526 Hungary is defeated at the Battle of Mohács; lands are divided between Turks and the Hapsburg Empire.

1563 The Council of Trent orders Roman Catholic churches to keep vital records.

1584 The Habsburg Empire adopts the Gregorian calendar.

1671 Hungary becomes a province of Austria.

1740 Maria Theresa becomes the empress of Austria-Hungary.

1754 The first census of Hapsburg territories takes place.

1780 The Slovak National Revival begins.

1781 The Holy Roman Emperor issues the Patent of Toleration, giving religious freedom to non-Catholic Christians.

1785 Serfdom is abolished in Slovakia.

1843 The Central Slovak dialect becomes the Slovak language standard.

1848 Serfdom is abolished in Austria-Hungary following a Hungarian rebellion.

1848 Slovaks launch a revolt against the Hapsburgs.

1861 Slovaks assert autonomy with the Memorandum of the Slovak Nation.

1867 The dual monarchy of Austria-Hungary forms.

1873 A cholera epidemic and crop failures spur Slovak emigration.

1918 Czechoslovakia, a new state comprising the Czech lands and Slovakia, gains independence from the dissolved Austria-Hungary.

1933 Germany gains control of Czechoslovakia.

1939 The Slovak Republic becomes independent of the Czech lands.

1944 Germans quash the Slovak National Uprising.

1969 The Soviet Union converts Czechoslovakia into a federation of the Czech Socialist Republic and the Slovak Socialist Republic, outlining modern borders of the two countries.

SLOVAKIA Fast Facts

OFFICIAL NAME: Slovenska Republika (Slovak Republic)

SHORT NAME: Slovensko (Slovakia)

CAPITAL CITY: Bratislava

AREA: 18,921 square miles

BORDERING COUNTRIES: Austria, the Czech Republic, Hungary, Poland, Ukraine

OFFICIAL LANGUAGE: Slovak

POPULATION: 5 million

MAJOR ETHNIC GROUPS: Slovak, Czech, Hungarian, Romany, Ruthenian, Ukrainian

MAJOR RELIGIONS: Roman Catholicism, Protestantism, Greek Catholicism, Orthodoxy

The modern Slovak Republic corresponds to the historical province of Slovakia, which was under Hungarian control from the 1500s until after World War I.

and all of the important Hungarian administrative, political, and religious institutions moved to Slovakia.

In the sixteenth century, Hungary, including Slovakia, became an associated state of the Habsburg Empire. Between 1867 and 1918, the Austrian (Habsburg) Empire was restructured into a double state called Austria-Hungary. In this state, Hungary, including Slovakia, had its own government, parliament, army, and citizenship. Inhabitants of Austria-Hungary were considered either Austrian or Hungarian citizens. Most Slovak citizens, having lived in the Hungarian portion of the empire, would have considered themselves Hungarian citizens. But others—even some in the same family—may have indicated Austrian citizenship instead.

For most genealogists, this time period holds the greatest significance for the research process. Because of the changing geographical and political borders, researching Slovak ancestors can often be challenging. You must be aware of both the Slovak and Hungarian name changes for towns, villages, and counties, and also take place-name changes into account when searching for documents such as church and civil vital records, census returns, and other important genealogical sources. Those searches will be addressed in later chapters.

For more detailed information on the history of Slovakia, consult the "Short Chronological History of Slovakia," prepared by Slovak historian Anton Hrnko <www.panorama.sk/go/clanky/39.asp?lang=en>.

CZECHOSLOVAKIA

The treaties ending World War I dissolved the Austro-Hungarian Empire, and part of the empire was carved out to create the independent state of Czechoslovakia in 1928. The new country consisted of Bohemia, Moravia, Slovakia, Ruthenia, and parts of the Polish province of Silesia. The new name was adopted to reflect the union of the Czech and Slovak territories. But the independence did not last long, and Slovakia's partnership with the Czechs was not an equal one.

World War II

In 1938, Nazi Germany annexed much of Bohemia and Moravia. Hitler seized the Sudetenland in Bohemia, insisting that the area rightly belonged to Germany due to its high concentration of ethnic Germans. Later, he took control of the entire country. The official government went into exile in England. Slovakia, although now officially "independent" of Czechoslovakia, became a German puppet state.

World War II was especially devastating for Czech Jews. Most were killed, and their records were destroyed in an attempt to wipe out any trace of them.

Communist Influence and the Velvet Divorce

As the war came to a close, Soviet forces came into Czechoslovakia, bringing with them Soviet influence that would persist long after Hitler's defeat. In 1945, Allied powers restored Czechoslovakia (minus the eastern region called Subcarpathian Rus'), but the region fell within the Soviet sphere of influence. Alexander Dubček led a brief period of reform in 1968 that was commonly known as the Prague Spring. But the Soviets crushed Dubček's efforts and continued to influence the Czech government until the late 1980s,

What is a Rusyn?

The term *Rusyn* refers to people from Carpathian Rus' (also called Ruthenia), an area on the southern and northern slopes of the Carpathian Mountains where the borders of Ukraine, Slovakia, and Poland meet.

Rusyns have never had their own state—since the sixth century, they've lived as minorities within various nations. Their homeland now sits mostly in Slovakia.

Rusyns have borne numerous self-imposed and assigned monikers, including Carpatho-Russian, Carpatho-Ukrainian, Rusnak, Ruthene, Ruthenian, and Uhro-Rusyn. The most appropriate designation is Carpatho-Rusyn, or simply Rusyn. They're not "just some kind of Slovak."

At least one hundred thousand people of Rusyn descent live in Slovakia today, but fewer than fifty thousand still identify as Rusyn in some way. Due to their lack of any firm geographic identity, Rusyns have been described as "the people from no man's land." To read more, go to **<www.carpathorusynsociety.org>**.

when the Soviet Union's Mikhail Gorbachev, with his ideas of *glasnost* ("openness") and *perestroika* ("restructuring"), relaxed the Soviet hold on satellite countries to allow for more freedom of expression.

In June 1990, the well-known dissident and poet Václav Havel was elected president of Czechoslovakia, but difficulties between the Czechs and Slovaks led Havel to resign in 1992. On January 1, 1993, the country divided to form two new nations, the Czech Republic and the Slovak Republic (Slovakia). The Czech Republic joined the European Union in 2004, but hasn't adopted the euro as its currency. The Slovak Republic joined the European Union in 2004 and adopted the euro as its currency in 2009.

AT A GLANCE: KEY EVENTS INFLUENCING CZECH AND SLOVAK GENEALOGY

Genealogically speaking, you should keep in mind these key dates and events as you search for your Czech and Slovak ancestors:

- **the creation of Austria-Hungary (1867):** A compromise instituted a dual monarchy. The two independent states shared a common ruler as emperor in Austria and king in Hungary.

- **World War I (1914–1918):** Austria-Hungary was defeated and split into separate entities based on nationality: Czechoslovakia, Yugoslavia, Galicia (to Poland), and

Transylvania (to Romania). Border changes may influence how your immigrant ancestor listed information on passenger lists and other North American records.

- **the end of World War II (1945):** Subcarpathian Rus' became part of Ukraine, and the eastern border of Poland moved westward so that Eastern Galicia became part of Ukraine (significant if your ancestors are Rusyn).

KEYS TO SUCCESS

✳ Know the key ethnic groups in your ancestors' homeland. Czech and Slovak history have been influenced especially by the Hungarians, Germans, and Russians, but also the Celts, Turks, and Serbs. If your ancestors hailed from the area of Carpathian Rus' (also called Ruthenia), your ancestry is likely Rusyn, which is different from Czech or Slovak.

✳ Learn the important dates that produced power shifts, border changes, and religious edicts in Czech and Slovak lands—you'll need to understand these to find the appropriate documentation for your ancestors. Modern Slovakia and the Czech Republic were ruled by the Habsburg Empire (later Austria-Hungary) for hundreds of years before gaining independence as Czechoslovakia after World War I.

✳ Study in particular the period preceding your Czech or Slovak ancestors' immigration. For many Americans, this is the era of the Austro-Hungarian dual monarchy, which lasted from 1867 to 1918.

PART 2

GETTING TO KNOW THE OLD COUNTRY

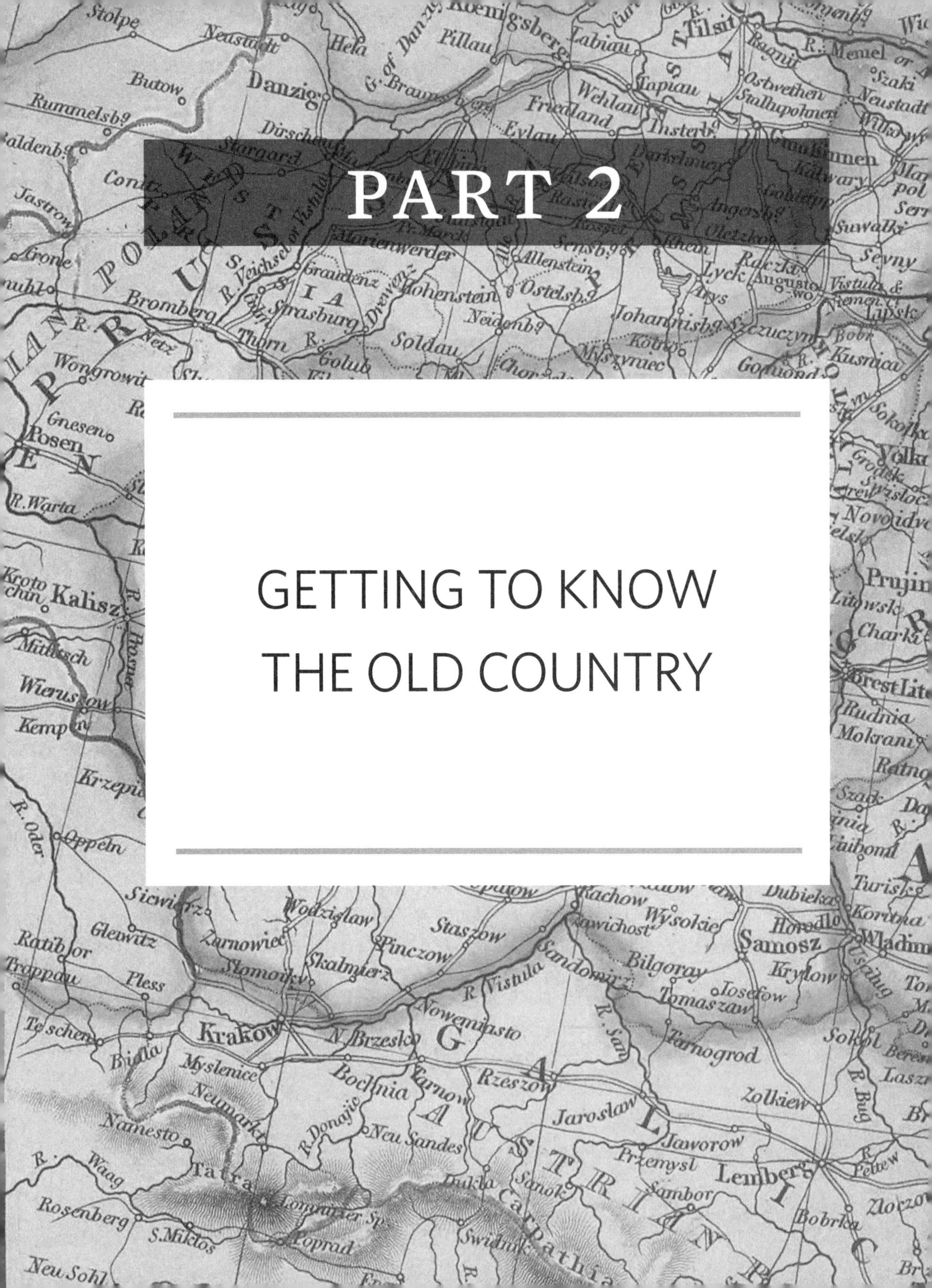

6

Understanding Eastern European Geography

Once you determine the specific place your ancestors came from, you'll need to research it: Verify the correct spelling, identify which country it's in now and when your ancestors lived there, and locate it on a map. You also will need to know what province, county, or district had jurisdiction over the place. Why is this so crucial? Your Polish, Czech, or Slovak ancestors' records are organized by locality. Without understanding the where, you can't unravel the who, what, when, and how of your family tree. This chapter will cover tools to help you get to know your ancestors' hometown.

HELPFUL GEOGRAPHIC RESOURCES

As you may have discovered, locating your ancestral town isn't necessarily as easy as searching for its name on Google Maps **<www.google.com/maps>**. Modern maps may not contain your ancestor's home village at all (or not by the name you know it). Your search might turn up many places with the same name—which of the nine (or more) Dubravas in Slovakia is your family's town? Or might it actually be Dubravica?

This is why you'll need to use a combination of geographical references—maps, atlases, and gazetteers, both modern and historical—to research your family's Eastern

European village. Let's first walk through the resources and how to access them; we'll recommend key references for each country later in the chapter.

Maps

In addition to telling you the location of your ancestral town, maps provide context for your research. Was your ancestor's village in a forest, in the mountains, or on a seacoast? Was it a suburb of a major city or far away from any other town? If you can't find your ancestors in that town, what nearby towns might have records? What are the closest administrative centers likely to have civil registrations?

The easiest place to begin is with online maps. You'll find a wide variety of modern and historical maps on the Internet; these are a few of my favorites for Eastern European research:

- David Rumsey Map Collection **<www.davidrumsey.com>**: The sixty-one thousand digitized historical maps here (see image **A** for an example) let you zoom in to an amazing level of detail. Click the link for Europe or search by country.

- Foundation for East European Family History Studies Map Library (FEEFHS) **<feefhs.org/maplibrary.html>**: View highly detailed historical maps of the Austro-Hungarian, German, and Russian empires that encompassed your ancestors' town. The FEEFHS Map Library also has links to other map sites and helpful articles.

- Google Earth **<www.google.com/earth>**: The most useful feature of this free tool for Polish, Czech, and Slovak genealogy is the ability to overlap historical maps onto the present-day map, letting you visualize border changes that occurred over time. Family Tree University's Google Earth for Genealogists course **<www.familytreeuniversity.com>** teaches you how to use the program step by step.

- Library of Congress **<www.loc.gov/maps/collections>**: Its online collection features a fraction of its five million maps and eighty thousand atlases. Search a country name to find maps of interest.

- Perry-Casteñeda Map Collection **<www.lib.utexas.edu/maps>**: You'll find useful modern and historical maps within this digital collection from the University of Texas at Austin.

- Maplandia **<www.maplandia.com>**: This searchable world gazetteer of two million places integrates with Google Maps to show you the location as well as its administrative divisions.

- Mapy: Specialized sites for the Czech Republic **<mapy.cz>**, Poland **<mapy.pl>**, and Slovakia **<mapy.sk>** give you a view of your ancestors' homeland.

The David Rumsey Map Collection website contains English-language historical maps of Eastern European countries. As this 1901 map of Austria-Hungary illustrates, it's important to look for period place-names on old maps: The labels *Czech* and *Slovakia* weren't present until after World War I, for example.

Of course, don't overlook offline maps—an extremely useful map might be sitting on a library shelf in printed or microfilm format. Check major public libraries' map collections, college and university libraries, and genealogical libraries such as the Allen County Public Library **<www.acpl.lib.in.us>** and FamilySearch's Family History Library **<www.familysearch.org>**. You can order microfilmed maps from FamilySearch for viewing at a local FamilySearch Center. See if other repositories lend the items you need through interlibrary loan.

Atlases

Most maps from Eastern Europe lack indexes to the towns they show—a helpful feature you'll typically find in atlases. Historical atlases are especially useful, as they describe the growth and development of countries. They show boundaries, migration routes, landowners, settlement patterns, military campaigns, and other historical information. While modern maps might not show Great-grandpa's village, historical atlases will give an accurate picture of the region during his time. One excellent atlas to have on your reference shelf is *The Palgrave Concise Historical Atlas of Eastern Europe* by Dennis P. Hupchick and Harold E. Cox (Palgrave Macmillan, 2001). Also bookmark these online atlases:

- Atlas of Austria-Hungary **<commons.wikimedia.org/wiki/Atlas_of_Austria-Hungary>**

- Atlas of Czechoslovakia **<commons.wikimedia.org/wiki/Atlas_of_Czechoslovakia>**

- *Atlas des Deutschen Reichs* **<www.library.wisc.edu/etext/ravenstein/home.html>**

- Historical Atlas of the Twentieth Century **<users.erols.com/mwhite28/20centry.htm>**

Consult the country-specific resources and search the FamilySearch catalog to find more. Atlases are typically categorized with maps.

Gazetteers

Gazetteers are geographical dictionaries that summarize and cross-reference villages, districts, and other geopolitical divisions. When you look up a place, you'll learn which administrative district it's in, as well as about local churches and other social statistics.

In addition to helping you locate your ancestral village, a gazetteer will give you the correct spelling (or alternate spellings) of its name and help you locate the associated religious parish so you can find church records. Some gazetteers even shed light on life in the ancestral village, including the village's population, physical size, religious composition, and history. Gazetteers often list civil records offices too, opening up new avenues of research.

You may also gain insight about the surrounding area: Gazetteers can describe the city or town's parent county, canals, mountain ranges, rivers, natural barriers to migration, and transportation networks that may have influenced your ancestors' decisions. Information about neighboring villages can also give clues about where "missing" ancestors may have come from or gone to. Be sure to check multiple gazetteers, as parish boundaries often changed.

FamilySearch has an excellent collection of Eastern European gazetteers. You can access them by checking the online catalog for microfilmed items you can borrow through

RESEARCH TIP

Find It on FamilySearch

To access FamilySearch resources recommended in this chapter, search the catalog **<www.familysearch.org/catalog-search>** for the item title. The catalog detail page will provide you with the film numbers so you can rent the film for viewing at a local FamilySearch Center. To order a film on FamilySearch.org, you'll need to set up an account and select your preferred center. Alternatively, you can search WorldCat **<www.worldcat.org>** to find nearby libraries that have the item or can receive it via interlibrary loan.

your local FamilySearch Center. You also can find gazetteers in reference sections of most libraries. Specific gazetteers for each country are recommended later in this chapter.

Whether or not you have Jewish ancestry, JewishGen **<www.jewishgen.org>** offers two helpful online gazetteers of sorts: The JewishGen Communities Database covers six thousand localities and the JewishGen Gazetteer (formerly called ShtetlSeeker) covers one million. The ability to search for similar-sounding locations is particularly useful.

Note that your results may not list some common name variations. You might also get hits on the name in multiple countries—for example, there is a Kučín in present-day Belarus, two places with this name in Slovakia, and other variations of this village name in Poland, Russia, Lithuania, and Croatia. Narrowing the search criteria by modern-day place can help.

When using the JewishGen Gazetteer, you may need to experiment with different variations of the search criteria in order to locate a place. Even then, keep in mind that these databases do not contain all localities in Eastern Europe, so you should also consult other print and online resources.

POLAND ADMINISTRATIVE DIVISIONS AND RESOURCES

Because of Poland's turbulent history, administrative jurisdictions have changed numerous times. Historically, *powiaty* (counties) were the basic geographic division; while those still exist, the government introduced *województwa* (literally, "voivodeships," but commonly called provinces) in 1975. In 1999, it consolidated Poland's forty-nine former *województwa* into sixteen. PolandGenWeb's map **<www.rootsweb.ancestry.com/~polwgw/polandgen.html>** can help you sort out that reshuffling. Parish boundaries have shifted over time, too—and they don't follow those of political jurisdictions.

The internal administrative structure of former Polish territory was different in each partition. In the Prussian partition (modern western Poland), the land was divided into provinces and then by *kreise* (similar to US counties), notably Poznań (*Posen*), West Prussia (*Prusy Zachodnie/Westpreussen*), East Prussia (*Prusy Wschodnie/Ostpreussen*), Pomerania (*Pomorze/Pommern*), and Silesia (*Śląsk/Schleisen*). The Austrian partition

Clues in Cadastral Maps

From the 1700s to the 1860s, the Habsburg Empire created a series of detailed maps for taxation and agricultural reforms. Called cadastral maps, these resources enable researchers to pinpoint the exact plot of land where the ancestral homestead was situated. They provide numerous details about eighteenth- and nineteenth-century life, including size and type of land, field plots, and individual yards. The government created three versions of these maps (a field sketch, a draft, and a full-color version), so at least one iteration is available for most villages.

Researchers interested in exploring cadastral maps should consult the Gesher Galicia Map Room <maps.geshergalicia.org> and its Cadastral Map and Landowner Records Project <www.geshergalicia.org/projects/cadastral-map-and-landowner-records>. Cadastral maps were also made in the modern Czech Republic and Slovakia. See Mollova mapova sbirka (Moll's Map Collection) <mapy.mzk.cz/mollova-sbirka> for maps from the Czech lands and Slovakia. Slovak researchers can also check out the Cadastral Portal online at <www.katasterportal.sk/kapor>.

(modern Ukraine and southeastern Poland) was divided into *powiaty*. In the Russian partition (parts of modern Lithuania, Belarus, and central and eastern Poland), land was divided into *gubernias* (provinces), then into *ujezds* (counties). *Gubernias* with large Polish populations were Łoznan, Suwałki, Siedice, Warsaw, Kielce, Lublin, Radom, and Płock. Many Polish speakers also lived in the western provinces.

Maps and Atlases

Begin orienting yourself to Polish geography with the Internet map of contemporary Poland <www.mapa.szukacz.pl>, the Polish Geographic Atlas <pgsa.org/polish-geographic-atlas>, and World Atlas Poland <www.worldatlas.com/webimage/countrys/europe/pl.htm>. Consider buying a modern road atlas of Poland, too; you'll find these on Amazon <www.amazon.com> and at other booksellers.

For historical maps, explore the online *Archiwum Map Wojskowego Instytutu Geograficznego 1919–1939* (Map Archive of the Military Geographical Institute) <www.mapywig.org>. And look for these two useful maps series on FamilySearch microfilm: *Karte des Deutschen Reiches* (Map of the German Empire) (Reichsamt für Landesaufnahme, 1914–1917) and *Mapa Polski (Taktyczna)* (Tactical Maps of Poland) (Wojskowego Instytutu Geograficzny, 1926–1938).

DEFINITION: *POLISH VILLAGE*

POWIAT/DISTRICT: *SŁUTSK*

PHYSICAL LOCATION: *ON THE RIGHT SIDE OF THE KLECK-PINSK ROAD*

DISTANCE FROM OTHER LANDMARKS: *2 MILES FROM THE POST OFFICE IN SIENIAWKI*

SIZE: *17 SETTLEMENTS*

DEFINITION: *WOODED HILL IN DOLINIAŃSKIM POWIAT/DISTRICT*

LOCATION INFO: *IN THE VICINITY OF TURZA WIELKA TOWNSHIP, EAST OF IT*

miasteczku starościńskiém urodził się w roku 1793, z ojca unickiego księdza, znakomity duchem obywatelskim, nauką i dowcipem, autor i poeta Ignacy Szydłowski, dzielny członek „Szubrawców" występujący w Brukowcu i w Tygodniku wileńskim pod pseudonimem „Gulbi".   *A. Jelski.*

Hajna, piękna i bystra rzeka w powiecie borysowskim, prawy dopływ Berezyny. Ma początek w okolicy miasteczka Hajny na podgórzu, płynie z początku w kierunku południowo-wschodni [...] wszy w siebi [...] razu na pół [...] — 5 wpada do Be [...] j Borysowa, o 3 w. wyżej wsi Wesołowo, wprost folw. Kryczyn. Ten zwrot gwałtowny Hajny w stronę północną jasno wskazuje niekorzystne pochylenie tej części kraju, jakoż rzeczywiście klimatyczne warunki tu są odmienne; zauważono w całej okolicy w porównaniu do innych obniżkę temperatury w ogóle i ostre wiatry, promienie bowiem słoneczne padają na ową płaszczyznę kraju ukośnie, wiatry zaś północne łatwo wyziębiają zwróconą ku sobie. Ztąd też jak świadczy E. Tyszkiewicz, nazwa miasteczka Ziębina, położonego w stronie ujścia Hajny, kędy uparte zimnice zwykłą są chorobą mieszkańców (ob. Opis pow. borys. str. 131). Długość rzeki wynosi około mil trzynastu, dość jest rybna, w górnym biegu ma brzegi malownicze, a od zwrotu na północ obfituje w łąki i bagna i tu w ostatnich dniach listopada 1812 r. w okolicach ujścia Hajny do Berezyny spełniły się straszne wypadki w czasie rejterady francuzów z pod Borysowa na Ziębin i dalej. Dno ma kamieniste w niektórych miejscach bagniste. Wyżej wsi Antopola na dnie rzeki znajdują się ogromne kamienie, które nie małą są przeszkodą dla spławiania drzewa. Dolina Hajny od początku do wsi Antopol wązka i ściśnięta wzgórzami; od wsi zaś Antopol rozszerza się i ku końcowi dochodzi do 4 wiorst szerok., wszędzie bagnista i trudna do przebycia. Na Hajnie są 4 młyny i 2 wiataraki a przy wsi Rudki była niegdyś fabryka żelaza wytapianego z rudy znajdowanej na brzegach tejże rzeki; fabryka ta dzisiaj nie istnieje. Po Hajnie spławia się drzewo, dziś w małej ilości, ponieważ lasy przyległe zniszczone; spław zaczyna się od wsi Antopol o 45 w. od ujścia. Płynie krętém korytem a na wiosnę rozlewa szeroko, po brzegach obszerne łąki obfitujące w bujną trawę. Z prawej strony Hajna przyjmuje rz. Meiaż a z lewej Cnę. Według Zielińskiego dopływy Zajelijanka, Usiaż, Derożnia z prawej strony, a z lewej Cna, Łowo-

Hajnik, potok górski w Magórze spiskiej, w obr. gm. Toporca (Topórcz); po krótkim, w kierunku wschodnim płynącym biegu, wynoszącym 2 kil., łączy się z potokiem Malergrund i tworzy rzekę Toporzec, lewy dopływ Popradu.   *Br. G.*

Hajnin, wś poleska, pow. słucki, z prawej strony drogi klecko-pińskiej, o 2 mile od st. p. Sieniawki, 17 osad.   *Al. Jel.*

Hajnów, niem. *Hainau*, miasto na Szląsku w okr. reg. lignickim, pow. złotogórsko-hajnowskim, o 11 mil od Wrocławia, o 2 i pół od Lignicy, nad rz. Deichsel. Książę Bolesław III nadał H. prawo miejskie lignickie 1333 roku; 1428 r. splądrowali miasto husyci, roku 1642 Szwedzi, 1813 Francuzi. Bywają w H. 4 jarmarki. Od H. do Spitzberga wzdłuż rz. Deichsel ciągnie się jednym rzędem 11 wsi, razem do 8000 mk.

Hajnowo, niem. *Hagenau*, wś, pow. morąski, st. p. Quittainen.

Hajowe, wzgórze lesiste w pow. doliniańskim, w obr. gm. Turza Wielka, na wschód od niej.   *Lu. Dz.*

Hajowniki, wś i folw. w północno-wschodniej stronie pow. zamojskiego, gm. i par. Skierbieszów, leżą w lesisto-górzystej miejscowości nad rz. Wotyka, odl. od Zamościa w. 28, Krasnegostawu w. 32, w 2 okr. sądowym. Liczą obecnie dom. dwor. 5, włośc. 34; ludność 113, prawosł. 166 i żydów 11, razem 290 mk., obszaru dwor. 877 mr. (własność Kiełczewskiego) i włośc. 334 mr. Gleba żytnia, żyzna, stan zamożności średni. Posiadają młyn wodny o 2 kam. Do folw. H. należała niegdyś wieś Lipiny, osad 11, rozl. mr. 178.   *T. Żuk.*

Hajsyn (Aysyn, Ajszyn), miasto główne powiatu tegoż nazwiska, gub. podolska, nad rz. Sobem, dopływem Bohu, o 260 wiorst od Kamieńca odległe, o 80 od stacyi kolei odeskokijowskiej Rachny; posiada urząd powiatowy, stacyą telegraficzną, kantor pocztowy 2 klasy, szkołę powiatową o 2 klasach, (mirowy) sąd pokoju i zjazd sędziów pokoju, szpital powiatowy; mieszk. do 10000, w tej liczbie chrześcian do 6000, reszta żydów; katolików według wykazów urzędowych do 300. Pod względem stanów: szlachty (z urzędnikami) 167, duchownych 25, reszta mieszczan. Jest tu cerkiew soborna, murowana, pod wezw. św. Mikołaja, licząca 3100 wiernych, uposażona 51 dz. ziemi. Kościoła katolickiego dotąd niema; parafia katolicka należy do odległej o kilka wiorst Kuny, dekanatu bracławskiego. Miasto dość porządnie zabudowane, błotne, jak wszystkie po większej części podolskie; domów liczy do 1500, po części drewnianych, synagoga i

The *Słownik* gazetteer provides details about your Polish ancestors' town. Entries will usually include a brief description of the locality, plus information about where it's located. The entries for Hajnin and Hajowe are annotated to show roughly what each section of the entry is describing, with the English translation in italics.

Gazetteers

The best gazetteer for Polish genealogy is *Słownik Geograficzny Królestwa Polskiego* (Geographical Dictionary of the Kingdom of Poland, or SGKP), a fifteen-volume gazetteer published between 1880 and 1902 by Filip Sulimierski. Like other gazetteers, *Słownik* provides a snapshot of your ancestor's life in a Polish village, including the town's geographic placement, information on a town's agriculture and trade, and historical surveys (image **B**).

Divisions of Partitioned Poland, 1772–1918

As we discussed in chapter 4, the parititions of Poland can be difficult to understand. In addition to knowing what part of Poland your ancestors lived in *during* the Partitions, you'll also need to know in what region their hometown ended up as governing partitions readministered the land. The list below explains how the administrative divisions of Partitioned Poland changed from the Three Partitions to Poland's independence in 1918. Note that some important divisions were created after the Partitions, namely the Duchy of Warsaw (1807–1815), the Grand Duchy/Province of Posen (1815–1918), "Congress Poland" (1815–1915), and the Province of Prussia (1829–1875). In 1815, the Duchy of Warsaw was broken up into the Grand Duchy of Posen (Prussia), the Free City of Kraków (administered by the three powers), and Congress Poland (Russia).

Austrian Partition

- Kingdom of Galicia and Lodomeria: 1772–1918
- New Galicia: 1795–1803 (to the Kingdom of Galicia and Lodomeria)

Prussian Partition

- East Prussia: 1772–1829 (to Province of Prussia), 1878–1918 (to Germany)
- New East Prussia: 1795–1807 (to the Duchy of Warsaw)
- New Silesia: 1795–1807 (to the Duchy of Warsaw)
- Netze District: 1772–1793 (to West Prussia)
- South Prussia: 1793–1807 (to the Duchy of Warsaw)
- West Prussia: 1772–1829 (to the Province of Prussia), 1878–1918

Russian Partition

During the Partitions, Russia organized its Polish lands by expanding existing or creating new *guberniyas* (governates), though this became part of the Duchy of Warsaw after 1807. In 1815, the Congress of Vienna created "Congress Poland" out of most of Russia's Polish territory and divided it into eight *voivodeships* (equivalent to provinces) and, later, eight similar *guberniyas*. These divisions largely remained the same until they were consolidated into five guberniyas in 1844, then ten in 1867. Congress Poland was incorporated into the Kingdom of Poland during World War I, then became part of independent Poland in 1918. Learn more at **<en. wikipedia.org/wiki/Administrative_division_of_Congress_Poland>**.

Beware Doctored Maps

Be cautious when using Soviet Union maps (including Ukraine) printed between 1930 and 1990. The Soviet Union falsified public maps of the country; rivers and streets may be misplaced, boundaries distorted, and geographical features omitted.

You can view the entire *Słownik* gazetteer online **<dir.icm.edu.pl/pl/Slownik_ geograficzny>**. The site is in Polish, but you can use Google Translate **<translate.google. com>** to view an English translation. The Polish Genealogical Society of America (PGSA) has translations of some of the *Słownik* entries and offers helpful tips for understanding entries **<pgsa.org/polish-history/translated-descriptions-of-polish-villages-and-provinces>**. Consult PolishRoots' detailed instructional guide before diving into this digitized version **<www.polishroots.org/Portals/0/pdf/How_to_use_Polish_Gazeteer_Online(rev.2011_02).pdf>**.

For researching Polish places between the world wars and later, consult these helpful gazetteers:

- *Skorowidz Miejscowości Rzeczypospolitej Polskiej* (Index to Place-names in the Republic of Poland) (Wydawnictwo Książnicy Naukowej, 1934): This work lists all localities in Poland within its borders at the time, arranged alphabetically. It covers territory now in Belarus, Lithuania, and Ukraine, but does not include western Polish towns that were part of Prussia in 1934. Jurisdictional information is given in columns, with parishes in the final column. You can access it online **<www.wbc.poznan.pl/ dlibra/docmetadata?id=12786&from=publication>** and on FamilySearch microfilm.

- *Spis Miejscowości Polskiej Rzeczypospolite Ludowej* (List of Place-names in the Polish People's Republic) (Wydawnictwa komunikacji i Łączności, 1967): This work is similar in format to the 1934 gazetteer. While it does not give the parish for each locality, it does provide the location of the civil registry office. It includes territory regained from Germany after World War II and is available on FamilySearch microfilm.

- *Wykaz Urzędowych Nazw Miejscowości i ich Części* (List of Official Names of Places and Their Subdivisions) **<ksng.gugik.gov.pl/urzedowe_nazwy_miejscowosci.php>**: This gazetteer lists modern Polish place-names and their associated jurisdictions in an easy-to-understand table format, with columns for *nazwa miejscowosci* (village name), *rodzaj* (type), *gmina* (community/sub-district), *powiat* (county), and *województwo* (province).

- Eastern Borderlands Places **<www.kami.net.pl/kresy>**: You can search this online gazetteer of eastern Polish localities for a place-name or browse by province. It covers both governmental and church jurisdictions.

See a complete listing of Poland gazetteers available through FamilySearch at **<www.familysearch.org/learn/wiki/en/Poland_Gazetteers>**.

Resources for Russian Poland

There are fewer resources for the areas of Poland once under Russian control than for those areas under Prussian or Austrian jurisdiction. One publication, *Skorowidz Krolestwa Polskiego* (Polish Kingdom Index) (W Drukarni, 1877), contains place-names for the various Polish communities that were ruled by Russia. You can view the gazetteer online at **<www.sbc.org.pl/dlibra/docmetadata?id=10795&from=publication>**; you'll need to have installed the Java plug-in **<www.java.com>** to view the two-volume collection. The Federation of East European Family History Studies (FEEFHS) also has a more general map of the Polish provinces of Russia in 1902, which is available online at **<feefhs.org/maplibrary/russian/re-polan.html>**.

Resources for Prussian Poland

For ancestors from the Polish provinces of Prussia (detailed in chapter 4), you'll be dealing with place-names in German and Polish. Consult Uwe-Karsten Krickhahn's *Kartenmeister* (German for "Map master") **<www.kartenmeister.com/preview/databaseuwe.asp>** to sort through German/Polish name changes for the German provinces of East Prussia, West Prussia, Posen, Pomerania, and Silesia. This database lists most towns and geographic features: mills, some bridges, battlefields, named trees, cenotaphs, etc. You can search by the German name or the current Polish, Russian, or Lithuanian name.

Another useful resource is *Atlas des Deutschen Reichs* **<uwdc.library.wisc.edu/collections/German/Ravenstein>**, a digitized version of Ludwig Ravenstein's 1883 *Atlas of the German Empire*. The atlas is color-coded and marks the locations of churches. An accompanying table gives statistics on the religious denominations found throughout the German Empire down to the *Regierungsbezirk* and *Kreis* administrative divisions.

The definitive gazetteer for German place-names is *Meyers Orts- und Verkehrs-Lexikon des Deutschen Reichs* (Meyer's Gazetteer and Directory of the German Empire), available on Ancestry.com and FamilySearch microfilm. For each town, this German gazetteer indicates the location of vital records offices, gives the former German province, and states whether it has its own parish or synagogue. For help using *Meyers Orts-*, see FamilySearch's tutorial **<www.familysearch.org/learn/wiki/en/Step-by-step_guide:_Using_Meyers_Gazetteer_Online>**.

Another helpful gazetteer is *Gemeindelexikon für das Königreich Preußen* (Verlag des Königlichen Statistischen Bureaus, 1887–1888). It has separate volumes for East Prussia,

West Prussia, Pomerania, Posen, and Silesia. Ancestry.com has a searchable version accessible to subscribers **<search.ancestry.com/search/DB.aspx?dbid=34415>**.

Resources for Austrian Poland (Galicia)

In addition to the aforementioned resources, two websites will help orient you to Galicia's place-name complexities—even the region itself has been called by various names throughout history. Genealogist Matthew Bielawa's website Genealogy of Halychyna/ Eastern Galicia **<www.halgal.com/galicia.html#eastgal>** provides a helpful breakdown of those names by time period, based on Paul Robert Magocsi's book *Galicia: A Historical Survey and Bibliographic Guide* (University of Toronto Press, 1983) and other helpful reference material. The website of Eötvös Loránd University's Department of Cartography and Geoinformatics in Hungary **<lazarus.elte.hu/hun/digkonyv/topo/3felmeres.htm>** offers a series of digitized historical maps of Austria-Hungary, including places in Galicia.

You should also consult *Gemeindelexikon von Galizien: Gemeindelexikon der im Reichsrate Vertretenen Königreiche und Länder* (Gazetteer of Galicia: Gazetteer of the Crown Lands and Territories Represented in the Imperial Council) (K.K. Statistische Zentralkommission, 1907), available on FamilySearch microfilm and online at **<wiki-de. genealogy.net/w/index.php?title=Datei:Oesterreich-12.djvu&page=1>**. In the gazetteer's appendix, you can use district and village names to determine the parish where the church records were kept for your ancestors' village.

CZECH REPUBLIC ADMINISTRATIVE DIVISIONS AND RESOURCES

Since 2000, the Czech Republic has consisted of thirteen regions (*kraje*, singular *kraj*) plus the capital city, Prague (Praha):

- Jihočeský (South Bohemia)
- Jihomoravský (South Moravia)
- Karlovarský
- Královéhradecký
- Liberecký
- Moravskoslezský (Moravia-Silesia)
- Olomoucký
- Pardubický
- Plzeňský (Pilsen)
- Středočeský (Central Bohemia)
- Ústecký

- Vysočina (Highlands Region)
- Zlínský

Those thirteen *kraje* encompass seventy-six districts (*okresy*); each *okres* is divided into municipalities (colloquially called *malé okresy*, or little districts). Note that some *kraje* have changed boundaries over time, meaning that records from these regions might be housed in another *kraje*. Visit **<www.wwjohnston.net/famhist/czech-research.htm>** for tips on how to search for local records.

Maps and Atlases

FamilySearch has an excellent collection of Czech maps and atlases; you'll find them in the catalog under the heading Czech Republic–Maps. Consider getting a modern road atlas to familiarize yourself with Czech geography; you can purchase one through an online bookseller or borrow one from a library.

A helpful historical atlas available through FamilySearch is *Militär-Landesaufnahme und Spezialkarte der österreichisch-ungarischen Monarchie* (Detailed Map of the Austro-Hungarian Empire) (Das Institut, 1875–1918). Visit Old Czech Maps **<oldmaps.geolab.cz>** to view old military survey maps going back to the mid-eighteenth century. Other websites of interest include Czech Vanished Localities **<www.zanikleobce.cz>** and Lexicon of Towns in North and Northwest Bohemia **<www.soalitomerice.cz/slovnik/slovnik.php>**.

Gazetteers

Aside from the possibility of multiple language variations, there's another potential stumbling block to locating your ancestral village: Many Czech localities have similar names that can be easily confused. The FamilySearch Wiki **<familysearch.org/learn/wiki/en/Czech_Republic_Gazetteers>** gives a great example of this: Kámen, Kamenec, Kamenice, Kamenička, Kameničky, Kamenka, Kamenná, and Kamenné are all separate Czech towns. Additionally, Czech grammatical endings can change place-name spellings. If your ancestors live "in Kamenka," they would say *v Kamence* in Czech, but to say they come "from Kamenka" in Czech is *z Kamenky*. Having a solid knowledge of counties and administrative districts can help you sort out these similar words. Use historical maps and gazetteers to compare documents you have for your ancestor to see which spelling is correct.

Not every village in the Czech Republic had its own parish. Often, several small villages belonged to one parish. Use the following gazetteers—all of which are available on FamilySearch microfilm—to determine the proper record-keeping jurisdiction.

- *Administratives Gemeindelexikon der Čechoslovakischen Republik* (Administrative Gazetteer of the Czechoslovak Republic) by Rudolf M. Rohrer (Statistischen

Staatsamte, 1927–28): This gazetteer gives information on all towns and villages in Czechoslovakia after 1918. It's arranged by political districts with one index for the entire country. Volume I covers Bohemia; volume II includes Moravia.

- *Gemeindelexikon der im Reichsrate Vertretenen Königreiche und Länder* (Gazetteer of the Crownlands and Territories Represented in the Imperial Council) (K.K. Hof- und Staatsdruckerei, 1905–1908): Based on a 1900 census, this gazetteer has a volume for each province of the Austrian Empire. Volumes are arranged by political district and subdivided into court districts, with an index to both German and local place-names at the end of the book. Volume IX covers Bohemia, volume X covers Moravia, and volume XI covers Silesia. You can access digitized versions of this gazetteer at **<www.familysearch.org/search/catalog/218291>**.

- *Místopisný slovník Československé republiky* by Břetislav Chromec (Tiskem a Nákladem Československého Kompasu, 1929): FamilySearch bases Czech place-names in its catalog on this gazetteer.

- *Ortslexikon der Böhmischen Länder, 1910–1965* (Gazetteer of the Bohemian Land, 1910–1965) by Heribert Strum (R. Oldenbourg Verlag, 1977): This resource has place-names in German, Czech, and Polish for easy reference.

- *Gemeindeverzeichnis für Mittel- und Ostdeutschland und die Früheren Deutschen Siedlungsgebiete im Ausland* (Gazetteer of Germany and of German Settlements in Europe and the Former German Settlements Abroad) (Verlag für Standesamtswesen, 1970): This gazetteer has an alphabetical listing of settlements with the numerical code next to each locality name. This code refers to the specific country, county, and district listed in the beginning of the book.

SLOVAKIA ADMINISTRATIVE DIVISIONS AND RESOURCES

Like its Czech neighbor, Slovakia is divided into *kraje* (regions), currently having eight (note that these names are spelled differently alone when including the word *region*):

- Banská Bystrica, or Banskobystrický Kraj
- Bratislava, or Bratislavský Kraj
- Košice, or Košický Kraj
- Nitra, or Nitriansky Kraj
- Prešov, or Prešovský Kraj
- Trenčín, or Trenčiansky Kraj
- Trnava, or Trnavský Kraj
- Žilina, or Žilinský Kraj

And similar to the Czech Republic, Slovakian *kraje* are divided into *okresy* (Slovakia has seventy-nine), which contain *obec* (municipalities) and, more significantly for researchers, *jaras* (county-like administrative districts). Civil records were housed in the registrars' offices of individual *jaras*, though accessing them requires handwritten permission from the person's Slovakian ancestor.

All localities in Slovakia have names both in Slovak and Hungarian, with many places also bearing German names. For instance, the capital, Bratislava, is *Pozsony* in Hungarian and *Pressburg* in German. In the area of Subcarpathian Russia, localities had names in Ukrainian.

Place-names are often misspelled in American sources. Difficult names got shortened and diacritical marks omitted. And take care not to confuse jurisdictions—Slovakia has a city *and* a region called Trenčín, for example. You'll encounter multiple villages with the same name or similar names, too, such as Jeskova Ves and Jeskova Ves nad Nitricou (the latter meaning "Jeskova Ves on the Nitra River"). As you should do in Czech research, seek corroborative evidence (i.e., information from multiple, independent documents) for the greatest accuracy, and double-check a town's spelling in historical resources to trace how a place-name might have changed over time or have been modified in records. Learn more about sorting out place-names at **<www.iabsi.com/gen/public/ancestral_village.htm>**.

Maps and Atlases

You'll want to have a current road atlas for the Slovak Republic so you can learn the lay of your ancestors' homeland and have an index to current place-names. Search for one on Amazon or another bookseller. The SuperNavigator website **<www.supernavigator. sk>** can help you narrow in on specific areas. Explore FamilySearch's holdings for microfilmed maps you can rent; look in the catalog under the heading Slovakia–Maps.

In the realm of historical cartography, remember that you're looking for maps of Hungary or Austria-Hungary, as Slovakia didn't exist independently in the nineteenth and early twentieth centuries. An excellent choice is the online *Osztrák-Magyar Monarchia vármegyéi* (Austria-Hungary 1910 County Maps) **<lazarus.elte.hu/hun/ maps/1910/1910ind.htm>** and Third Military Mapping Survey of Austria-Hungary **<lazarus.elte.hu/hun/digkonyv/topo/3felmeres.htm>**.

Gazetteers

The helpful *German Towns in Slovakia & Upper Hungary: A Genealogical Gazetteer* by Duncan B. Gardiner (Family Historian, 1991) was created specifically for family history researchers. Check for availability via interlibrary loan. You also should consult *Návzy Obcí na Slovensku za Ostatných Dvesto Rokov* (Place-names in Slovakia During the Last

54. Megye — *Comitat:* Trencsén.

1) Járás — *Bezirk:* **Csacza.**

1. **Csacza** (Csatsa, Csácza, Csottza, Tschatza), RK. 3640 Nyitra, ág. 6 —, ref. 3 —, IZR. 349, egyéb 2 —.
2. **Cserne**, RK. 1497 Nyitra, izr. 7 Csacza.
3. **Dunajó**, rk. 422 Ohodnicza, izr. 7 Kisucza-Ujhely.
4. **Horelicz**, rk. 970 Csacza, ág. 5 —, izr. 2 Csacza.
5. **Olesna**, rk. 1368 Turzovka, ág. 4 —, izr. 6 Turzovka.
6. **Oscsadnicza**, RK. 2979 Nyitra, izr. 15 Csacza.
7. **Podviszoka**, rk. 431 Turzovka, izr. 6 Turzovka.
8. **Rakova**, RK. 2722 Nyitra, ág. 1 —, izr. 29 —.
9. **Szkalite**, RK. 2129 Nyitra, ág. 1 —, izr. 10 —.
10. **Szorcsinovecz**, rk. 1245 Cserne, ág. 3 —, izr. 6 —.
11. **Sztasko**, RK. 1159 Nyitra, izr. 12 Csacza.
12. **Turzovka** (Turzófalva), RK. 6789 Nyitra, IZR. 163.
13. **Zákopcse**, RK. 2269 Nyitra, izr. 38 Csacza.

Járási összeg : — *Gesammtsumme des Bezirkes:* rk. 27620 Nyitra, ág. 20 Dunáninnen, ref. 3 Tiszántul, izr. 645 III., egyéb 2 —.

2) Járás — *Bezirk:* **Kisucza-Ujhely.**

1. **Besztercze (Ó-)**, RK. 2581 Nyitra, IZR. 101.
2. **Besztercze (Uj-)**, RK. 2939 Nyitra, izr. 15 Ó-Besztercze.
3. **Brodnó** (Bradnó), RK. 458 Nyitra, izr. 4 —.
4. **Budatin**, rk. 393 Brodnó, ág. 4 —, izr. 23 Zsolna.
5. **Budatin** (Lehota-), rk. 379 Brodnó, izr. — Zsolna.
6. **Chmecz**, rk. 540 Nagy-Divina, izr. 7 Zsolna.
7. **Divina (Kis-)** (Divinka), rk. 114 Nagy-Divina, izr. 17 Zsolna.
8. **Divina (Nagy-)**, RK. 1197 Nyitra, izr. 22 Zsolna.

44*

This page from Volume 1 of the Dvorzsák Gazetteer indexes localities within the Cszaka and Kisucza districts (*járás*) of Trencsén county (*megye*). You can see name variations in parentheses.

Two Hundred Years) by Milan Majtán (Slovenskej Akademie Vied, 1972) on FamilySearch microfilm or in print form via interlibrary loan.

Because of Slovakia's historical ties to Hungary, you will also be looking at Hungarian gazetteers. These are typically organized by county, district, and village. The most useful Hungarian gazetteer for genealogists is *Magyarország helységnévtára tekintettel a közigazgatási, népességi és hitfelekezeti viszonyokra* (Gazetteer of Hungary with Administrative, Populational, and Ecclesiastical Circumstances) by János Dvorzsák (Havi Füzetek Kiadóhivatala, 1877), known as the Dvorzsák Gazetteer for short (image **C**). The entire gazetteer is available on FamilySearch microfilm; volume 1 is online through the University of Pécs <kt.lib.pte.hu/cgi-bin/kt.cgi?konyvtar/kt03110501/tartalom.html>.

Here's how the Dvorzsák Gazetteer works: Volume 1 indexes all Hungarian communities, with cross-references for variant names, by county and district. Counties are numbered at the heads of the pages. Additional names for the locality are in parentheses. Use the numbers from the index in volume 1 to find the entry for your town in volume 2, which gives specific information about the locality. The names of farmsteads, settlements, and mills that belong to the locality are sometimes listed within brackets. Population figures by religion follow. For help, consult Bill Tarkulich's excellent Dvorzsák Gazetteer tutorial <www.iabsi.com/gen/public/dvorzsak_gazetteer.htm>. Jordan Auslander's handy *Genea-logical Gazetteer of the Kingdom of Hungary* (Avotaynu, 2005) and the Hungarian Village Finder <www.hungarianvillagefinder.com> are both based on the Dvorzsák Gazetteer.

CARPATHO-RUSYN RESOURCES

The Carpatho-Rusyn Society provides a list of Carpatho-Rusyn villages located within modern Slovakia, Ukraine, and Romania, based on the 1910 Hungarian census for the Prešov region and Subcarpathian Rus' <www.carpatho-rusyn.org/villages.htm>. Data for the Lemko region—villages located in what is today southeastern Poland—are based on the 1921 Polish census.

You may also wish to purchase a copy of *Carpatho-Rusyn Settlement: A Map and Gazetteer* by Paul Robert Magocsi, available from <www.rusynmedia.org>. This large-scale wall map displays more than fourteen hundred villages and towns with majority Carpatho-Rusyn populations in the early 1900s, with Rusyn areas indicated clearly in color. It shows the present-day borders of Poland, Slovakia, Ukraine, Romania, and Hungary, as well as the pre-World War I Hungarian county and Austrian district boundaries. The gazetteer portion lists forty-five hundred current village and town names with cross-references to alternate names in Croatian, Hungarian, Polish, Romanian, Rusyn, Serbian, Slovak, or Ukrainian.

KEYS TO SUCCESS

* Begin by using online map libraries and modern atlases to familiarize yourself with the geography of your ancestor's homeland.

* Move on to printed and microfilmed resources to get a more detailed picture of a particular location.

* Know the administrative districts of your ancestors' country. This will help you identify the locations of genealogical records.

* Consult gazetteers (geographical dictionaries) to learn important details about your ancestor's village, including which administrative districts it's in, as well as information about churches the locals attended.

7

Language, Surnames, and Given Names

Names are a common roadblock in Polish, Czech, and Slovak genealogical research. It could be you don't have a consistent or correct spelling. More often, you know the right name but can't seem to find it in an index. Such name stumpers can be the result of foreign spelling, foreign accents, bad handwriting, nicknames, and name changes. Playing the "name game" is inevitable in Eastern European genealogy, as the name you know your ancestor by or see in North American records may or may not be the one he or she used back home.

As you will see, language—whether Polish, Czech, Slovak, Latin, Hungarian, German, or Russian—plays an important role when determining and deciphering names. This chapter will look at how the Polish, Czech, and Slovak languages relate to surnames and naming patterns, as well as ways to work around these potential roadblocks. Be sure to have your Name Variants Worksheet from chapter 3 handy to piece together your family's name puzzles.

SURNAME RESEARCH BASICS

Surnames were created out of necessity—they came about gradually as populations grew and contact between isolated groups of people increased. People were generally referred to by their first names. Last names developed to distinguish one person from another. For example, a small village could have many young men named Jan. To avoid confusion, the local populace would attach a descriptor to distinguish one Jan from another. Surnames usually fall into four basic categories:

- **occupation:** Trades or professions were perhaps the most common basis for surnames, such as *Sedlák,* which means "landowning farmer"; *Kucharski,* "cook"; or *Dvořák,* "landowner."

- **physical characteristics:** These could be complimentary (*Wilczek,* for "wolf") or not (*Cibuľka* means "little onion").

- **geography:** Also called habitational names, geography-based surnames relate to places or landmarks, as in *Slezák* ("Silesian"), *Zaleski* (derived from *za,* meaning "behind" or "beyond").

- **father's name:** Called patronyms, these surnames were created by adding a suffix to the father's name. For example, *Janáček* means "little Jan" (son of John); *Piotrowski* and its variant *Pietrowski* are both patronymic versions of *Piotr.*

Some examples of the surnames from my own family tree include *Figlyar* (trickster, jokester) and *Alzo* (from *also,* meaning "lower"). Nicknames may have been added to further distinguish people. In addition, surnames take different forms with the language and culture.

In the 1800s and earlier, spelling was not standardized as it is today. As a result, multiple phonetic variations to a name's spelling were common. Due to colloquialisms and regional dialects, name spellings changed depending on where you were. You may likely discover different spellings or versions of the family name. For example, my grandfather spelled his name *Figlar,* but one of his brothers spelled it *Figler.* Another family name, *Straka,* appears as *Sztraka* (Hungarian spelling) and in American records as *Stracha* or *Strake.*

How to Overcome Name Obstacles

Teasing your Polish, Czech, or Slovak ancestors' names out of online databases can be challenging. When you're confused about where to look next, keep these five factors in mind.

SOUNDS

Be aware of the way the immigrant's original language sounded, because it may account for some of the incorrect spellings you will encounter. For instance, a *ch* combination in one language may sound like an English *ck* or *k* instead. In German, the sound of an initial consonant *b* often sounds like a *p.* Take these pronunciations as well as unique letters into consideration when looking at indexes or search results.

NICKNAMES, MIDDLE NAMES, AND FOREIGN NAMES

Don't overlook your ancestors' nicknames, middle names, or native first names from their home country. *Ludwig, Louis, Lewis*, or *Lou* could all be correct first names for one individual. Some researchers get stumped looking for Uncle Bill or Aunt Stella only to discover that they should have been looking for *Bolesław* or *Stanisława*.

LANGUAGE STANDARDS

When last names were being standardized, each language usually had a single word for commonly used descriptors—for instance, a miller using his profession as a surname would have had *Müller* in German or *Molnár* in Hungarian. As a result, individuals found ways of personalizing their surnames. While the main Slovak surname for miller was *Mlynár*, some Slovaks used the variations *Mlynarčík, Mlynarovič, Mlynárik, Mlynka, Mlynkovič, Minár, Minárik, Minarovič, Mlynček, Mlynčár*, and *Mlynský* to distinguish themselves.

PHONETICS

Some online search forms allow for phonetic name searches. One such option is Soundex, a phonetically based surname "code" that captures similar-sounding names. Soundex is an American invention, however, and doesn't always handle Eastern European surnames well. Alternative Soundex schemes have been developed to overcome this, most notably the Daitch-Mokotoff Soundex system. If a website offers options for Soundex or "sounds like" searches, give those a try.

FOREIGN LETTERS

The Polish, Czech, and Slovak languages have letters that the English alphabet does not, and those letters' pronunciations can create roadblocks for English speakers. For example, the Polish *Ł/ł* often confuses non-Poles—it's pronounced like an English *W*. It may be transcribed as *L/l* in English, or the lowercase version may become the similar-looking lowercase *t*. Similar issues occur with the Polish *ą*—pronounced *ahn* but often transcribed as a simple *a* in English. Remember these letters, too, when you're searching foreign-language indexes and websites—they may be the reason you're not finding what you are looking for.

Resources for Researching Names

In addition to the search tactics we've covered, these resources will help you in tracking down your ancestor's surname.

ONE-NAME STUDIES

One-name studies will likely be one of your first resources in searching for your ancestor's records. Generally, a surname's one-name study encompasses all known variants of that surname and follows that name's occurrences throughout history. One-name studies are especially popular in Great Britain, but you can find some for Slavic surnames. Search the Guild of One-Name Studies' website <www.one-name.org> or use the alphabetical name listing to peruse registered names <www.guild-dev.org/namelist.html>. You can also register with the guild (there is a sliding-scale membership fee based on country) and, if you're so inclined, add a study name. Other general resources include the RootsWeb Surname Resources page <resources.rootsweb.ancestry.com/surnames> and Cyndi's List: Research <www.cyndislist.com/personal>.

DNA STUDIES

Surnames may be wrong, but DNA doesn't lie. A Y-DNA test can show whether two same-named men are related, and if so, estimate the number of generations that separate them from their most recent common ancestor. Family Tree DNA <www.familytreedna.com> is the leading Y-DNA testing company; check its website for surname studies. Those with Czech roots will want to read about the Czech American DNA study at <www.cgsi.org/content/czech-american-dna-study-leo-baca>, which has a listing of surnames that have participated in the study. In chapter 13, you will learn more about using DNA as a tool when you get stuck.

POLISH SURNAMES AND NAMING PATTERNS

Polish surnames developed around the practices described earlier in this chapter. Some Polish surnames are unique to certain regions, while others are found throughout the country. To determine the frequency of a particular Polish surname and its geographical distribution by province, consult *Słownik Nazwisk Współcześnie w Polsce Używanych* (Dictionary of Surnames Currently Used in Poland) edited by Kazimierz Rymut (Polska Akademia Nauk/Instytut Języka Polskiego, 1992). Compiled from a 1990 Polish government database, this was the first comprehensive compilation of Polish surnames, covering 94 percent of the population. This Polish-language work is searchable at <www.herby.com.pl/indexslo.html>. Before using it, consult William F. Hoffman's step-by-step guide

Study Your Surnames

Refer to the following free resources for help with surname meanings and distributions:

- **Ancestry.com <www.ancestry.com/learn/facts>**: Find out interesting facts about your surname, including meaning and history, where in the United States the name is prevalent, and when immigrants with that surname arrived. This is useful for common Polish, Czech, or Slovak surnames (such as *Novak* or *Kowalski*), but not for rarer surnames (including mine, *Alzo*).

- **Behind the Name <www.behindthename.com>**: This website covers the etymology and history of first names (including Polish, Czech, and Slovak versions); for surnames, go to **<surnames.behindthename.com>**.

- **English Versions of Foreign Names <freepages.genealogy.rootsweb.ancestry. com/~atpc/genealogy/surnames/cref-given-names.pdf>**: While admittedly incomplete and missing some sources, this page shows you first names in Polish, Czech, Slovak, and other languages.

- **FamilySearch Wiki <familysearch.org/learn/wiki/en/Surname_ Distribution_ Maps>**: See maps depicting how various surnames are distributed geographically—that is, areas where a name is most common.

- **Locate My Name <www.locatemyname.com>**: Find the distribution of your surnames across countries and regions. A high concentration of one surname in a place indicates that many members of the same family lived there, or even that the name might have originated there. The site also has information on first names, but states that "this is mainly used for entertainment and curiosity and it has no historical value."

- **Moikrewni.pl <www.moikrewni.pl/mapa>**: Covering more than three hundred thousand Polish names, this cross-sectional map shows the breakdown of the name in all districts. Enter a name in the search bar or click the first letter of the name in the navigation bar.

- **Origin and Distribution of Czech Surnames <zlimpkk.tripod.com/Genealogy/czech-surnames.html>**: Read an informative article adapted from "Jak vznikla naše příjmení" (How did our surnames come into being) in the book *Naše Příjmení* (Our Surnames) by Dobrava Moldanová (Mladá Fronta, 1983).

- **Origins of Last Names (Slovakia and Hungary) <www.pitt.edu/~votruba/qsonhist/ lastnamesslovakiahungary.html>**: Prepared by a professor of Slavic languages at the University of Pittsburgh, this site gives the origins of the most common surnames in Slovakia and Hungary.

Top Ten Polish Surnames

These are the most common surnames in Poland today.

Name	Meaning/Translation
Nowak	newman
Kowalski	smith (from *kowal*)
Wiśniewski	cherry (from *wiśnia*)
Wójcik	from *wójt* (the chief officer of a municipality) and the popular name Wojciech, from *wojak* (warrior)
Kowalczyk	patronymic of smith (from *kowal*)
Kamiński	stone (from *kamień*)
Lewandowski	lavender (from *lawenda*)
Zieliński	green (from *zielony*, or *ziele*, which means "herb")
Szymański	patronymic of Simon (from *Szymon*)
Woźniak	usher (from *woźny*)

<www.jri-poland.org/slownik.htm> to learn how to enter names for best results and interpret the results. You'll also want to use Google Translate **<translate.google.com>** to convert the site to rough English.

As we discussed earlier, it was common for Polish immigrants to "translate" their first and last names to English equivalents or alter the spellings to look more American after they settled in their new home. To trace your family in Poland, you need to figure out the original Polish names. Consulting the surname databases described here can help you "repair" personal and place-names recorded incorrectly in American sources. It also helps to gain familiarity with Polish language basics: When you know the sounds associated with certain letters and letter combinations, you'll be able to devise alternative search terms.

You'll also need to know Polish naming practices. Polish Roman Catholics, for example, would often name a child after a saint whose feast day was celebrated on or near the baby's date of birth or baptism. Several books can help you find the proper spellings of surnames and determine given names in German, Hebrew, Latin, Polish, Russian, and Ukrainian: *Polish Surnames: Origins and Meanings,* second edition by William F. Hoffman (Polish Genealogical Society of America, 1997) and *First Names of the Polish Commonwealth: Origins and Meanings* by William F. Hoffman and George W. Helon (Polish Genealogical Society of America, 1998). In addition, *Going Home: A Guide to Polish-Amer-*

ican Family History Research by Jonathan D. Shea (Language and Lineage Press, 2008) includes an index of first names most often seen in Polish research, prepared by Hoffman.

Polish letters with diacritical (accent) marks—*ą, ć, ę, ł, ń, ó, ś, ź,* and *ż*—were often misinterpreted (even in parts of the old country, where records weren't kept in Polish). You might find the given name *Władysław* transcribed as *Wtadystaw*, or the surname *Zdziebko* transcribed as *Fdziebko* because the *Z* was written in the European manner with a slash through the middle, making it look like an *F*. See appendix A for help with the Polish language, and chapter 14 for an example of how the spelling of Polish surnames can change (even beyond the grave).

CZECH AND SLOVAK SURNAMES AND NAMING PATTERNS

The countries surrounding the modern Czech and Slovak republics (Germany, Hungary, and Poland) strongly influenced local names. As in those cultures, Czech and Slovak names generally consist of a given name and a surname. In the Czech lands, the state typically only

Top Ten Czech Surnames

These are the most common surnames in the Czech Republic today.

Name	Meaning/Translation
Novák	new (from *nový*)
Svoboda	freedom
Novotný	new (from *nový*)
Dvořák	grange owner
Černý	black
Procházka	walk
Kučera	curl
Veselý	cheerful
Horák	highlander
Němec	German

Top Ten Slovak Surnames

These are the most common surnames in Slovakia today.

Name	Meaning/Translation
Horváth	Croatian (from the Croatian *Hrvat*)
Kováč	smith
Varga	leatherworker or cobbler (from the Hungarian *varga*)
Tóth	Slovak (from Hungarian *tót*)
Nagy	large (from the Hungarian *nagy*)
Baláž	blessed (from the Hungarian variant of the Latin name *Blasius*)
Szabó	tailor (from the Hungarian *szabó*)
Molnár	miller (from the Hungarian *molnár*)
Balog	left-handed (from the Hungarian *balkezes*)
Lukáč	Luke

Slovak women's surnames often carry the suffix -ova, as shown on this tombstone for Maria and Mikuláš Fenčak in Poša, Slovakia.

recognized these two names, though parents might choose additional names (e.g., middle names) at baptism and individuals may adopt new supplementary names at confirmation (e.g., confirmation names). Most Slovaks also do not have an official middle name. And as in other Western cultures, women in the Czech Republic and Slovakia typically adopted their husbands' surnames upon marriage.

Surname spellings often vary in grammatical context. For example, male Czech surnames may end in -*ovec* or -*úv*, while Slovak names may end in -*ula* or other suffixes. You may encounter patronymic surnames derived from the father's name, such as *Štěpánek* (meaning "little Stephen," indicating a forefather named Stephen); other surnames reflect social status (*Král*, meaning "king"), personal features (*Straka*, meaning "bird" or "magpie"), or trade/occupation (*Bača*, meaning "shepherd"). Czech and Slovak female surnames typically have the suffix -*ova* at the end (such as *Fenčakova* in Slovak, as shown in image **A**). Learn more about surnames in books from the Czechoslovak Genealogical Society International <**www.cgsi.org/store/books?topic_id=31**>.

Like Poles, Czech and Slovak Orthodox and Catholic families frequently named their children for saints. Visit Behind the Name for explanations of common Czech and Slovak given names. Also, learn to recognize regional and cultural translations: Great-great-

Re-create Spelling Mistakes

Having trouble finding your ancestor's name in an index? Try writing out the name in the style of script used at the time. Would a handwritten *P* resemble an *F*? Or perhaps a *J* appears to you as a *Y*? This will help you find variations to try when searching databases and print records.

grandma might appear as *Elizabeth* on her naturalization application, *Alžbeta* in Slovak parish registers, and *Erzsébet* in Hungarian census returns.

Learning Czech and Slovak naming patterns and practices will help you more easily spot spelling variations and transcription errors in records. As you can see from the sidebar of common Slovak surnames, Slovakia's eight hundred years under Hungarian rule heavily influenced the frequency of surnames. The Slovakian and Hungarian languages exchanged words, phrases, and naming patterns with each other and with other surrounding languages, notably Croatian. This "borrowing" of names (as well as migrations of people within the Hungarian empire) caused a mixture of Slavic names. See <**www.pitt. edu/~votruba/qsonhist/lastnamesslovakiahungary.html**> for more on the intermingling of Slavic languages. Note that Hungarians typically put the surname before the given (first) name, so your Slovak ancestors may be sorted by their surname in some records.

KEYS TO SUCCESS

* Learn naming conventions and patterns to help you distinguish your ancestors from others in the same village or town.

* Research the origin of your ancestors' surnames for clues to their lives, appearances, or places of origin, even previous generations' names. Surnames often reflected characteristics of the people or family they described, with origins in place-names, physical characteristics, geography, or the father's name. Czech and Slovak surnames may also show German, Hungarian, and Polish influences.

* Brush up on the basics of your ancestors' language to untangle garbled transcriptions.

* Chart variations of your ancestors' first names and surnames for easy reference when you search online databases and print indexes.

PART 3

TRACING YOUR FAMILY IN POLAND, THE CZECH REPUBLIC, AND SLOVAKIA

8

Vital Records

I n the quest to learn more about your Polish, Czech, or Slovak ancestors, one of your primary goals is likely going to be crossing the pond to find details about an immigrant before he arrived in North America, as well as about the family members who stayed behind. The good news is that Europe has many excellent sources to research. Researchers in the United States and Canada rely heavily on census records, land records, wills, and probates to build a pedigree of their families in North America. In many instances, this is because there is nothing better available. But in Europe, the availability of vital records greatly improves your chances of finding those generational links necessary to work back through history.

Vital records are resources that document basic information about people at important points in their life, such as birth and death. These include religious records (baptisms, marriages, deaths/burials, and confirmations) and civil registration (records of births, marriages, and deaths maintained by government authorities). If you're lucky enough to find surviving vital records for your ancestor, they're excellent sources for names, dates, and places of births, marriages, and deaths, making them essential for genealogical research. While civil registration is a relatively new phenomenon (most countries only mandated universal civil registration in the nineteenth century), some church records date back as early as the 1600s.

In Eastern Europe, vital records are typically kept at the local level—sometimes at a regional archive and in other instances with local registry offices. Therefore, as discussed in earlier chapters, establishing the town or village of origin of an immigrant ancestor is the key to your success. In addition, you'll need basic foreign-language skills, as these records are written in a number of languages: Latin, Polish, Czech, Slovak, Hungarian, German, Ukrainian (Ruthene dialect), Old Church Slavonic, Russian Hebrew, and Yiddish.

In this chapter, we'll discuss the different kinds of vital records, what information about your ancestors you can expect to find in them, and how to locate them in Poland, the Czech Republic, and Slovakia.

TYPES OF RECORDS

To identify which records you may be looking for, you'll need to know when the government in your ancestor's country instituted civil registration. Before that date, the vital records available to you will be those kept by churches and synagogues, so these registers are the records of choice for documenting most Eastern Europeans before the late nineteenth century. Unlike in the United States, virtually every Christian resident in Europe was recorded in and belonged to a church—usually the one endorsed by the state. Some eastern states had two or three churches, but a large majority of residents belonged to just one denomination in each locality: Catholicism, Orthodoxy, or a sect of Protestantism (e.g., Lutheranism or Reformed). Other members of the population belonged to smaller church denominations (such as Mennonites and Baptists) or practiced other religions (such as Judaism).

Don't forget to broaden your search. Once you've found records for your target ancestor, search for his siblings, then for his parents' marriage record. You will then need to search for the relevant deaths, bearing in mind that many children died in infancy and many mothers in childbirth. Repeat this process for other families or generations.

Unfortunately, vital records are not available for all Eastern European locations, as some have been destroyed and others lost over the years. In addition, they may not include everyone who lived in a particular parish—every town had some persons of other faiths—and the fields, especially in earlier records, may not be complete. In addition, records that are available may only be accessible onsite or through a professional researcher.

While the appearance of vital records and the information in them will vary by time and location, most civil registrations and church records in Eastern Europe share certain

Baptismal records, such as this 1897 excerpt of Greek Catholic register from Posa, Slovakia, contain valuable information about a child's birth, legitimacy, and parents. Erzsébet Fencsák's entry is indicated by a box.

194. This happened in Warsaw in the parish of the Holy Cross on the tenth day of May in the year one-thousand eight-hundred sixty-three at the hour of five forty-five in the afternoon. We make it known that in the presence of witnesses Ignacy Iwanowicz, a police prison guard thirty-two years of age, and Józef Trawiński, a master craftsman shoemaker forty-three years of age, residing in Warsaw, on this day a religious marriage was contracted between Stanisław Piątkowski, an unmarried man, twenty-one years of age, a valet in Warsaw, residing at one-thousand seven-hundred seventy-one Letter A [St. Jerski?] Street, born in the town of [Mochilawo?] of the married couple the deceased Ludwik and Benigna née Kosecka Piątkowski, and Apolonia Konopka, an unmarried woman, twenty-one years of age, a maidservant in Warsaw, residing at two-thousand seven-hundred seventy-nine Aleksandrya Street, born in the village of Konopki in the Augustów Gubernia of the married couple the deceased Stanisław and Rozalia née Karwowska Konopka. This wedding was preceded by three readings of the banns here in Warsaw in the parish of the Holy Cross, St. John, and the Birth of the Virgin Mary on the twenty-sixth of April, the third and tenth of May in this same year. The newlyweds stated that they had made no prenuptial agreement between them. This document was read aloud to the newlyweds and witnesses and was signed by the bridegroom and by us because the bride and the witnesses do not write.

Civil marriage records, such as this one recording the marriage of Poles Stanislaw Piątkowski and Apolonia Konopka in 1863, can contain interesting information about your ancestors. A rough translation is on the right.

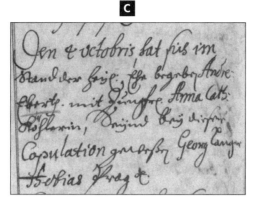

This Czech marriage record from 1876 is in German and translates roughly to: "On October 4, Andreas Eberth and the virgin Anna Catharina Löhlerin betook themselves to the holy marital status. Georg Langer and Thobias Prag witnessed this marriage."

characteristics. In this next section, we'll discuss the major kinds of vital records and what you can expect to find in them.

Birth and Baptismal Records

In most Christian churches, children were baptized shortly after birth, making baptismal records (image 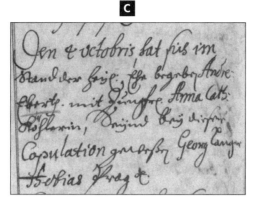) the best resource for information on when your ancestor was born. These records nearly always include the date of baptism, name of the child, the name of the child's father, and the place of birth (often inferred as the parish, if not given directly). Other data such as the date of child's birth, the mother's given name, the father's occupation, the names of the sponsors (e.g., godparents), if the father was deceased at the time of birth or baptism, and the name of officiant (usually the pastor or minister). Sometimes you will also see the following: the mother's maiden name, the parents' house number, the sponsors' village and relationship to the child, and the time of day of the birth. Occasionally you may also see how many previous children the child's parents had (or had baptized), the father's or mother's age, or the occupations of witnesses. Likewise, civil authorities recorded your ancestor's infancy in birth registers, which mirrored the information provided by baptismal records: the date the entry was recorded; the child's name; the place and date of birth; and the ages and residence of the parents. Until the mid-twentieth century, these records also included the parents' religion and the name of any witnesses.

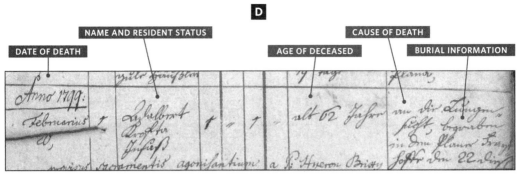

This (church) death record is in German and from a 1799 Czech registry. It reveals that on February 20, 1799, Adalbert Krofta (age 62) died of tuberculosis (*lungensucht*) and that he was buried in Planá on February 22.

Marriage Records

As in modern Western culture, weddings in Eastern Europe were opportunities for celebration with the community as couples began their married life. Marriage records, both civil (image **B**) and church (image **C**), will typically include the date of marriage, the names and residence of the bride and groom, the groom's occupation, and the place where the ceremony took place (often inferred as the parish, if not given directly). Civil records generally have less additional information than their church counterparts, containing just the names and residences of parents and witnesses and (until 1948) the bride and groom's religion. Church records, however, also will usually contain the name of the officiant (usually the pastor or minister) and the names, occupations, and statuses (e.g., alive, dead, widower) of the fathers of the groom and bride, plus information about previous spouses (if any). While less likely, church records may also contain the ages and birthplaces of the bride and groom, the bride's occupation, and the names and statuses (e.g., alive, dead, widowed) of the mothers of the bride and groom.

Confirmation Records

Baptism, marriage services, and burial rites aren't the only church records your ancestor may have left behind. As part of their initiation into full Christian life, followers of many Christian denominations (including Roman Catholics, Eastern Orthodox Christians, and some Protestants) underwent confirmation, in which members of the church who have come of age profess their faith as adults. While difficult to find (many ceremonies weren't recorded and few of those that were have survived), confirmation records can provide helpful clues and a snapshot of your ancestor's youth, including the date of the ceremony (which was usually performed for many individuals at once) and the names of the child and his or her father. In addition, these records may include the child's age (or date of birth) or the family's residence.

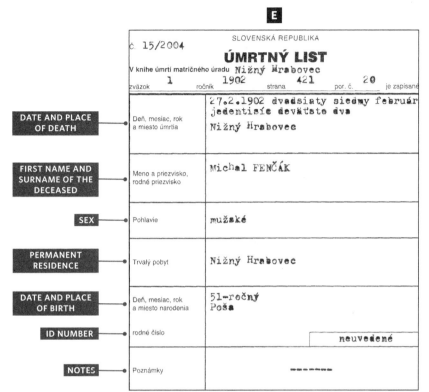

E

SLOVENSKÁ REPUBLIKA

č. 15/2004

ÚMRTNÝ LIST

V knihe úmrtí matričného úradu Nižný Hrabovec

| zväzok 1 | ročník 1902 | strana 421 | por. č. 20 | je zapísané |

DATE AND PLACE OF DEATH	Deň, mesiac, rok a miesto úmrtia	27.2.1902 dvadsiaty siedmy február jedentisíc devätsto dva Nižný Hrabovec
FIRST NAME AND SURNAME OF THE DECEASED	Meno a priezvisko, rodné priezvisko	Michal FENČÁK
SEX	Pohlavie	mužské
PERMANENT RESIDENCE	Trvalý pobyt	Nižný Hrabovec
DATE AND PLACE OF BIRTH	Deň, mesiac, rok a miesto narodenia	51-ročný Poša
ID NUMBER	rodné číslo	neuvedené
NOTES	Poznámky	--------

This 1902 *úmrtný list* (death certificate) for Michal Fenčák is obtained from Nižný Hrabovec, a village in Slovakia.

Death and Burial Records

Records were taken at the end of an ancestor's life by religious (image **D**) and civil (image **E**) institutions to document both the physical (death) and the sacramental (rites of burial). Both kinds of record will nearly always include the date of burial or death and the name and a description (age, occupation, marital status, etc.) of the deceased. Depending on the deceased's age, records might list information about the deceased's father (if she was a child) or spouse and/or surviving children (if he was an adult who married). Sometimes you will also find a woman's maiden name, the residence of the deceased (given as a village or house number), information about the deceased adult's parents, and (perhaps most morbidly interesting) the cause of death. Church records may also contain more detailed information about any surviving children, the time of day when the death occurred, or a funeral sermon.

Because records in Eastern Europe can be difficult to find, it's helpful to understand who kept the records, under what government, and where these records can be found in modern-day Poland, Czech Republic, or Slovakia. Here's a breakdown for each country.

POLAND

As discussed throughout this book, Poland's tumultuous history affects what resources are available for genealogists. Indeed, the format, language, content, and availability of vital records in Poland varies greatly by partition (see chapter 4). However, certain characteristics apply to most Polish vital records. As was the case in the Czech Republic and Slovakia, vital records were administered by the local church or synagogue (rather than the civil government) for centuries, with Catholic clergymen, sometimes acting as registrars for the state, keeping separate registers for each religion. Indeed, most parts of Poland didn't have strictly civil registration until the nineteenth century. The Prussian government began requesting copies of religious vital documents in 1794 but didn't begin its own civil registration until 1874. Likewise, Napoleon III mandated civil registration when he controlled Polish lands in 1808, and the registration continued in Russia-held Poland even after Napoleon's defeat. However, Galicia/Austrian-held Poland had no direct civil registration until Poland's independence in 1918.

In addition, the ruling governments of each partition typically had guidelines regarding what information would be contained in records and even how it would be presented. While the records' formatting can sometimes be confusing, becoming familiar with how records are structured will help you read them more adeptly. Records in Galicia, for example, were usually in Latin and in a columnar format (i.e., set up with columns for each field like US census records) while German-Polish records were in Latin, German, or Polish. Even more confusingly, most of the Russian partition recorded information in paragraph format (i.e., written out in a block of text) and in one of three languages (Latin or Polish until 1867, see image **F**; Russian after 1867) while the eastern portion used columnar format in Russian (after 1850).

Generally speaking, records older than one hundred years are in the state archives while more recent records (which are restricted to only direct-line descendants) are in local vital records offices.

Your first step in finding vital records is seeing if they're located on the Web. The Polish national state archives has digitized many of its available records and made them searchable online at <www.szukajwarchiwach.pl>. In addition, individual parishes and dioceses may have recorded information in their own archives. You can browse a directory of parishes and dioceses at <www.opoka.org.pl/struktury_kosciola/diecezje/index.html>. The *Polskie Towarzystwo Genealogiczne* (Polish Genealogical Society) has also indexed vital

This 1868 Polish language birth record from the Parish at Przytuly, Province of Lomza, is representative of the paragraph style of birth records found in Russian Poland. A rough translation: "This took place on the 21st of February 1868 in the church village of Przytuly at ten o'clock in the morning. Aleksander Kryszczynski appeared, age 30, a farmer in Chrzanowo Cyprki and in the presence of the witnesses Jan Cendrowski, age 60, and Pawel Kaminski, age 40, both farmers residing in Chrzanowo Cyprki, declared that a child of the male sex was born in Chrzanowo Cyprki on the nineteenth day of the current month and year at ten o'clock in the evening to him and his lawful wife Karolina nee Leoszewska, age 28. The child was given the name *Franciszek* today at his holy baptism. The godparents were Feliks Golembiewski and Ewa Okonska. This document was read to those appearing and signed only by me, as they do not know how to write. Signature of Rev. S Kollak, Assistant Pastor and Registrar of VItal Records."

records that are available from many different Polish sites <www.geneteka.genealodzy.pl>. While some of the sites listed in this index will provide a link to a digitized version of the record, others will provide only the year and record number of an individual record. In addition, the Polish state archives databases <www.archiwa.gov.pl> and BASIA (*Baza Systemu Indeksacji Archiwalnej*, or the Archival Database Indexing System), developed by the Wielkopolska Genealogical Society <www.basia.famula.pl/en>, boasts large indices that can help you locate where your ancestor's records might be. Jewish researchers can also search **<www.jri-poland.org>**, while other websites offer resources for more niche groups (marriage records from the city of Poznan at the Poznan Project **<www.poznan-project.psnc.pl>**; records from eastern interwar Poland in modern Ukraine at AGAD **<www.agad.gov.pl/inwentarze/testy.html>**).

Once you've exhausted your online options, consider requesting letters from records offices in Europe. In addition to the state archives system, each town's Urząd Stanu Cywilnego (Vital Statistics Office), or USC, houses records seized by the Communist government when it took power in 1945 that are less than one hundred years old. Records held here are restricted to direct-line descendants and are moved to the state archives once they reach one hundred years old. Depending on where your ancestors lived in historic Polish lands, the records you're looking for may instead be held by governments of modern neighboring countries, including Belarus, Germany, Lithuania, Russia, and Ukraine. See appendixes E and F for specific places to write and appendix G for information on writing request letters. In addition, genealogist and tour guide Lukasz Bielecki has developed a website **<www.donhoward.net/genpoland>** with information on how to request birth, marriage, and death certificates from Poland.

THE CZECH REPUBLIC

The Austrian government began civil registration in 1869; before then, all records were kept by religious authorities. And when it comes to religion in the Czech Republic—well, it's complicated. As throughout Europe, Protestants and Catholics clashed in the Czech lands, and the government allowed only Roman Catholicism in the Czech lands for hundreds of years. With the Patent of Toleration in 1781, Protestants came out of hiding, but

The Greek Catholic Church

The interplay between Orthodox, Greek Catholic, and Roman Catholic churches (three important religious institutions in Slovakia) can be confusing. The Orthodox Church definitively split from the Roman Catholic Church in 1054, but the Greek Catholic Church (Uniate, or Byzantine in America) was a part of the Orthodox Church that reunited with Rome in the mid-1600s in order to gain legal recognition. While still belonging to the (Roman) Catholic Church, the Byzantines maintained a great deal of independence, with unique rituals, services in Greek, and (except in the United States) married priests. As a result, Greek Catholics are officially called "Catholics of the Byzantine Rite" rather than "Catholics of the Roman Rite." Most Balkan Slavs (Bulgarians, Serbians, etc.) and Eastern Slavs (Russians, Ukrainians, Belorussians, Rusyns) remained Orthodox Christians but later, under various political pressures, united or reunited with Rome (hence the name "Uniates").

the majority of the country remained Catholic. Indeed, all vital events until 1849 were recorded in Catholic registers; Protestants who refused the Catholic authority simply weren't recorded. Following the Catholic Hapsburg monarchy's decline, the Catholic Church's influence waned and people began declaring themselves "without confession" (*bez vyznání*) or as belonging to the new Czechoslovak (Hussite) church. Despite these trends, don't assume anything about your ancestor's religion or what records might be available. Even if you think your ancestor went against the establishment when it came to religion, you should still investigate vital records kept by the church.

Czech vital records are usually in one of three languages: Czech, German, or Latin. Often one parish has records written in all three. Records from one state regional archive (*statní oblastní*) may favor one or more languages. For example, records from Litoměřice are usually written in German or Latin, while records from Plzeň or Třeboň are usually written in Czech, German, and Latin equally. To learn more, and to view additional sample Czech Church records, go to **<www.familysearch.org/learn/wiki/en/ Czech_Republic_Church_Books_(FamilySearch_Historical_Records)>**.

The Czech Republic has an extensive state archives system. In addition to the National Archives (*Narodni Archiv*) **<www.nacr.cz>** in Praha/Prague, seven regional archives document the history of different sections of the modern country: Brno (southern Moravia), Litoměřice (northern Moravia), Opava (northern Moravia), Plzeň (western Bohemia) Praha/Prague (middle Bohemia), Třeboň (southern Bohemia), and Zamrsk (eastern Bohemia). Czech church registers, plus early cadastral maps, architectural plans, court records, administrative papers, and other historical documents, are accessible at the appropriate archive in the Czech Republic should you choose to travel there or hire a private researcher. Note that privacy laws restrict access to birth records for one hundred years and death records for seventy-five years, except for immediate family members.

Records from these regional archives are now being made available online, but most are not yet indexed. FamilySearch.org has selected records from certain archives. Click on the link with the magnifying glass that says Browse All Published Collections, then select Continental Europe and Czech Republic. You will want to keep checking back with these resources, as they're periodically updated. Due to privacy laws, recent records may not be displayed.

In addition, the Třeboň archive itself is putting images of its records online at **<digi. ceskearchivy.cz/index_main.php?lang=en>**, and you must register for an account to view them. In addition, a Prague population registration from 1850 to 1914, available through the national archives in Prague **<digi.nacr.cz/prihlasky2>**, might be helpful as well.

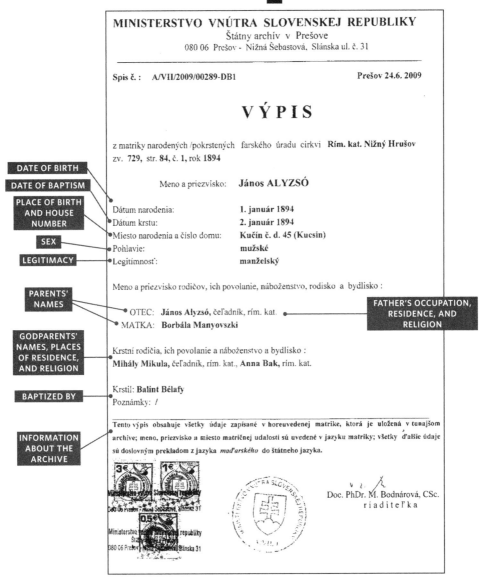

G

MINISTERSTVO VNÚTRA SLOVENSKEJ REPUBLIKY
Štátny archív v Prešove
080 06 Prešov - Nižná Šebastová, Slánska ul. č. 31

Spis č. :   A/VII/2009/00289-DB1   Prešov 24.6. 2009

VÝPIS

z matriky narodených /pokrstených farského úradu cirkvi **Rím. kat. Nižný Hrušov**
zv. 729, str. 84, č. 1, rok 1894

DATE OF BIRTH

DATE OF BAPTISM

Meno a priezvisko: **János ALYZSÓ**

PLACE OF BIRTH AND HOUSE NUMBER

Dátum narodenia: **1. január 1894**
Dátum krstu: **2. január 1894**
Miesto narodenia a číslo domu: **Kučín č. d. 45 (Kucsin)**

SEX

Pohlavie: **mužské**

LEGITIMACY

Legitimnosť: **manželský**

Meno a priezvisko rodičov, ich povolanie, náboženstvo, rodisko a bydlisko :

PARENTS' NAMES

OTEC: **János Alyzsó**, čeľadník, rím. kat.
MATKA: **Borbála Manyovszki**

FATHER'S OCCUPATION, RESIDENCE, AND RELIGION

GODPARENTS' NAMES, PLACES OF RESIDENCE, AND RELIGION

Krstní rodičia, ich povolanie a náboženstvo a bydlisko :
Mihály Mikula, čeľadník, rím. kat., **Anna Bak,** rím. kat.

BAPTIZED BY

Krstil: **Balint Bélafy**
Poznámky: /

INFORMATION ABOUT THE ARCHIVE

Tento výpis obsahuje všetky údaje zapísané v horeuvedenej matrike, ktorá je uložená v tunajšom archíve; meno, priezvisko a miesto matričnej udalosti sú uvedené v jazyku matriky; všetky ďalšie údaje sú doslovným prekladom z jazyka *maďarského* do štátneho jazyka.

Doc. PhDr. M. Bodnárová, CSc.
r i a d i t e ľ k a

This transcript of a *matriky* record for János Alzsó, born January 1, 1894, was obtained from correspondence with the Prešov archives in Slovakia. According to the record, both János' father and godfather listed their occupation as groomer or servant (*čeľadník*).

SLOVAKIA

Before 1895, different churches and Jewish congregations recorded births, marriages, and deaths in parish and/or synagogue registers. The Hungarian government first instituted civil vital records in 1895, largely to better handle baptismal records of children born to families of mixed religions. Since then, there have been two concurrent systems of civil and church/synagogue vital records, as imperial law also required that the parish registers record births, deaths, and marriages separately for each village in the parish.

The earliest church register from Slovakia (Košice) began in 1587. Some Catholic registers date from the early and mid-1600s, but most are from the early 1700s. Protestant churches usually did not begin to maintain parish registers until the late 1600s, and Catholic priests were ordered to record Protestants in their books in 1730. It wasn't until 1787 that they were authorized to keep registers independent of Catholic control. Greek Catholic parishes started keeping records in the mid-eighteenth century. If you are searching for Jewish ancestors, look in Catholic books because, until 1868, Jews can often be found in those registers.

Most church records more than one hundred years old are now kept in state regional archives, and later records are maintained in the vital records sections of local city offices. Until 1950, when the government instituted civil registration in state archives (*štátne archívy*), the churches held all of the official village records for birth, marriage, and deaths. Church records from before 1895 were transferred to the state archives (with some exceptions) while most later records are still held in parish offices.

Slovakia has seven state archives, located in Bystrica, Bratislava, Bytča, Košice, Levoča, Nitra, and Prešov **<www.minv.sk/swift_data/source/verejna_sprava/pictures/statny_archiv_sr/ p19-01-09.jpg>**. These archives hold most pre-1900 parish books and so are the most important for Slovak researchers. In addition to early parish books, the state archives house an enormous amount of important material including early cadastral maps, architectural plans, historical documents, court records, administrative papers, and more. The archives maintain extensive catalogs of their holdings, but these are not yet online.

Slovak church registers (image **G**) are also accessible to those who hire a private researcher to visit the archives for them or who can visit the archives in Slovakia themselves and research the records in person. Privacy laws may apply; a reliable professional researcher will be able to advise you.

In general, you will want to look for your ancestors' parish to determine which branch of the state archives to search—but be aware that some villages' church records were kept in different parishes or larger, nearby towns. Specialty maps such as the *Všetky kostoly Slovenska* (church locator map) **<dennikn.sk/160769/kostoly-slovenska-mapa-fotky>** are

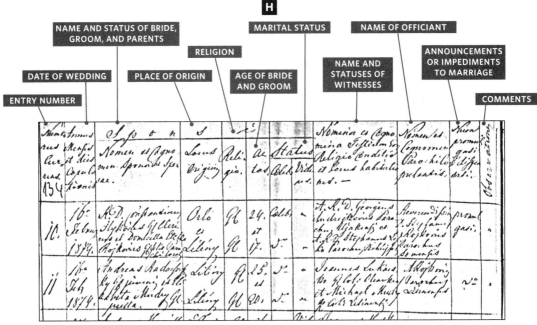

H

NAME AND STATUS OF BRIDE, GROOM, AND PARENTS

DATE OF WEDDING

ENTRY NUMBER

PLACE OF ORIGIN

RELIGION

MARITAL STATUS

AGE OF BRIDE AND GROOM

NAME AND STATUSES OF WITNESSES

NAME OF OFFICIANT

ANNOUNCEMENTS OR IMPEDIMENTS TO MARRIAGE

COMMENTS

Once you familiarize yourself with their columnar structure, church marriage registers, such as this 1874 excerpt from Slovakia, provide valuable information about the bride and groom and their parents and witnesses.

Reading Tabular Records

Before the 1800s, most records were written freehand, which can look intimidating at first glance. While it can be frustrating to search for a surname in records of this format, you can still do so. Some ruling governments instituted specific rules on how these records would be presented. For example, the Hungarians, who ruled Slovakia, attempted to put some discipline into record keeping with a tabular recording method (though the actual date of this standardization varies by parish). Most of these records (images **H** and **I**) are written in Magyar (Hungarian), Ukrainian, Slovak, or sometimes Cyrillic (a Greek-based language that incorporates Slavic sounds).

When you first see this type of record, you may feel intimidated by the language. But, once you identify the column headings, the data contained therein is fairly standard: dates, given names, surnames, or place-names. Some of these words are not presently in use and may not be found in modern-day dictionaries or in translation tools such as Google Translate. You can find language translation aids on the FamilySearch Wiki **<www.familysearch.org/learn/wiki/en/Category:Word_List>** or by visiting **<www.iabsi.com/gen/public/CensusMain.htm#feudal>**. Also see appendixes A, B, and C for help with the Polish, Czech, and Slovak languages.

ENTRY NUMBER

DATE OF DEATH

PLACE OF ORIGIN AND RESIDENCE

GIVEN LAST RIGHTS?

AGE OF DECEASED

PLACE AND DAY OF BURIAL

NAME OF BURIAL PERSON

NAME AND STATUS OF DECEASED

GENDER (MALE IS LEFT)

CAUSE OF DEATH

COMMENTS

Handwriting can be difficult to decipher in old records, such as this 1879 Slovakian death register. But learning what information each column contains is an important first step to making sense of these valuable records.

useful for finding your ancestor's parish in Europe. In addition, you may find it helpful to consult the *Matričný Slovník: Pomôcka na Zapisovanie Údajov do Cirkevných Matrík* (Parish Registers' Vocabulary: Tool for Recording Data in Parish Registers) (Spolok svätého Vojtecha, 1999), which you can locate via WorldCat <www.worldcat.org>.

The Genealogical Society of Utah (associated with FamilySearch) began microfilming Slovak archive vital records in 1991. Although the microfilming is not complete, most of the films are now available through the FamilySearch Centers. FamilySearch also has the following collection online: Slovakia, Church and Synagogue Books, 1592–1910. Click the Learn More button to access a FamilySearch Wiki article on Slovak Church and Synagogue Books and see Slovak record examples at <www.familysearch.org/learn/wiki/en/Slovakia_Church_and_Synagogue_Books_(FamilySearch_Historical_Records)>. On FamilySearch.org, click the magnifying glass labeled Browse All Published Collections, then Continental Europe and Slovakia, or go directly to Slovakia, Church and Synagogue Books, 1592–1910 <www.familysearch.org/search/collection/1554443>. FamilySearch.org also has a handy tool that indicates the number of records, the places and years covered, and the type of event being covered in each resource <www.familysearch.org/learn/wiki/en/Slovakia_Church_and_Synagogue_Books_(FamilySearch_Historical_Records)_Coverage_Table>.

✷ Make finding vital records (such as birth/baptism, marriage, and death/burial) your first genealogical priority, as these resources can give you the most basic information about your ancestor and serve as a springboard for future Eastern European research.

✷ Take the time to learn in what year the region your ancestor lived in mandated civil registration. This will help you identify what records you should be looking for, as churches were the primary keeper of vital records for centuries.

✷ Brush up on your Polish, Czech, and Slovak history (see chapters 4 and 5) and language (see chapter 7 and appendixes A, B, and C) to help you make sense of the records you find.

✷ Exhaust all online resources before writing to archives overseas for records, as many are held by smaller local archives and are restricted to those who can prove direct-line descent.

VITAL RECORDS CHECKLIST

Ancestor's name: _____

Ancestor's maiden name (if female): _____

Residence/location(s): _____

Religion (if known): _____

Fill in the following information as you discover it and confirm it in your research.

Birth

Date birth records started in birthplace: _____

Date of birth: _____ Birthplace: _____

Mother's name: _____

Father's name: _____

Source(s): _____

Marriage

Date marriage records started in marriage place: _____

Date of marriage: _____ Place of marriage: _____

Spouse's name: _____

Source(s): _____

Death/Burial

Date death records started in death place: _____

Date of death: _____ Place of death: _____

Cause of death: _____

Source(s): _____

Date of burial: _____ Place of burial: _____

Cemetery name: _____

9

Census Records

As you learned in chapter 8, church registers are the most popular and useful sources for tracing most Eastern European ancestors. Often these are the only records in which you will find information about your Polish, Czech, or Slovak ancestors and their families in the old country. When census records are available, however, they can be useful, especially in the absence of church and vital records for your locality.

As you probably learned from exploring US or Canadian census records for your ancestors, the prime value of census records is for grouping families together. In Eastern Europe, censuses were usually taken for tax and military conscription purposes. Searching census records can be hit or miss depending on the country, the region, and whether or not registers have been preserved. Because of shifting borders and the destruction of records during wartime hostilities, only relatively small portions of certain record groups survived in many instances. Therefore, you should check registers of births, marriages, and deaths (not census records) first, opposite of what genealogists typically do when looking at North American records for their ancestors.

This chapter will provide an overview of what census records are available, where to find them, and which censuses will be most applicable to your research.

CENSUS RECORDS IN POLAND

The different types of population counts in Polish history have been lustrums (*lustracje, which were historically taken every five years*), household tax registers (*rejestry podatkowe*: 1675), Prussian population surveys (*przeglądy*: 1789, 1793, and 1797), and municipal revisions (*spisy ludności*: 1619, 1765, and 1792). The earliest were parish censuses taken in 1567, 1676, and 1775.

In Russian Poland (Kingdom of Poland), the government's Statistical Department within the General Administration Department (*Oddział Statystyczny przy Wydziale Administracji Ogólnej*) was founded in 1847 to oversee the collection of statistical reports, including censuses.

Contents of Polish censuses vary according to the censuses and their purposes. For example, the 1793 census for South Prussia (the area taken by Prussia in the 1793 partition) includes names of adult males and widows, the number of people in each household and their householders, but no ages.

Some censuses include specific information. For example, the 1790–1792 census of Poznan (*Posen*) and Kraków includes school-age children as well as adults and has dates of birth, marriage, and death. Later census records are more standard and include names of heads of family and their children in chronological order, sex, ages or dates and places of birth, civil status, occupations, duration of residency, and so on. For larger cities in Poland, you can find street addresses in city, occupational, or business directories; civil certificates of birth, marriages, and deaths; church records of christenings, burials, and marriages; and taxation records.

Census records for nineteenth-century Poland largely were not preserved (in some instances only compiled information remains) and as such are not available for research. Fragments from limited time periods exist in various archives.

Some census records still exist in archives but are usually not available to researchers. Some censuses are in the Main Archives of Ancient Documents (*Archiwum Główne Akt Dawnych*, or AGAD) in Warsaw; various district and municipal archives, such as Płock and Kraków; or even local parishes. Most Polish census records are missing, so you may have to contact various archives in the vicinity of the town where your ancestor lived.

RESEARCH TIP

Get Street Smart

Finding the street where your ancestor lived will help you search other kinds of records, such as civil registrations and church records (see chapter 8).

Familysearch has copies of census records for very few towns in Poland. You will find them in the FamilySearch Catalog under Poland (Province), then (Town) Census. In addition, Ancestry.com has a database of 1939 Jewish census records from Będzin at **<search. ancestry.com/search/db.aspx?dbid=1516>**.

From 1772 to 1773, Prussia conducted a land tax census (*Marburger Auszüge*) of all the Polish lands that it acquired in West Prussia to determine the heads of household, obtain a count of family members, and tax the new households. The paper census was held in the Herder Institute in Marburg, Germany. Microfilm copies are held in the Scientific Institute in Turin, Poland, and a digital index of the Polish heads of household enumerated in this census is available from the Odessa Digital Library collections at **<www.odessa3.org/ collections/land/wprussia>**.

You also may occasionally come across preserved population registers that list family members in each household along with their birth dates, parents' names, birthplaces, and marital status. These registers were updated on a continual basis, recording any changes in family composition or residence. If extant, these registers are housed in the national

Poland Population Censuses

The following is a list of Polish censuses provided by The Polish Genealogy Project **<www. polishgeno.com/?page_id=10>**. While some genealogists might find them helpful, they are not available online and are only accessible through on-site research in the archives or with the assistance of a professional researcher.

- **Poland, 1789:** first nationwide census of population
- **Poland, 1808–1810:** first (complete) general censuses of population in the Grand Duchy of Warsaw
- **Prussia, 1840:** first general census of the population of the Grand Duchy of Poznan (then surveyed every three to five years until 1914)
- **Austria, 1857:** first general census of population in Galicia; conducted again in 1869, 1880, 1890, 1900, and 1910
- **Russia, 1897:** general census of population in the Congress Poland (the only one carried in that area until World War I)
- **Poland, 1921:** first general census of the population of post-WWI Poland; conducted again in 1931
- **German-occupied Poland, 1943:** summary census of population
- **Poland, 1946:** first summary census of the population of post-WWII Poland; conducted again in 1950, 1960, 1970, 1978, 1988, and 2002

archives. You can search a database of this material listed by locality on the *Ewidencje Ludności w Archiwaliach* (Registers of Population in Archival Materials) database **<baza. archiwa.gov.pl/sezam/ela.php?l=en>**. This database comprises information on all population registers (lists, rolls, indexes, etc.) found in archival materials of all branches of the Polish national archives. Note that this database does not contain information on parish registers and civil registration nor any lists of names or information on specific people or places. There are other censuses that might be useful for statistical purposes like the 1921 Polish census or the 1897 compilation of localities in Galicia by Jan Bigo. See the Poland Population Censuses sidebar for a list.

Keep in mind that while census records can provide information when other records are missing, proceed with caution when using the information, since it may have been given to a census taker by any member of the family or a neighbor and could be incorrect.

CENSUS RECORDS IN THE CZECH REPUBLIC

In the Czech Republic, the first censuses were taken beginning in 1158 but have only been preserved in fragments. The records are at the national archives in Prague (no inventory has been published) and are all in Latin.

The first census to record people by name (and therefore to be the most useful to genealogists) was the *Soupis poddaných podle víry z roku 1651* (Register of People by Denomination of 1651). The Catholic Habsburg rulers ordered the 1651 census of the Czech lands to determine the religion of the people and the prospects of their conversion. This census was taken to obtain religious information in preparation for the Hapsburgs bringing the country back in line with Roman Catholicism (see chapter 5). Some entire estates are conspicuously missing from the census (presumably Protestant families fearing persecution), but it appears that the overwhelming majority of the populace of Bohemia was recorded.

The 1651 census, which was recorded in German, lists the names of all heads of household, along with names of spouses, children, and servants. Also listed are occupation, age, religion (i.e., whether Catholic or not), and if not Catholic, whether there was hope/no hope of conversion. View a sample page of the 1651 census on FamilySearch.org **<www. familysearch.org/learn/wiki/en/File:1651_census_of_Podebrady.jpg>**.

Summaries also remain of a 1702 count of all people over the age of ten. Though most of them have been lost, censuses were carried out in 1754 and 1762 with revisions every few years, plus population counts in 1770 and 1776 that were largely for military purposes. FamilySearch's Family History Library (FHL) holds some books containing surviving names of Prague residents from the 1770 census. The first true, comprehensive census was conducted in 1857. To learn more, consult the example on the Czech Census Searchers website **<www.czechfamilytree.com/1857census.htm>**. Various censuses were

Surviving census records, such as this 1880 excerpt from the Bruntál district in the Czech Republic, can help you group families together.

subsequently taken regularly (1869, 1880, 1890, various intervals during the 1900s, and 2001). Beginning in 1724, a periodical census of Jews was taken.

While many of the census records in the Czech Republic have been preserved, most of the returns with lists of inhabitants have been lost. In most cases, only summary information from the censuses is available. You will find the contents of Czech census records vary. Some censuses list only the head of household, conscription number of the house, and information on taxable property. Many census returns from the 1800s give house number, head of household, names of members of the household (including servants), ages, occupations, religions, and relationships to the head of household; some also give date and place of birth. An 1869 census holds the greatest amount of information on each family (although censuses as early as 1825 to 1840 may list birthplace, which is the most important piece of information). Each person in the household is listed with his or her sex, birth year, marital status, occupation, religion, and other information. View sample images (image **A**) along with English translations of the column headings on FamilySearch.org <www.familysearch.org/learn/wiki/en/Czech_Republic_Census#1869_Census>.

Generally, surviving census records are stored in district archives (*okresní archívy*) and city archives (*městské archívy*). Census returns are usually not stored in the state regional archives (*státní oblastní archívy*). See chapter 8 for information on these archives.

Some census returns have been published. The FHL has published copies of the Prague census and parts of the 1651 and 1770 censuses. FamilySearch.org has an unindexed collection of more than three million census record images from the Czech Republic covering select areas from 1800 to 1945 at **<www.familysearch.org/search/ collection/1930345>**. You also can browse censuses from 1857 to 1921 on subscription site Ancestry.com at **<search.ancestry.com/search/db.aspx?dbid=60253>**.

Presently, other census materials may be researched in person at the Czech archives, or you may be able to hire a private researcher to search the records for you.

CENSUS RECORDS IN SLOVAKIA

In Slovakia, censuses were taken in the same manner as those conducted in the Czech lands, but according to Hungarian law. Again, these censuses were mostly used for statistical purposes (e.g., taxation and conscription). The first census of the inhabitants of the Kingdom of Hungary took place between 1784 and 1785. Other Hungarian censuses were conducted in 1808, 1828, 1848 (Jews only), 1850, 1857, 1869, 1880, 1890, 1900, and 1910. Under the Czechoslovak government, Slovakia had censuses in 1921, then every ten years from 1930 to 1980, then again in 1991.

Census contents vary. Some censuses list only the head of household, conscription number of house, and taxable property. Many nineteenth-century census returns give house number, head of household, names of members of the household (including servants), ages, occupations, religions, and relationships to the head of household; some also give date and place of birth.

Because most censuses are geographically limited or focus solely on landowners, the 1869 Hungarian census is perhaps the most valuable for genealogical researchers. In some instances, you may be able to obtain at least the year of birth for some of your ancestors when the information is not available in church records. The data listed in each entry include each occupant's name, birth date, birthplace, occupation, religion, ethnicity, literacy, and other items. Also noted is a detailed inventory of livestock, probably your ancestor's most valued asset.

Note that this census does not cover all of Slovakia, but only the regions Bytča, Banská Bystrica, and Nitra. Note, too, that because the collection consists of census records created during the period of the Hungarian Empire, the census forms in this record are written in Hungarian and (primarily) German. The 1869 Hungarian census is in FamilySearch. org's digitized collections **<www.familysearch.org/search/collection/1986782>**, as well as on Ancestry.com **<search.ancestry.com/search/db.aspx?dbid=60145>**. At the time of this writing, the collections are not searchable by name, but you can browse the collections'

Browsing on FamilySearch.org

While some records on FamilySearch.org aren't currently indexed and keyword searchable, they're still worth examining if you believe your ancestors' records may be hiding in them. When viewing an unindexed collection, go through the images one by one and compare the information listed with what you already know about your ancestors, such as their names, ages at the time of the census, and hometowns, to determine if the census image you're viewing contains a match. Because these records are handwritten, you may have to read around marks that obscure the information made by the clerks who compiled the census data. To learn more about browsing unindexed records, read the *Unofficial Guide to FamilySearch.org* by Dana McCullough (Family Tree Books, 2015) **<www.shopfamilytree.com/unofficial-guide-familysearch>**.

images. To learn more and view a sample 1869 census record go to **<www.familysearch.org/learn/wiki/en/Slovakia,_Census,_1869_(FamilySearch_Historical_Records)>**.

The best place to begin looking for Slovak censuses is the FHL. Census returns are listed in the FamilySearch Catalog under Hungary—Census and Slovakia—Census. To learn more, consult *Hungarian Census Returns* by Daniel Schlyter (1982), available in book form at the FHL and on microfiche. Another useful resource with detailed explanations and examples of the Magyar (Hungarian) censuses is the Slovak Genealogy Research Strategies website **<www.iabsi.com/gen/public/CensusMain.htm>**.

Additional Slovak Census Resources

Slovak researchers may find other, more unique censuses helpful as well. For example, a 1775 Ubarial census defined the goods and services that a serf was obligated to give the feudal lord and included the names of landowners and serfs. Microfilm copies of these censuses are found at the FHL, which you can locate via the FamilySearch Catalog under Slovakia, then Slovakia—Taxation. Note that this census uses old Magyar village names. To view an example, see **<www.iabsi.com/gen/public/census_1775_1828_examples.htm#1775>**.

Likewise, an 1828 land and property holder census documents less than 20 percent of the total Kingdom of Hungary population. Organized by village, this census is written in Latin and has three components for each listed village: a title sheet (village and key village individuals), an enumeration sheet (each head of household), and an observation sheet. You can access the 1828 census via FamilySearch microfilm. While FamilySearch has not indexed villages mentioned in the census, the Slovakia Genealogy Research Strategies website listed earlier provides a helpful list of "Villages named in the 1828 Hungarian

Census," produced by genealogist John Adam. Using this document is the only quick way to locate a village on the census, as the census contains all Hungarian counties (rather than just Slovakia). To view a sample of the 1828 census, see **<www.iabsi.com/gen/public/ census_1775_1828_examples.htm>**.

Finally, a special 1848 census of Jews in Hungary is available at the national archives of Hungary **<www.mnl.gov.hu>** and FamilySearch **<www.familysearch.org/search/cat alog/352982?availability=Family%20History%20Library>**. In addition, JewishGen has transcribed many of these records. See its 1848 census page **<www.jewishgen.org/ Hungary/1848Introduction.htm>** for details, as well as the collection on Ancestry.com **<search.ancestry.com/search/db.aspx?dbid=1382>**.

KEYS TO SUCCESS

✴ Turn to census records in the absence of church and civil vital records for your locality. When available, they could help you retrieve details about an ancestor such as birth date and birthplace and information on other family members.

✴ Know what resources for census records are available. Censuses have limited availability in Poland, with many available only through specific archives. In the Czech Republic, censuses with the most genealogical value include the Register of People by Denomination of 1651 and the 1869 census. The 1869 Hungarian census may prove to be the most valuable census for Slovak researchers.

✴ Utilize FamilySearch's online collections, microfilms, and printed sources before you attempt to contact an archive in Poland, the Czech Republic, or Slovakia or spend money hiring a researcher to obtain census or other records.

10

Military Records

Military records are often considered a secondary resource for genealogical researchers exploring roots in Poland, the Czech Republic, and Slovakia. Why? Because they are not easy records to locate. If you can locate these records, however, you could enhance your understanding of both the time period during which he lived as well as insight into his personal and family life.

To find military records for the Austro-Hungarian Army, you first need to determine where and how to look for them, since they were kept at different locations throughout history and were kept differently for the various states within the empire. (Review chapters 4 and 5 to understand the history of the Austrian Empire and the subsequent Austro-Hungarian Empire.) Also consider that the army not only protected the country against external threats, but also maintained control of the various ethnic groups within its borders. There is a useful timeline of historical maps to aid you in further understanding the history of Hungary at **<www.zum.de/whkmla/histatlas/eceurope/haxhungary.html>**.

There are a few other general principles to keep in mind when searching for military records. The time period in which your ancestors lived is perhaps the most important, as this determines whether your ancestor served during the Partitions of Poland or the Austro-Hungarian rule over the Czech and Slovak republics (see the timeline of War in

TIMELINE War in Eastern Europe

The modern Poland, Czech Republic, and Slovakia have been at the crossroads of various conflicts for centuries, and understanding when some of these conflicts occurred can be crucial to identifying and finding military records that your ancestors can be found in. Check out this timeline of major military conflicts that your ancestors may have fought since 1700:

1701-1714 War of the Spanish Succession: Powers collide over the future of the Spanish Empire following the death of King Charles II.

1718-1720 War of the Quadruple Alliance: Great Britain, France, the Holy Roman Empire (including Austria), and the Dutch Republic curb Spain's expansionist plans.

1733-1738 War of the Polish Succession: Hapsburgs and Bourbons struggle over who will rule as the next Polish king.

1740-1748 War of the Austrian Succession: European states protest the succession of Maria Theresa as empress of the Hapsburg Empire.

1756-1763 Seven Years' War: Disputes between France and Great Britain in the New World spill over into Europe, where the major powers collide.

1803-1815 Napoleonic Wars: European powers unite to defeat France under Napoleon III.

1863-1864 January Uprising: Poles rebel against the Imperial Russian Army.

1914-1919 World War I: Allied Powers square off against the Central Powers (Germany, Austria-Hungary, Bulgaria, and the Ottoman Empire). Nations (including Poland and Czechoslovakia) battle for independence and over territory from the dissolved Austria-Hungarian Empire.

1917-1922 Russian Civil War: Revolutionaries overthrow the czarist government and, later, the Communist party takes control.

1939-1945 World War II: Allied Powers fight to defeat fascist Italy and Nazi Germany.

1968 Warsaw Pact Invasion: The Soviet Union and Warsaw Pact states invade Czechoslovakia to quash the Prague Spring.

Eastern Europe). Next, you will need to know how the process of conscription worked and the regiment/military unit your ancestor served in, though finding this information is not always an easy task. Finally, you will need to become familiar with the types of records (e.g., muster sheets, personnel sheets, military citations), which vary by regiment and period. The following is a brief summary of what to expect with military research in Poland, the Czech Republic, and Slovakia, and some of the key military records you might be able to locate for your ancestors.

POLAND

Poland's tumultuous history is reflected in the availability of its military records. In his book *Going Home: A Guide to Polish-American Family History Research* (Language and Lineage Press, 2008), Jonathan D. Shea writes that military records from Poland (if they exist) are most likely to be draft lists, while actual service records will more likely be held by the countries ruling Poland at the time. Shea explains that the latter kinds of records (if extant) will be in Russian or Austrian archives, and that most Prussian military records were destroyed during Allied bombing raids in World War II. To find strictly "Polish" military materials, you will need to look in the Central Military Archives (*Centralne Archiwum Wojskowe*) in Warsaw <www.wp.mil.pl>. These holdings generally cover Poland's history from its independence after World War I to the present. You can find details of the archive's holdings in *Centralne Archiwum Wojskowe: 1918–1998; tradycje, historia, współczesność służby archiwalnej Wojska Polskiego* by Wanda Krystyna Roman (Marszałek, 1999). A search on WorldCat <www.worldcat.org> will help you find a copy in a library nearest to you. Fragments of pre-induction records containing personal information can sometimes be found in various regional archives. You can search the archives on SEZAM <baza.archiwa.gov.pl/sezam/sezam.php?l=en> (or printed guides) to find the proper record group.

Before you do this, however, you should gain an understanding of the draft system. The partitioning powers began mandatory conscription at different times: Russia in 1874, Prussia in 1816, and Austria in 1868. You can learn more about the draft system in "Russian Military Records from the Kingdom of Poland as a Source for Genealogical Research" by Michal Kopczynski from the University of Warsaw. Contact the Polish Genealogical Society of Connecticut and the Northeast about obtaining a copy <www.pgsctne.org/Publications/Publication Spring 2000 to Fall 2002.aspx>.

According to Shea, it is sometimes also possible to locate draft records from the period of the Second Republic (independent Poland 1918–1939) in the state's archive system. These registers are in the record groups of the *starosta* (chief administrative officer). The records deal with individuals over age twenty-one and contain data about the recruit, such as the names of his parents and his place of residence, occupation, level of education, marital status, and condition of health. While only men were drafted, you may find the name of the draftee's female relatives (e.g., his wife) in these records. Note that in some cases, nobility, government officials, and clergymen were exempt. Use the SEZAM database on the Polish state archives website to learn more. If your family's origins lie in Galicia, you will also need to examine the military records generated by the Austro-Hungarian Empire (see section below). Learn more at <www.polishroots.com/Resources/austrian_recruit/tabid/204/Default.aspx> or on the FamilySearch Wiki entry on Polish military records <www.familysearch.org/learn/wiki/en/Poland_Military_Records>.

Twentieth-Century Wartime Records

Hitler's campaign to destroy the Polish nation and Soviet atrocities during World War II generated large bodies of records containing personal data of individuals murdered, imprisoned, or deported. These included

- **concentration camp records**, which are housed at the sites of the former Nazi death camps. Check individual camp websites such as the Auschwitz-Birkenau Memorial and Museum **<www.auschwitz.org>** and JewishGen **<www.Jewishgen.org>**.

- **Yizkor books (books of remembrance)**, which were published after World War II by Jewish Holocaust survivors and often contain name lists and histories of pre-war Jewish Communities **<www.jewishgen.org/yizkor>**.

- **the International Tracing Service**, located in Bad Arolsen, Germany, which has a forty-six-million-card file on Holocaust victims, displaced persons, and camp survivors **<www.its-arolsen.org/en/homepage/index.html>**.

- **repatriation records**, which are found in Poland's state archives and contain personal data on those resettled or deported in the period following World War II.

In addition, Polish army and air force units joined the British in fighting the Nazis during World War II. Check with the UK national archives **<www.nationalarchives.gov.uk/ help-with-your-research/research-guides/royal-air-force-personnel>** for documents from this era if you believe your ancestor may have fought with them. Additionally, after the war, Polish army veterans served with the US Army in Europe, so look for documentation in the appropriate archives. There might be monuments or records in town archives or churches. Also try to connect with historians who specialize in a battle, country, or unit, and check for area war cemeteries.

Don't forget about the index to Haller's Army records, available through the Polish Genealogical Society of America **<www.pgsa.org>**. Named after its commanding general, this Polish army in France comprised nearly twenty thousand Polish immigrants to America that were fighting for Poland's independence during World War I.

THE CZECH REPUBLIC AND SLOVAKIA

Because the modern Czech and Slovak Republics were once under foreign control (see chapter 5), you'll have to review Eastern European history to know which country's armed forces your ancestor might have served in.

Know Your Ancestor's Draft Eligibility

After 1802, the term of military service in the Austrian army was reduced to ten years, but many were still exempt from having to serve. In 1868, a universal conscription went into effect, and every male citizen was obligated to serve three years of active military duty.

Austro-Hungarian Military Records

Military records of Czechs and Slovaks fall under Austria-Hungary until after World War I. In Austria-Hungary, conscription requirements varied over time and national need. In the 1890s, for example, men entered the army at age twenty and were released at age twenty-three with a subsequent nine years in reserves. For later time periods, refer to the resources in the Toolkit: Resources for Military Records sidebar.

In order to successfully research military records for a Czech or Slovak ancestor, you should also understand the administrative and political structure of the Austro-Hungarian Empire. Before 1867, the records of soldiers from across the empire (including Galicia, the modern Czech regions, and Hungary/modern Slovakia) resided in the Vienna War Archives. Once the empire formally became a dual Austro-Hungarian government, records were administered and maintained by either the Austrian (Galicia, Czech lands) or the Hungarian (Slovakia) government. The Empire's successor states (Poland, Czechoslovakia, and other Eastern European countries including Romania, Yugoslavia, and Ukraine) then assumed record-keeping duties following Austria-Hungary's defeat and disbandment in World War I. Learn more in Carl Kotlarchik's "A Guide for Locating Austro-Hungarian Military Records" **<www.ahmilitary.blogspot.com>**. You also can learn more about the army at **<www.austro-hungarian-army.co.uk>**.

Modern Resources

Despite foreign rule for hundreds of years, some records are available in the modern Czech Republic and Slovakia. In the Czech Republic, muster rolls and qualification lists are available from the 1700s through 1915. Military records also have been microfilmed by the FamilySearch. The films are mostly of Austrian records, but some Hungarian records (which, again, include modern Slovakia) are available. These include alphabetically arranged lists of officers and some common soldiers who were not ethnically German. These records are only of value if you know the regiment your ancestor belonged to. Consult *Das Österreichische Heer* for more information **<www.kuk-wehrmacht.de/regiment>**.

Toolkit: Resources for Military Records

The search for an ancestor's military records in the former Austro-Hungarian Empire can be a daunting task. Here is a list of eight essential resources to consult before you begin:

1. "An Introduction to Austrian Military Records" by Steven W. Blodgett, *FEEFHS Journal* Vol. IX, 2001 **<feefhs.org/journal/9/blodgett.pdf>**

2. "Austro-Hungarian Land Forces 1848–1918" by Glenn Jewison and Jorg C. Steiner **<www.austro-hungarian-army.co.uk/index.htm>**

3. "Czech Military Records" by Steven Blodgett, *FEEFHS Journal*, Vol. VII, 1999 **<www.feefhs.org>**

4. "Military Records at the LDS" by Karen Hobbs. Program/Syllabus, 2003 Czechoslovak Genealogical Society International Conference **<www.cgsi.org>**

5. *Fighting Troops of the Austro-Hungarian Army 1868–1914* by James Lucas (Hippocrene Books, 1987)

6. Austro-Hungarian Military Mailing List at RootsWeb **<lists.rootsweb.ancestry.com/index/other/Military:_Europe/AUSTRO-HUNGARIAN-MILITARY.html>**

7. List of Kriegsarchiv holdings **<www.genealogienetz.de/reg/AUT/krainf-e.htm>**

8. Austrian Military Regiment Garrisons within Galicia **<www.polishroots.org/Resources/austrian_garrison/tabid/341/Default.aspx>**

Once you have determined your ancestor's regiment, you can look for his *Grundbuchblätter* personnel records, which contain valuable information. From these records, you can learn the soldier's birth year and location, marital status, civilian occupation, religion, dates of service, description of duties, promotions (if any), and date of discharge.

Military records for soldiers coming from the Czech regions of Bohemia, Moravia, and Silesia from 1820 to 1864 are located at the *Kriegsarchiv* (Austrian State Archives) in Vienna **<www.oesta.gv.at>**. Each is arranged alphabetically by surname and given name.

Keep in mind that finding copies of later resources can be complicated, if not impossible. According to the director of the Kriegsarchiv, *Grundbuchblätter* records of soldiers born from 1865 to 1900 in the Austro-Hungarian Empire were scattered among its successor states following World War I. As a result, the Kriegsarchiv only holds records for soldiers born between 1865 and 1900 who lived within the post-WWI Austrian Republic, while records from other parts of the Empire were kept separately. Many of them have been destroyed, though some records of Czech soldiers born between 1887 and 1900 survive in the Czech Historical Military Archives in Prague.

A

B

First page:

Read carefully the following admonition.
Lack of knowledge (ignorance) does not prevent from criminal consequences.

State Emblem

Military card

First and last name of the card holder:
Figlyar Yan

Year of birth: *1896*
Years of military service: *1918-1920/573*

The organization die and military district's attorney sign:

Hometown local commander office
Signature

Dismantle station
The departure of the person whose name is written above is registered.

On the red seals is written:
Infantry regiment's commander

The sign of military card owner

seal

Jan Figlyar's military book (*Vojenska Knizka*) provides valuable information about him such as year of birth.

As this translation depicts, military passports display their subjects' names, years of birth, and durations of military service.

Unfortunately, records for the remaining regions of the Empire are not organized alphabetically by name. To find these records, you must first determine the regimental number using charts showing where infantry regiments recruited in the various regions of the Empire over different time periods. Sources for these charts include

- "An Introduction to Austrian Military Records," by Steven W. Blodgett, from the *FEEFHS Journal* in 2001 <feefhs.org/journal/9/blodgett.pdf>.

- *Geschichte der k. und k. Wehrmacht[viii]* (History of the Austro-Hungarian Armed Forces) by Alphons Wrede (L.W. Seidel & Son, 1898).

- *Dislokations-Verzeichnis des k.u.k. Heeres und der k.u.k. Marine, 1649–1914* (Location Index for Recruitment into the Imperial and Royal Austrian Army and Navy Troops) by Otto Kasperkowitz (Genealogical Society of Utah, 1978).

Other records of interest may include the pre-1820 *Musterlisten und Standestabellen* (Muster Rolls and Formation Tables), records for officers, and information for other types of units within the army beyond those of the infantry, including the *Jägers* (riflemen), the artillery, the engineers, and the cavalry. Additional types of Czech military records are well described at Czech Census Searchers <www.czechfamilytree.com/military.htm>. For locating

A község és a lajstromában előforduló számnak megnevezése	Sors-szám	A hadkötelezett családi-, kereszt- vagy utó- s egyéb mellékneve	Születési éve	Születési helye (járás és megye)	Vallása és állapota (nőt-len, nős, van-e gyermeke vagy nincs?)	Olvasásban	Irásban	zenében	tornászatban	Művészete, üzlete mestersége, egyéb életmódja	Az ap családi reszt- után
							jártas-e ?				
1	2	3	4	5	6	7	8	9	10	11	
Kladzán	230	*Gesperik Mihály*	*1853.*	*Kladzán*	*nős nőtlen*					*belkötű*	
Póssa	231	*Fencsák Mihály*	"	*Póssa*	*GC*					"	

This cropped page shows the 1873 entry (second row) for Mihály Fencsák, from Póssa, Slovakia. Details include parents' first names, height and chest size, religion, and "weak returned" as the decision of the committee for induction or transfer.

the records of individuals who were born before Czechoslovakia became a state but served in the Czechoslovak army, see information from Slovak genealogy professional researcher Peter Nagy at <www.iabsi.com/gen/public/military_records_in_upper_hungar.htm>.

Refer back to <www.ahmilitary.blogspot.com> to learn more about the discrepancies among these different charting resources and for detailed descriptions and sample images of many different types of Austrian and Hungarian military documents. In addition, see the Toolkit: Resources for Military Records sidebar for additional resources.

The FHL has individual soldiers' records for both Austrian and Hungarian armies until 1870, including military church books for both armies until 1920 and a listing of WWI casualties. WWI records of individual soldiers are only available from the Kriegsarchiv in Vienna.

Records of soldiers who served 1870 to 1914 are more likely to be found in military archives in Prague or Bratislava if the records survived World War II. When the FamilySearch Catalog shows nothing later than 1870, ask the Vienna War Archives if anything is available. The reply will suggest an appropriate national archive when it cannot help.

In addition, Bill Tarkulich gives a great overview entitled "Military Records in Upper Hungary (Slovakia)" on his website <www.iabsi.com/gen/public/military_records_in_upper_hungar.htm> that includes images of military documents issued at different time periods including sample muster lists, *kmenový* (personnel) lists, military citations, and military passports (images **A** and **B**).

Be sure to scour home and family sources, too. Ask your relatives if they have any similar papers that an immigrant ancestor may have brought with him proving service in the Austro-Hungarian military. For example, I have a book from my grandfather (image **C**).

Austrian Military Records from FamilySearch

There are more than twenty-six hundred titles for Austrian military records in the FamilySearch Catalog. About half of them are personnel and regimental records, and the other half are military church books. These records are accessible on film and online <www.familysearch.org/search/catalog> or via a private search in the archives. All of the records are in German and use German place-names when available (for example, *Slowakai* for Slovakia). Cities, towns, and villages also may have German place names (refer to gazetteers). Search the FamilySearch Catalog under Austria—Military Records or Hungary—Military Records. If you don't find the records from Prague in the catalog, you can hire a private researcher to do a search for you.

KEYS TO SUCCESS

✳ Consider how war affected (and even documented) your ancestors' lives. Military records can provide additional family details and give you a bigger picture of what your ancestors experienced. Other wartime records, such as those from concentration camps, records of displaced persons, police lists of those trying to dodge conscription, war memorials, and cemeteries, can also provide useful information.

✳ Brush up on your Austro-Hungarian and Polish history before you search for your ancestor's military service records.

✳ Determine the regiment your ancestor belonged to so you can locate military records for your him. Charts in books and online resources can help you determine the recruiting districts.

✳ Look for *Grundbuchblätter* personnel sheets for your ancestor. Check the FamilySearch Catalog for microfilmed copies of the records; if none are available, hire a professional researcher to check the appropriate archive.

11

Other Record Resources

While home sources, US census records, maps, gazetteers, and church records are crucial to conducting your research, using them is just scratching the surface of learning about your Polish, Czech, or Slovak ancestors. A bevy of resources you might not have considered can answer your research questions and flesh out the ancestors you're investigating. While these "genealogical gems" may not be accessible by a few clicks of the mouse and may take some digging to find, the family history payout can be huge if you find your ancestors in a book, periodical, cemetery, list, telephone directory, or other document. In this chapter, I'll discuss some lesser-known resources and records available to Eastern European researchers.

STATESIDE RESOURCES

Though more and more records are available online each day, don't overlook nineteenth- and twentieth-century sources that were originally available in print, especially those you can access from North America.

Newspapers

The website Chronicling America: Historic American Newspapers **<chroniclingamerica. loc.gov>** (a joint project of the Library of Congress and National Endowment for the Humanities) provides a bibliography of all US newspapers, including those in states with large Polish, Czech, and Slovak immigrant populations. Search results on this site include the names and dates of publication for the newspapers and also what repositories have copies (paper or microfilm) of parts or all of the paper's run.

Other newspapers have been digitized as part of the Google News **<news.google.com/ newspapers>** project. While you are not likely to find Polish, Czech, or Slovak press offerings here, it is worth checking for newspapers covering those Polish, Czech, or Slovak "cluster communities" discussed in previous chapters. Many of these old newspapers have been scanned and placed online where they are keyword-searchable. You can find an overview of American ethnic newspapers on Readex **<www.readex.com/content/ american-ethnic-newspapers>**.

Compiled Genealogies and Periodicals

If you are lucky, you might come across a compiled genealogy of your family. While Polish, Czech, and Slovak families may not have done this as frequently as the English, the Germans, or other ethnic groups, you could find your ancestors mentioned in genealogical societies' publications.

Most genealogical and historical societies in North America and in Poland, the Czech Republic, and Slovakia publish periodicals—usually in the form of magazines and newsletters. The articles often include

- family genealogies and pedigrees

- transcripts of church records, migration lists, and cemetery records

- helpful articles on research methodology

- information about local records, archives, and services

- book advertisements and book reviews

RESEARCH TIP

Find Periodicals in the Family History Library

The Family History Library (FHL) has some collections of genealogical material for Polish, Czech, and Slovak families. These may include published and unpublished collections of family histories and lineages as well as periodicals. For general searches in the FamilySearch Catalog, search by Place, then look under GENEALOGY—PERIODICALS or GENEALOGY—PERIODICALS—INDEXES.

- research advertisements
- queries or requests for information about specific ancestors that can help you contact other interested researchers.

Copies of periodicals are available from the local societies that publish them. Major archives with genealogical collections have copies of some periodicals, particularly those representing the area they serve.

The Periodical Source Index, known as PERSI, is the leading index for English-language magazines and journals relating to genealogy. Most of PERSI's articles come from periodicals covering the United States and Canada, which will help with your Polish, Czech, or Slovak research on this side of the ocean. PERSI is crucial in identifying research, records, and transcriptions you might not find in any other print or online source, as well as locating "orphan" data—information relating to locations distinct from the periodicals they appear in. It's a good idea to obtain the entire article for any additional information it includes, such as notes and sources, related family data, and important background and contextual information.

You can search PERSI via Findmypast **<www.findmypast.com>** or at a library. Note that PERSI doesn't have the actual articles—rather, it has the title, date, and other information that will help you find the article of interest. Findmypast is working with the Federation of Genealogical Societies **<www.fgs.org>** to make the digital images of articles in PERSI accessible. If the articles you would like to study are not yet available online, try searching your local library's online catalog or searching WorldCat **<www.worldcat.org>** to generate a list of libraries near you that own a particular item you would like to access. You also can order a copy of a PERSI periodical article by completing an Article Request Form through the Allen County Public Library's Genealogy Center **<www.acpl.lib.in.us/database/graphics/order_form.html>**.

Libraries and Historical Societies

Collections housed in local libraries can contain "one-of-a-kind" books, documents, photographs, postcards, compiled genealogies, local histories, and other ephemera. In some communities, you could discover that some local government records, such as school censuses or voting records, may have been deposited in these collections. College and university libraries (especially those with master's and doctoral programs in Slavic languages) often contain excellent Polish, Czech, or Slovak materials in their collections. While it is unlikely that there will be dedicated genealogical materials in these collections, it's still worth exploring them for books or resources on Slavic topics. A simple Google search can help you locate them. Specialty libraries, such as the Carnegie Library of Pittsburgh **<www.carnegielibrary.org>**, may have material as well.

Look for Books

Be on the lookout for books dedicated to Polish, Czech, and Slovak immigrants or focused on the areas where they settled—for example, *History of Czechs in America* by Dr. Jan Habenicht (1996) and *History of Slovaks in America* (2007) by Konstantin Culen, both published by the Czechoslovak Genealogical Society International. In addition, a number of photographic histories chronicling Czech, Polish, and Slovak communities in the United States have been compiled by local authors and published in the Images of America Series by Arcadia Publishing. Search the catalog at **<www.arcadiapublishing.com>** to find a complete current listing.

Also, Google Books **<books.google.com>** and the Internet Archive **<www.archive.org>** have unique publications. For example, the Internet Archive provides access to digital versions of *Praktiný slovensko-anglický tluma* (Practical English Slovak Dictionary) by Paul K. Kadak (G. Klein & Son, 1905) **<www.archive.org/details/praktinslovens00kadauoft>**.

Ethnic Institutes and Museums

Aside from libraries, a number of ethnic organizations and institutions have ethnic archival and book collections. The Balch Institute for Ethnic Studies at the Historical Society of Pennsylvania in Philadelphia and the Immigration History Research Center (IHRC) in Minneapolis have been mentioned in previous chapters, but there are other organizations and societies that focus on Polish, Czech, and Slovak materials.

Polish researchers will want to explore the Polish Museum of America in Chicago **<www.polishmuseumofamerica.org>** and the Central Archives of Polonia at the Polish Mission located in Orchard Lake, Michigan **<www.polishmission.com>**. Smaller Polish-centric archives focus on specific organizations or time periods (mostly post-WWII). These include the Polish Falcons of America in Pittsburgh **<www.polishfalcons.org>** and the Polish collection of the Hoover Institution at Stanford University in California **<www.hoover.org>**, along with the Józef Piłsudski Institute of America **<www.pilsudski.org>**, and

---

RESEARCH TIP

Skim Digitized Polish Archives

Polish researchers interested in the Hoover Archives' WWII-era Polish archival collections housed at Stanford University can now access more than 1.5 million pages of digitized documents online thanks to Poland's National Digital Archives (*Narodowe Archiwum Cyfrowe*) **<www.szukajwarchiwach.pl>**. Consult the finding aid at **<www.oac.cdlib.org/findaid/ark:/13030/tf1489n4nr>**.

the Polish Institute of Arts and Sciences of America <www.piasa.org>, which has archival materials from the Polish Army Veterans Association of America <www.piasa.org/archivesabroad/swap.html> in New York City.

In addition, for those seeking information on Polish Jews, the YIVO Institute for Jewish Research <www.yivo.org> in New York City holds more than twenty-four million documents, photographs, recordings, posters, films, videotapes, and more, as well as the largest collection of Yiddish-language materials in the world. The Senator John Heinz History Center in Pittsburgh <www.heinzhistorycenter.org> and the Pember Library & Museum <www.thepember.com> in Granville, New York, are examples of other institutions with exhibits and information on various Slavic groups.

Czech and Slovak researchers have a museum dedicated to celebrating their cultures—the National Czech and Slovak Museum located in Cedar Rapids, Iowa <www.ncsml.org>. The museum's multilingual library collection includes books, periodicals, and multimedia and archival materials. While the items are noncirculating, it could be worth planning a research trip to explore the materials in person if you find something of interest in the online catalog.

In addition, the Czechoslovak Society of Arts & Sciences (SVU) <www.svu2000.org> is an independent nonprofit international cultural organization bringing together people from around the world who have an interest in the Czech Republic and/or Slovakia, their histories, peoples, and their cultural and intellectual contributions. While SVU doesn't have a physical library (the SVU Archive was acquired by the IHRC in 2002), its website has a plethora of information, including links to the Czech & Slovak American Archivalia <www.svu2000.org/archivalia>.

Other Czech and Slovak collections include the Czech Center Museum in Houston <www.czechcenter.org>, the Czech Heritage Project at the University of Nebraska-Lincoln <www.unl.edu/czechheritage/home>, and the Slovak Institute in Cleveland <www.slovakinstitute.com>.

Ethnic Genealogical Societies

Genealogical societies may offer some of the more unique resources related to your Polish, Czech, or Slovak heritage and can help connect you with others who may be researching the same surnames or localities.

Membership in these societies typically provides a good value for your money due to benefits such as "members-only" access to unique record sets, databases, publications, and message boards, plus discounts on society-published books or registration fees for conferences and workshops. Many also offer online and offline networking opportunities with members around the world.

Polish, Czech, and Slovak Genealogical Societies

Organized Polish genealogical societies began in the late 1970s and early 1980s. The first were started in Illinois, Texas, Michigan, and Connecticut, and others were subsequently established in Massachusetts, New York, Ohio, Wisconsin, and California. Each of these organizations operates independently and separately. Some of these societies have their own dedicated projects ranging from cemetery indexing to society and union records. See appendix H for a list of societies.

Here's a list of other ethnic genealogical societies that may provide helpful resources:

- East European Genealogical Society **<www.eegsociety.org>**
- The Foundation for East European Family History Studies **<www.feefhs.org>**
- Jewish Genealogical Society of Greater Washington **<www.jewishgen.org/jgsgw>**
- Polish Genealogical Society of America **<www.pgsa.org>**
- Czechoslovak Genealogical Society International **<www.cgsi.org>**

One benefit, in particular, is surname lists. Genealogical societies often have surname lists or projects. You also may find lists published by individual researchers or other groups. The PolishOrigins website **<www.polishorigins.com>** is one example where you can search for people whose forefathers had the same surnames as your ancestors. You can add your own surnames by registering on the site for free. There is also a surnames database on The Polish Genealogy Project **<www.polishgeno.com>**. The SVU has links to Czech and Slovak surname lists and sites online at **<www.svu2000.org/publications/genealogy/c5gd1list8.htm>**. The Slovak Pride Database **<www.slovakpride.homestead.com>**, run by Helene Cincebeaux, has more than twenty-five thousand surnames and villages. Learn more about how to research your ancestors' surnames in chapter 7.

FOREIGN AND ONLINE RESOURCES

In addition to scouring stateside resources, you also can turn to your ancestor's homeland to learn more about his life and times. Check out these sources from Europe, as well as resources online.

Parish Censuses

As discussed in chapter 9, religion was a crucial part of our ancestors' lives, having a tangible role from their birth to their death. Most Christians belonged to a church, and some of these institutions conducted their own parish censuses. While civil records might not have survived (as they largely didn't in Poland, for example), parish censuses (image **A**)

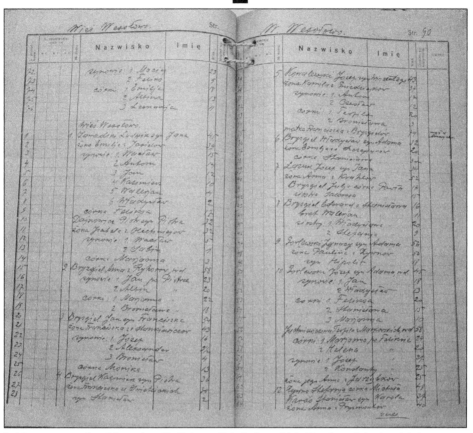

Parish censuses, such as this one from the Dabrowa Bialostocka parish in Wesolowo, Poland, contain key information about parishoners.

can be great resources if you can find them. At minimum, they recorded the name and age of the parishes heads of the household and the names and ages of the residents in his house (including servants and farmhands). Some of these schedules even included birth, marriage, and death dates or accounts of military service or immigration. You can't find parish censuses in either ecclesiastical or state archives, depending on your ancestor's location and whether the records survived.

Population Registers

In some European countries, such as Poland, the government required its citizens to register their place of residence, and these records can provide your ancestor's name, birth date and birthplace, family relationship, parents' name, and marital status. Many of these registers are still in local offices, but you can search online databases to find records that have survived. The Polish archives system has such a resource in the ELA database **<baza. archiwa.gov.pl/sezam/ela.php?l=en>**, though the ELA simply lists what registers are available and does not contain individual records. These kinds of records were less centralized in the Czech Republic and Slovakia, so check with individual records offices or consult a professional researcher to see if registers exist for your ancestor's community.

Land Records

Land records are one of the next best sources. The primary advantage of using land records is that they go back further in time than the parish registers of births, marriages, and deaths. Often, the same land was passed from generation to generation, so it is possible to assemble much of your family tree from viewing land records. Land records may be deposited in various archives (e.g., at the national or regional archives or at the town level). These more local records are not uniform, however, so you should check with the archivist to make sure you're searching in the correct places. Try perusing the FamilySearch.org online collections, or search the FamilySearch Catalog under Place (Poland, the Czech Republic, or Slovakia), then click on Land and Property. You also can go to the FamilySearch Wiki pages **<www.familysearch.org/learn/wiki/en/Main_Page>** for each country to learn more about land. A database of land records from 1450 to 1889 from the Czech Republic is available at **<www.familysearch.org/search/collection/1918632>**.

Tax Lists

Just as we do, our ancestors paid taxes, and documents left behind by the taxation process are another potential source of ancestor information. In Poland, you will find revision lists that contain personal data on household members. Consult with individual archives to see if any other records are available. Austrian tax records (*Berní ruly*) were first compiled in 1654, then again in 1684, 1746, 1757, and 1792. These tax lists include only the heads of families who own taxable property or have a trade, and they are helpful when an ancestor is known to have been in a taxable status. Tax lists are in various archives but not readily available to researchers. The FHL has a collection of unindexed tax lists, written in Czech. Search the FamilySearch Catalog under Czech Republic—Land and Property or Slovakia—Land and Property for more specifics on available records.

City Directories

Before there were telephone books (and before most people had telephones!), city directories were the best year-by-year compilations of residents in urban areas. Both Ancestry. com **<www.ancestry.com>** and Fold3 **<www.fold3.com>** have US city directories as part of their subscription packages. Also check with the libraries and historical and genealogical societies noted earlier in this chapter. Others can be located using the Online Historical Directories Website <**www.sites.google.com/site/onlinedirectorysite**>.

For city directories across the pond, consult the Library of Congress website (European Reading Room) for indexes and digitized versions of European address/telephone directories <**www.loc.gov/rr/european/tel.html**>; click the link for Poland or Former Czechoslovakia. PolishRoots.org <**www.polishroots.org**> has information on Polish city directories, as does the Polish Genealogy Project <**www.polishgeno.com**>.

Local Town or Village Histories

Individual towns or villages may also have published histories (images **B** and **C**). Search for the town or village name on Google, as your ancestors' names could be mentioned in these narratives. While it could be a challenge to obtain a copy if you don't have any living relatives in the town or village, you can always try contacting the local historian or perhaps

B

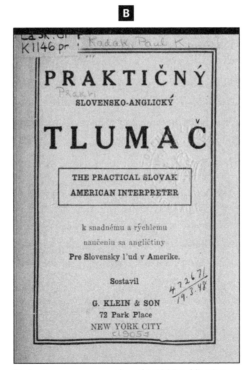

Find unique resources such as this 1905 publication *Praktiný slovensko-anglický tluma* (The Practical English Slovak Dictionary) on the Internet Archive.

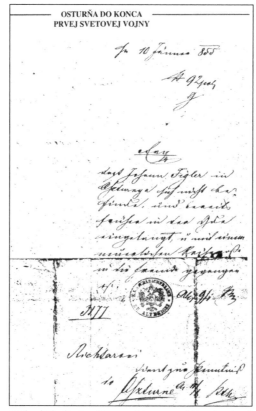

With a little digging, it is possible you could locate a book published about your ancestral town. This letter from the book *Dejiny Osturne* mentions one of my Figler ancestors.

the mayor of the town. For example, my maternal grandfather's family is mentioned in a book (*Dejiny Osturne*) about Osturňa, Slovakia, that was published by historians there. I was able to obtain a printed copy of this book from another genealogist who had organized a tour to the village in 2006. Look for local histories stateside as well as those from the American town where your immigrant ancestors settled, some of which are available at the FHL.

Researchers should also be aware of scholarly organizations or learned societies in Poland, the Czech Republic, and Slovakia. These organizations are typically composed of both academicians and history buffs from various fields of learning, and their mission is to fully document and record the history of their region. Many of these societies issue journals, but they are typically written in the native language (sometimes containing summaries in English or other languages) and most likely will not be available in US libraries.

To locate websites and other information for learned societies, search *Towarzystwo naukowe* (Polish), *genealogická společnost* (Czech), or *Slovenske ucene tovarisstvo* (Slovak).

Internet Telephone Directories

Because Polish, Czech, or Slovak families tended to be large, it's likely your immigrant grandmother or great-grandfather left behind a sibling or two when immigrating to America. Those siblings' descendants—your distant cousins—could help you fill in the blanks in your family tree. A Polish, Czech, or Slovak telephone directory is probably your best tool for trying to find currently living (close or distant) family members. Start with directories listed on PolandGenWeb **<www.rootsweb.com/~polwgw/wp.html>** or in the Czech Telephone Directory **<phone.fin.cz>**, Phonebook of the World **<phonebookoftheworld.com/czechrepublic>**, and Search Czech **<www.search-czech.com/people/czech-phone-directory.html>**. Slovak researchers can consult the Slovak Telephone Directory (Telefónny Zoznam SR) found on Infobel to look up phone numbers for individuals or companies in modern Slovakia **<www.infobel.com/en/world/WorldTeldir.aspx?page=/eng/euro/sk&qSelLang=EN>**. If online searches come up empty, look for a printed telephone book (both larger provincial or county-wide and smaller ones) covering your ancestral region—most libraries have them—and write to people with your surname. Because of privacy laws and language or formatting issues, you may wish to consult with a native-language speaker or professional researcher for assistance when using foreign telephone directories.

Memorial Websites

In addition to indexed cemetery lists published by societies or organizations, you can search online for and post photos and information about your ancestors' burial places. Some sites to explore include

- **BillionGraves <www.billiongraves.com>**: This site uses modern technology to capture images of headstones with the headstone's GPS location.

- **Find A Grave <www.findagrave.com>**: Search more than 132 million grave records. Use the pull-down search by country list to see included cemeteries for Poland, the Czech Republic, and Slovakia.

- **Foundation for Documentation of Jewish Cemeteries in Poland <www.cemetery.jewish.org.pl>**: This site serves as a database of Jewish cemeteries in Poland.

- **Interment.net <www.interment.net>**: Search and browse cemetery burial records from thousands of cemeteries across the world. Browse certain cemeteries by province in Bohemia, Moravia, and Poland.

- **StonePics—Cemeteries of the Czech Republic <czech.stonepics.com>:** This site has a database of more than 118,000 records of names, and information about cemeteries and gravestones in the Czech Republic.

- **Virtual Cemeteries of Slovakia <www.cemetery.sk/english>:** This database lists burials in cemeteries throughout Slovakia. An English version is available.

Foreign Libraries

Just as local libraries in the United States or Canada serve as repositories of articles, artifacts, books, manuscripts, photographs, and more, the same holds true for libraries in Poland, the Czech Republic, and Slovakia.

The *Informator o Bibliotekach i Ośrodkach Informacji* (A Guide to Polish Libraries and Information Centers) <mak.bn.org.pl> lists more than two thousand libraries in Poland and identifies the features of their collections, subject area strengths, and the total number of volumes the library possesses (including microfilm, microfiche, and CDs). You can also search library databases on *Biblioteka Narodwa* <mak.bn.org.pl/fidkar>.

Czech researchers can get a listing of libraries in the Czech Republic at <www.expats.cz/prague/directory/libraries> and at Cyndi's List <www.cyndislist.com/czech/libraries>, while those looking for libraries in Slovakia can check Cyndi's List or the website of the Slovak National Library (*Slovenská národná knižnica*) <www.snk.sk/en>. The University of Illinois at Urbana-Champaign has a National Bibliography of Czech and Slovak on its website <www.library.illinois.edu/spx/webct/nationalbib/natbibczechslovak2.html>.

KEYS TO SUCCESS

✳ Remember to search for one-of-a-kind resources (letters, photographs, and other ephemera) in libraries (especially those with dedicated Slavic collections), historical societies, ethnic genealogical societies, and museums.

✳ Consult FamilySearch resources and state, regional, or local archives for land records, tax records, city directories, and other errata.

✳ Search for compiled genealogies through genealogical societies and PERSI.

✳ Perform a Google search to see if your ancestral town or village—or the town where your ancestors settled in America—has a website that may include its history, or contact the mayor or priest to see if a published local history exists and how you can obtain a copy.

✳ Plug your ancestors' names into virtual cemetery websites—you never know what results will turn up.

12

Heritage Travel and On-site Research

No matter how convenient it may be these days to research ancestors without leaving home, you probably still dream of visiting your family's homeland. You're yearning to see where your ancestors lived, stand in the church where Great-grandpa was baptized, enjoy traditional cuisine, and understand what life was like for your ancestors before they made the journey to America. With heritage travel, you have an opportunity to go beyond the same old research strategies and discover those details you can't get from online databases, books, or microfilm.

For more than fifteen years, I imagined what it would be like to actually set foot in Milpoš, the Eastern Slovakian birthplace of my maternal grandmother. I'd seen pictures of this tiny village while doing genealogy research and watched tourists' videos on YouTube **<www.youtube.com>**, so I thought I knew what to expect when I finally traveled there. But I never could have predicted all that I learned and experienced on my trip to Milpoš (image **A**).

Visiting your ancestor's homeland like I did can provide a wealth of information. If your own bucket list includes a visit to your ancestral homeland, this chapter will help you plan the heritage trip of your dreams.

PLANNING YOUR VISIT TO POLAND, THE CZECH REPUBLIC, OR SLOVAKIA

Once you've decided that you want to make a heritage trip to the old country, start planning. Travel in Europe can be daunting and expensive, but you'll make the most out of your trip by thinking ahead and using the following tips.

Determine Your Destinations and Book Your Trip

First, consider the places you want to visit, your length of stay, and what you hope to accomplish. Then you'll need to get your passport, visa, and airline ticket. Note the sooner you book your airline reservations and accommodations, the better. Use travel sites such as Kayak <www.kayak.com> and FareCompare <www.farecompare.com> to compare flights and prices. For help, contact a travel agent who specializes in the area you want to go and ask genealogy buddies for references.

You could also consider a group trip sponsored by an organization. For example, the Carpatho-Rusyn Society <www.carpathorusynsociety.org> and the Polish Genealogical Society of Connecticut and the Northeast <www.pgsctne.org> frequently offer such excursions. For more than twenty-five years, Helene Cincebeaux has been offering an experience called Treasure of Slovakia Tours <www.our-slovakia.com>, though her tours will often go to other Central European countries. One caveat: Before you book a group tour, ask if you can build time in for personal research or side trips to your ancestral village. The Czechoslovak Genealogical Society International has more information about heritage tours on its website <www.cgsi.org/research/travel-resources>.

In addition, get to know the locations you're planning to visit. Google the town or city to find its website, check travel books and websites, and read travel reviews online. Use Google Maps <www.google.com/maps> to determine how long it takes to get around by car, public transit (if available), or walking. Look for information about the currency, ATM availability, and local laws (in Slovakia, for example, "rowdy behavior" is illegal between 10 P.M. and 6 A.M., so you'll want keep the toasts and celebrating with family members in check).

RESEARCH TIP

Collect Your Change

To help save for your trip, consider stashing away an envelope labeled *Genealogy Fund* where you can toss in loose change and extra dollar bills throughout the year. It adds up, and it's a good visual reminder of your goal to travel to an ancestor's hometown.

I visited my maternal grandmother's village of Milpoš, Slovakia, in June 2010. I was delighted to have a copy of *Three Slovak Women,* another of my books, with me.

The more you know about your ancestral homeland, the less stressed you will feel once you get there. Before you go, enlist the help of a local tour guide and/or professional researcher, invest in good maps (GPS may not work in remote locations), consult town/archive websites, and contact family and other individuals.

Set a Budget

Unless you've hit the lottery, you'll likely have limited funds to spend on your trip. To set a budget, list potential expenses, including airfare, lodging, meals, transportation, travel insurance, and fees for travel documents. Don't forget to build in incidentals, such as parking, copying costs, research service fees, snacks, souvenirs, tips, sightseeing admission fees, and other discretionary spending.

Remember to budget for the services of a researcher/guide who can provide transportation and, when necessary, be your translator (not everyone you meet will speak English—especially relatives in remote villages and even some archival staff). Download a free Research Trip Budget Worksheet at **<www.familytreemagazine.com/upload/images/PDF/travelbudget.pdf>**.

Scope Out Archives in Advance

Do some advance preparation before you make the journey over to Poland, the Czech Republic, or Slovakia. First, make sure you've learned all you can from US resources. Then, check out the archives abroad. We covered the archival structure in Poland, the

Czech Republic, and Slovakia in chapter 8, so you're well on your way to completing this step. Search the archive's online catalog to see if your ancestor might be listed and what items you may be interested in. Avoid disappointment by learning about record losses and privacy restrictions ahead of time. This will prevent you from wasting time and money searching for information that doesn't exist (such as records destroyed in a war) or is unavailable (e.g., due to privacy laws).

Remember that some archives have online finding aids you can refer to and that, while many records are listed in the online catalog, additional materials may be indexed in the finding aids at the individual archive. Once at the archive, try to access that finding aid if available, or have a copy you can use electronically on your computer, tablet, or smartphone.

Also bear in mind that, as at all archives in North America or Europe, you must follow certain procedures. For example, you may have to make reservations to visit repositories,

Tips for a Successful Trip

- **Have realistic expectations.** If you're a fan of the TV series *Who Do You Think You Are?*, you're likely hoping for that amazing discovery or joyous family reunion. With any luck it could happen to you, but you may not find exactly what you're looking for. You might make sad, shocking, or otherwise unpleasant discoveries or run out of time. While you hope your long-lost cousins will embrace you and share with you all you want to know, be prepared for the possibility you won't find family living in the area or that some doors may remain closed (literally or figuratively).

- **Expect the unexpected.** Build in wiggle room to rest or for prolonged or impromptu family visits or emergencies. Weather also could cause problems. Beware of limited windows of opportunity. For example, the parish priest may only be able to see you in the evening on your day of arrival because he will be away during the remainder of your visit. You might be exhausted, but you would not want to pass up the opportunity to view those church books!

- **Share your experiences.** Social media makes it easy to share your discoveries and experiences with family members at home: Post photographs, video, and stories on Facebook, Google+ **<plus.google.com>**, Instagram **<www.instagram.com>**, Twitter **<www.twitter.com>**, YouTube, or on a blog. Remember that "in the moment" posting may not always be practical due to limited Internet access. Plus, it may not be a good idea to let the world know you're away from home. To capture feelings while they're fresh, you could set up a private blog and publish posts when you get home.

- **Enjoy.** Remember to have fun and enjoy the moment!

archives, or churches or register at the office just outside the reading room of an archive in order to view records. You may also need to fill out request slips for books you are interested in. Know what years of records a book contains so you can prioritize your requests. In addition, be wary of the institution's hours of operation: Some archives close for a month in the summer, and many have a morning session, then close for lunch and end the day at 3 P.M. You may have to return another day to get the copies you have ordered or return later in the afternoon when ledgers become available. Check the archive's website for hours, policies (such as a five-books-per-day limit), instructions for copying records, and other pertinent information. If you employ a guide, he can help with this.

In addition to helping you decipher the rules of a particular archive, a guide can also translate for you if you're visiting a place where English isn't widely spoken. Get cost estimates up front and clearly communicate with the guide about what services you will receive.

Even if you have a guide, there will be times when you're not with him and will need to communicate with family and the staff at hotels, restaurants, and archives. Having a basic understanding of the native language in the country you're visiting will help you more easily navigate the country and give you a richer experience. Download translation apps for your tablet or smartphone or enroll in courses at your local college or adult education centers. Additional affordable options include watching language-focused videos on YouTube or reading travelers' language books like Lonely Planet's *Eastern Europe Phrasebook & Dictionary* **<shop.lonelyplanet.com/europe/eastern-europe-phrasebook-5>**.

Meet Locals and Relatives

You should plan to spend some time exploring your ancestral town, and a contact in the town may give you more knowledge of the area. Before you go, consider reaching out to the mayor or priest/rabbi, or search for possible relatives in the village. Use online telephone directories such as Infobel **<www.infobel.com>** or Phonebook of the World **<www.phonebookoftheworld.com>** to search for surnames and take the list with you so you can call people once you get there. If the town/village has a website, you often can find at least the mayor's name listed there.

You also might find local relatives by searching for surnames and places on Facebook **<www.facebook.com>**. Also, check out my website **<www.immersiongenealogy.com>** for more advice on how you can experience firsthand the customs and traditions of your ancestors, as well as discover more details about where and how your ancestors lived, worked, and worshipped during your trip to your ancestral homeland.

Create an Itinerary

Regardless of whether your trip to Eastern Europe is the first of many or a once-in-a-life-time experience, you will want to make the most out of every precious minute you have in your ancestor's homeland. As such, put together an itinerary and an outline of your research goals to maximize your time. While neither has to be set in stone, these will add some structure to your trip. Your excitement and emotions will be running high as you get acquainted with the new surroundings, meet new cousins, and fend off jet lag. Having a plan will help you remember what you want to accomplish and who you are supposed to meet when. But remember to be flexible, too, and don't overbook yourself—you never know when a relative or local will invite you for a meal or introduce you to other family members.

Make your itinerary by creating a document or spreadsheet on your computer or using Evernote <www.evernote.com> to create a virtual notebook to make lists. You should initially schedule everything (e.g., visits with relatives, time for cemetery exploration and researching in the archives), but be flexible. Realize you may not get to do everything, so have a "dream list" and a secondary plan. Create a contact list (family, professional researcher/tour guide, parish priest, mayor, archives, etc.) and gather documents such as lodging and airplane ticket confirmations.. Use online trip planning tools and apps such as Tripit <www.tripit.com>, TouristEye <www.touristeye.com>, TripAdvisor <www.tripadvisor.com>, TripCase <travel.tripcase.com>, and WorldMate <www.worldmate.com>. Whatever method or app you use, be sure you can access it offline in case you are in remote areas with spotty or no wi-fi service.

Pack Carefully

Give yourself a few weeks to pack so you can get necessities you don't already have. You'll want a sturdy suitcase, the necessary amount of clothing, comfortable walking shoes, travel-size toiletries, and other personal items, such as prescription medications (bring extra in case of travel delays).

Consult your airline for checked and carry-on baggage rules, and see Transportation Security Administration (TSA) regulations. If you plan to travel by train or other public transportation in your ancestral homeland, check those baggage rules, too. If possible, try to fit what you need into an airline-approved carry-on with wheels. Because you'll want to travel as lightly as possible, you may want to forgo bulky research binders and other heavy items. But do bring along your family tree information in some format—either digital or print—so you can refer to it as you research.

You also may want to be selective about the electronic devices you take, because there's always the risk you'll lose them or they'll be stolen. Leave room for gifts and other

Make Safety Your First STEP

When traveling to a foreign country, enroll in the Smart Traveler Enrollment Program (STEP), a free service of the US Department of State's Bureau of Consular Affairs **<step.state.gov/step>** that allows US citizens and nationals traveling abroad to register their trip with the nearest US embassy or consulate. Through this program, you can receive important information from the embassy about safety conditions in your destination country, get travel alerts and warnings, and help the embassy (and friends and family) contact you in case of an emergency.

souvenirs you'll acquire during your travels. Use the Foreign Research Trip Packing List at the end of this chapter for more suggestions.

In addition, consider purchasing a prepaid credit card such as Visa Travel Money or MasterCard Prepaid and a small amount of foreign currency in advance—*złoty* for Poland, *korunas* for the Czech Republic, and euros for Slovakia. Check with your bank or the Automobile Association of America (AAA) **<www.aaa.com>** first for the currency and pre-paid cards, as international currency kiosks at larger airports and local banks may charge a conversion fee. Rick Steves has good advice on getting cash abroad **<www.ricksteves.com/travel-tips/money>**.

If you're traveling to a country with less-than-stellar hospital facilities or you have health problems that might flare up during your trip, consider getting insurance. Check with your health insurance provider to learn if it offers international travel coverage. AAA offers various insurance plans for its members, too. MedjetAssist **<www.medjetassist.com>** provides additional coverage for medical evacuation flights from anywhere in the world.

KEYS TO SUCCESS

❋ Start planning your dream trip early (at least six months in advance), and make sure you set a budget and start saving in advance.

❋ Exhaust resources at home before you venture to Poland, the Czech Republic, or Slovakia. Doing as much research as possible in the United States or Canada will better prepare you to request records from parishes in the old country.

❋ Make contacts in the ancestral village (relatives, the mayor, or the local priest/rabbi) in advance of your trip to enrich your experience.

❋ Share your experiences via a blog or social media to let your family or other researchers vicariously walk in your ancestors' footsteps and maybe inspire them to plan their own heritage trip one day.

FOREIGN RESEARCH TRIP PACKING LIST

First, here's what *not* to take along on your heritage travel trip: your original files, photos, or documents. But do make room in your suitcase for these items.

Essentials

- paper or tablet device for note-taking
- pencils and pencil sharpener or mechanical pencil with plenty of refills (pens are forbidden in many libraries and archives)
- smartphone and/or tablet, along with charging cables, to use for taking photos, accessing the Internet, etc. (if you plan to make calls or text on your phone, make sure you have the appropriate plan from your carrier and the appropriate technology built-in to use it internationally)
- camera (and/or camcorder), flash, tripod and batteries; consider investing in a close-up lens for copying documents (ask permission before photographing in archives)
- maps
- change (in local currency) for photocopiers
- essential charts and lists of what information you want to find where
- business cards with your name, address, and e-mail address to leave behind
- file folders
- comfortable shoes (preferably thick-soled shoes that can stand up to cobblestone streets)
- magnifying glass
- passport and/or visa and a photocopy of each
- local currency and/or prepaid credit cards
- plug adaptor and/or voltage converter (see **<www.worldstandards.eu/electricity/plug-voltage-by-country>**)
- little souvenirs or postcards from home you can leave as thank-you gifts
- proper clothing—nix the white sneakers, sweatpants, and sports-logo shirts
- umbrella

Other Handy Items

- rice paper and crayons for tombstone rubbings (ask permission before attempting this)
- tape recorder for dictating notes or for taping an onsite translator (if not already on your mobile device)
- laptop computer with copies of your files
- handheld scanner
- gloves and trowel for clearing around tombstones, plus a plastic trash bag to kneel on

PART 4

ADVANCED SOURCES AND STRATEGIES

13

Putting It All Together

This book has presented a variety of sources and strategies you can use to uncover answers about your Polish, Czech, or Slovak ancestry. Of course, each of your ancestors experienced unique life circumstances that affect the research path you'll follow—you can't count on any one record or research technique to provide answers every time. The process for each family and ancestor will be a bit different. To illustrate this point, this chapter contains three examples of successful Eastern European genealogy research—one Polish, one Czech, and one Slovak—to show you how real-life genealogists have overcome the types of roadblocks you'll encounter.

NAME CHANGES CASE STUDY: "WHAT'S THE POINT(KOUSKI)?"

Avid genealogist Donna Pointkouski of Palmyra, New Jersey, has traced her family roots back to Poland's Mazowsze and Wielkopolski provinces since beginning her research in 1989. In this case study, adapted from a post titled "How Do You Spell That?" on her *What's Past Is Prologue* blog **<pastprologue.wordpress.com>**, Pointkouski recounts the perils of having a perplexing Polish surname.

＊　＊　＊

Even James Pointkouski's tombstone has a variant surname spelling: The carver goofed by substituting a *w* for the *u*, then corrected the mistake on the stone.

I ALMOST FELT SORRY FOR THE TELEMARKETERS calling my parents when I was young. I'd answer the phone and hear, "Hi, can I speak to Mr. ... uh, Mr. Po-, er, ah, Mr. P-p-pint, er, Mr. Portkonski?" I'd pause for dramatic effect, then respond, "No, I'm sorry, there is no one here by that name."

But worse than the telemarketers was the need to spell my name—all the time. Even my parents talked about changing our surname for a while. We considered my mother's equally Polish maiden name, *Pater*, because it seemed easier. For a while, *Perry* was in contention just because we liked it. Until my father called in a pizza order and the clerk asked, "What's the name?" My dad grinned and responded, "Perry!" But then the clerk asked, "How do you spell that?"

By now you might wonder why we feel no allegiance to our moniker. The answer is simple: It's not our true name. My grandfather James made it up. If he had invented a name that was easier to spell and pronounce, I'd thank him. As I delved into the family's history and gained pride in my Polish heritage, I was disappointed I couldn't have the "real" name that he changed slightly. Unfortunately, the nonlegal change was made just prior to all of today's rules, records, and federal regulations, and now I am one of only eight people on earth born a Pointkouski.

James' parents were Jan Piątkowski and Rozalia Kizeweter. Jan was a leather worker, and the family lived in Warsaw. Jan was born in Warsaw, and Rozalia's family moved there from just outside the city when she was a girl. They had a son, Józef, born in November 1903, and a daughter, Janina, born in December 1905. Shortly after Janina's birth, the family decided to leave one big city for another. Jan immigrated to Philadelphia in March 1906 with his sister's husband, Ludwik Czarkowski. Rozalia and the children followed in November. In America, their first names were Anglicized to John, Rose, Joseph, and Jean. But the last name changed slightly, too. In English, the Polish letter *ą* does not exist—so *Piątkowski* became *Piontkowski*.

That's the name my grandfather, my father, my brother and I should all bear. But the name change game continued with my grandfather.

James was the surprise baby, born in Philadelphia on July 6, 1910. His father was thirty-nine years old and his mother was forty-four, old by 1910 standards. On James' official Pennsylvania birth certificate, the name is listed as *Ganus Kincoski*. I assume *Ganus* is what became of James when spoken with a heavy Polish accent. Kincoski was apparently an alias my great-grandfather used, temporarily, attempting to hide from either law enforcement or people he owed money. Other than around 1910, John always used *Piontkowski*, his correct surname, on legal records.

By the time James, or "Jimmy," reached adulthood, he tweaked his surname further. As early as 1933, James changed a few letters and—*voilà!*—the surname *Pointkouski* was unofficially and unceremoniously born.

James' older brother, Joe, changed his name, too (also not legally). I always thought Joe had more sense, though, for the name he chose was a lot easier to spell: *Perk*. Ironically, I recently got to speak to one of Joe's daughters, who complained of being teased in school and called "Percolator"—to which she yelled back at her bully, "My real name is Pointkouski!"

My grandfather apparently tried this name for a while: He refers to himself as Perk in a letter to my grandmother in 1933, and a photograph of my father in 1936 is labeled *Jimmy Perk* on the back. But on all legal documents, my grandfather continued to use *Pointkouski*.

I remember my grandfather from my childhood, but I didn't see him very often. I wish I knew him better, and longer, because he passed away before I could ever think to ask him why our name is spelled the way it is. James died on February 13, 1980, at the age of sixty-nine.

In what I refer to as "The Final Misspelling," the monument maker accidentally carved a *w* into James' tombstone and corrected it to a *u*. A larger, correctly spelled stone is also in place.

Gradually, despite wishing I got to use my real Polish name *Piątkowski* (as a female, my name in Poland would be *Piątkowska*), this English major has embraced the permanent misspelling and is proud to be a Pointkouski—even if you can't spell it.

IMMIGRANT CASE STUDY: "GIVE ME YOUR TIRED, YOUR *PODRUH*"

Lee James of Olympia, Washington, shares the following case study detailing how he traced his Czech immigrant ancestors. James, a retired research engineer of forty years, has redirected his research to genealogy. The story is adapted from "The Emigration Sage of the Family of Tomáš Kohout," an article originally published in the December 2010 issue of the Czechoslovak Genealogical Society International's journal, *Naše Rodina* (Our Family).

* * *

MY MATERNAL GREAT-GRANDFATHER TOMÁŠ KOHOUT was a *podruh* (a landless peasant farmhand) who lived in the southern Bohemian village of Hamr, about four miles south-southeast of Veselí nad Lužnicí in the Tábor region. Tomáš was born on November 1, 1837, in nearby Višný (modern spelling: *Vyšné*) to a woodcarver and his wife. In 1867, he married Marie Kalát (or *Kalátová*), a woman ten years his junior.

As a landless peasant, Tomáš Kohout had a bleak future in the Bohemia of the 1860s and 1870s. Because Bohemian families often had many children, not every son could inherit land from his parents, making property scarce and expensive. Coupled with a partial crop failure and other factors, this caused consumer prices to rise, making it harder for farmers to make ends meet. So when Tomáš' father-in-law, Vojtěch Kalát, a *domkář* (a householder or "cottager") who owned house No. 10 and an adjoining field, sold his house to his son in 1873, any chance of land ownership (and thus economic prosperity) for Tomáš ended.

Further, the Austrian Empire—which controlled Bohemia—was engaged in a two-front war against Prussia and Italy in 1866. Tomáš served in the Austrian army on the Italian front. Although a final peace treaty was signed, the victorious Prussians kept occupation forces in Bohemia long enough to visit every community and demand their pro-rata share of war reparations. A war veteran like Tomáš might not have been treated well by the occupying Prussians.

Such postwar troubles probably factored into many Bohemians' immigration to America in the coming years. Clearly, Tomáš and Marie were seeking a better life in America when they decided to emigrate.

Austria's government, which considered its inhabitants (especially the working segment) part of the national wealth, opposed emigration—as did the Czech bourgeoisie, which feared rising Germanization of the Czech populace, and the Catholic Church, which worried that emigrants would lose their Catholic belief in the new country. Consequently, Austria placed legal obstacles upon emigration. The Kohout family had to meet several conditions before they could legally move to America, including meeting military commitments. According to his discharge papers, Tomáš served ten years, two months, and eighteen days in the Austrian Army, most of which was served in the Reserves with one month of active service in the War of 1866. Hence, he had fulfilled his military requirement for emigration. It was also necessary for him to be a Catholic in good standing, be law abiding, owe no debts or taxes, and demonstrate that he had sufficient funds to get to America.

The preparation of an application for emigration permit indicates that Tomáš met the government's requirements. I'm lucky to have two pages of Tomáš' file from the Jindřichův Hradec district archives—in general, the Czech archives did not consider application for emigration permits to be of permanent value, and most of them were lost, misplaced, stolen, or burned for heat during the communist era. Tomáš' file was found in an unmarked, unindexed box in the archives' basement. Tomáš was issued a passport on April 21, 1873.

Tomáš, Marie, and their first two living sons, Josef and Václav (another son, Jan, died in 1871), emigrated in May 1873. Most emigrating Czech families used the German ports of Bremen or Hamburg, and family legend has it that they departed at Bremen and arrived at New York. Unfortunately, Bremen's passenger lists for 1832 to 1908 were destroyed due to lack of space. I've checked the Hamburg passenger lists on Ancestry.com and Leo Baca's published *Czech Immigration Passenger Lists* (Old Homestead, 2000), but I have not located a passenger list for this Kohout family and so can't confirm.

The Kohouts settled first in Pittsburgh, where Tomáš worked at the Carnegie Steel Company for a little more than a year. It was a difficult, degrading job, and the family soon moved to Cleveland to seek better work. Cleveland city directories for 1875 to 1876 and 1877 to 1878 list their address as 150 Rhodes Avenue in an area called the near West Side, or *Kuba*, that was home to many Czech immigrants. Family legend has it that Tomáš worked on the Lake Erie docks, and the city directories list Tomáš's occupation as *laborer*. Tomáš declared his intention to become a US citizen before the Cuyahoga County probate court in 1874; he signed his name with an *X*. My maternal grandmother, Katherine Kalat Kohout, was born in Cleveland on November 27, 1876, and baptized at nearby St. Procop Church a day later.

Sometime before the 1880 federal census (June 1), the Kohout family moved from Cleveland to the town of Woodbine in Boyer Township, Iowa (they appear there in that census). Marie Kohout (née Kalátová) had a younger sister, Anna, who had previously moved to the same county with her husband, Charles Mickish. This probably influenced Tomáš and Marie, as Czech immigrants tended to move to communities containing other Czechs. The Harrison County, Iowa, circuit court granted Thomas (he had by now Americanized his first name) his final citizenship papers on October 16, 1885. Thomas was a laborer for either the Chicago & North Western Railway or the Illinois Central Railroad, both of which operated through Woodbine; both the 1880 federal census and the 1885 Iowa state census show his occupation as a railroad laborer. On November 24,

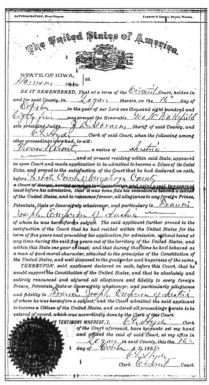

The Kohout family carried this *Reisepass* (passport, on the left) with them to America. The strip of paper (at right) is Tomáš' application for an emigration permit. Originally a single sheet that was separated, both items contain information in German about Tomáš Kohout's physical characteristics, year of birth, and region, Budweis (*České Budějovice*).

The circuit court of Harrison County, Iowa, issued Thomas' final US citizenship papers on October 16, 1885.

1884, Thomas purchased a building lot on Weare Street in Woodbine, upon which he subsequently built a house. To a *podruh* like Thomas, who had little or no chance of ever purchasing property in the old country, owning property in America must have felt like a real triumph. Three more children were born to Thomas and Mary (she had also Americanized her name) in Iowa: Thomas T., Marie, and Anna.

Tomáš apparently was not literate in either Czech or English—he signed his name with an *X* and stated in the 1880 federal census that he could neither read nor write. Marie, however, was somewhat literate in Czech and later in English: I have seen her personal prayer book written in Czech, and federal and state census records show she could read and write in English. As a member of a somewhat higher social class than her husband, it is not surprising that Marie was more literate—she likely had at least some education.

Tomáš likely had a difficult time adjusting to life in America. As an illiterate laborer, he had fewer job opportunities than better-educated immigrants or those with trade skills.

Thomas Kohout filed this document in 1874, declaring his intention to become a citizen of the United States and signing his name with an X.

In addition, earlier Irish and Germans immigrants had already taken many of the jobs for which Tomáš might have been qualified. Many Czech immigrants had never traveled more than a few miles from their home village. To such people, life in America—whether in a big city or small town—must have been a bewildering experience. Learning a new language and strange customs undoubtedly added to the confusion, and immigrants were usually homesick for the old country and its customs.

All of these pressures must have eventually gotten to Tomáš Kohout, because he took his own life by hanging on March 16, 1891. By doing so, he left Marie, just a few months shy of her forty-fourth birthday, a widow with several dependent children at home to support and raise. Although she was literate, she had apparently never worked outside the home and was not particularly well-prepared to support her family. Although every federal (1880, 1900, and 1910) and Iowa census (1885, 1895, and 1905) shows no occupation for Marie other than "keeping house," she managed to raise and educate her children.

Marie died on November 12, 1912. Her obituary stated: "No sacrifice was too great for her if only her children might have a better chance, and this was the real reason of their coming to America. She was a devoted wife and a self-sacrificing mother and a splendid neighbor."

Thus, the emigration saga of this Kohout family ended differently for Tomáš and Marie. Both left Bohemia with great expectations in search of the American Dream for themselves and their children. It appears that Tomáš may have fallen short in his search, but Marie and her children achieved it admirably in spite of great difficulties.

CLUSTER CASE STUDY: "MATVIJAS ARE EVERYWHERE!"

John Matviya of New Alexandria, Pennsylvania, has been exploring his Slovak family tree for more than three decades—starting in an era when communist policies and hostilities posed a true brick wall for American genealogy searchers. His story, a version of which was originally published in the December 2004 issue of *Naše Rodina*, shows how studying not just your ancestors, but others in their village, can extend your family tree.

* * *

WHEN I BEGAN MY FAMILY RESEARCH, finding the names of my father's grandparents seemed impossible. Not only was Czechoslovakia a foreign country and behind the Iron Curtain, I had always been told that my grandfather was born illegitimately and that my grandmother was an orphan. "Forget it," I was told, even by my own father. Information was just not available back in those days.

All I had to go on were my grandfather's naturalization papers from the county courthouse and a few word-of-mouth facts and stories. My grandfather Andrew Matviya's application for a certificate of arrival listed the villages in Austria-Hungary where he and my grandmother were born (Milpoš and Yakovin) and married (Sabinov). It also erroneously listed his mother's maiden name as *Susan Miserak*, although she was born a Matvija. My father told me that his father's father was a "prominent man" in the village named Figura. That was all I knew until I visited Slovakia in June 2000.

At the end of a business trip to Prague and Brno in the Czech Republic, I boarded a train for Košice in eastern Slovakia. Unlike Prague, where many people spoke English or German, Košice had few Western tourists and therefore few English speakers. I would have been totally lost had it not been for a local woman I met in Pittsburgh the previous summer. Slavka, my Slovak friend, wanted to ensure a pleasant visit to Košice and eastern Slovakia. Along with her boyfriend and youngest son, she drove me from Košice to the three villages listed in my grandfather's papers, more than an hour north in the foothills of the Carpathian Mountains.

We first climbed the single lane road to Jakovany where my grandmother Mary Kočis was born. As would become the pattern, my interpreters first approached people working in their garden and asked them if they knew anyone with my grandparent's last name. We were directed up the road to the home of Juri (George) Kočis. There we stood outside the gate while Slavka's friend reviewed with George the names in my small family tree. When George recognized one, his garden gate opened wide. He invited us to sit at a lawn table while George showed me his own papers and pictures—including a birth certificate of his grandfather Michael, which listed Michael's parents as the same couple known to be my grandmother's parents. George and I realized we were second cousins. To celebrate

Errors in Andrew Matviya's application for a certificate of arrival indicate that someone else filled out the form. Despite the mistakes, the record contained helpful clues.

our meeting, George poured us a large shot of homemade plum brandy (*slivovitz*), then a second. I wrote down as much of the family information as he could provide. Before leaving the village, George sent me to another second cousin, Michael Kočis. Once he knew we were related, Michael was equally friendly; he shared more photos and information, along with smoked ham, bread, and *pivo*, a local beer.

We moved on from to my grandfather's birth village, Milpoš, two valleys to the west. When the two women in their garden heard the question, "Do you know where any Matvijas live?" they laughed and told my friend, "Go knock on any door—Matvijas are everywhere!"

While Slavka's friend went to seek out someone who might know of my grandfather, she and I meandered around the small cemetery behind the town's Greek Catholic church. The first stone I came upon bore the name *Jan Matvija* (my own name in Slovak). A nearby stone was marked *Andrew Matvija*. Not only I did I see many stones bearing my last name, but others with the surnames of *Miserak* and *Figura*. Apparently, just as many people with these names still lived in the village, but none were old enough to remember my grandfather or his mother. I was just another Matvija, and in their world, "Matvijas are everywhere!"

All I expected from this trip was to visit my grandparents' villages, and I had already found so much more. To my surprise, even more was yet to come. Slavka called Sunday night to say that she was sending her sixteen-year-old son, Kuba, to help me find the state archives in Prešov and serve as my interpreter on Monday. He was fantastic at both. Kuba did all of the talking, and soon I was looking through books of nineteenth-century birth and death records. I found the baptismal records of not only my grandmother and her brother, but more of their siblings and even their godparents. I also was shown a village census from 1869 that listed the birth years of my grandmother's parents and the name of her grandmother, Anna Kočis, born in 1789.

Reading through the birth records of Milpoš' Greek Catholic church, I soon found my grandfather's name and birth date, along with the name of his mother, Susana Matvija (no father was listed).

Other records showed that two years after my grandfather's birth in 1883, Susana married Mathias Miserak. After giving birth to four more children who did not survive beyond their second birthdays, Susana herself died. Mathias remarried within a year. Suddenly the names started to make sense. No wonder no one in today's Milpoš knew of my grandfather: he probably lived with a family called *Miserak*, then moved in with his grandparents. Few Matvijas would have had contact with him.

The 1869 census listed Susana's parents: John Matvija and Anna Surin. My visit to the archives had confirmed the names and birth dates of my great-great-grandparents.

Not long after my trip to Slovakia, I acquired the microfilm of those same church records and the 1869 Hungarian census at my local FamilySearch Center. Understanding the utility in being aware of family "clusters," I transcribed all the Milpoš records into a database and began compiling a village "family tree." The census showed that Milpoš had only thirty-five houses in 1869. Susana Matvija's family lived in house No. 25. Her father was occupied as a tenant farmer, as were all but two of the "heads of household" in the village. Those two were "land owners," and in house No. 29 was John Figura, a "prominent man" just four houses away from Susana's. This Figura had three sons about the same age as Susana. I suspected that one of them was my great-grandfather, but it would be another ten years before I learned that DNA might help me prove it.

A Y-DNA test would help only if other close male relatives from my paternal line also tested. For years, I posted queries to genetic bulletin boards and Facebook, seeking men with the surname *Figura*. Finally I got a response from two Slovaks, one named Joseph Figura, the other Nick Adzima (whose mother was a Figura). Joseph could take

This Greek Catholic birth register lists the birth and baptismal dates for Andrew, the *illeg*, plus his mother's name and birth information and the names of his godparents.

the Y-DNA test, but Nick had the paperwork to help: a document trail showing that his mother descended from John Figura of Milpoš.

While building this family tree, we were also building trust and convincing ourselves that we were all cousins. Both DNA and paper records confirmed that the Figuras and I were second cousins, once removed, but which Figura is my great-grandfather?

Despite visiting the homeland, networking and cooperating with distant cousins, and taking DNA tests, I still don't have all the answers. Heritage travel, DNA testing, and traditional genealogy have all helped me learn about my family's history, but I still have questions about my ancestors. That's the great thing about genealogy—you're never finished.

14

What to Do When You Get Stuck

As you search for your Polish, Czech, and Slovak ancestors, you'll inevitably hit a "brick wall"—the bane of every genealogist's existence. A brick wall is that seemingly unsolvable research problem, when you can't find answers anywhere you look. You're also bound to run into common pitfalls that stall your research progress: false leads (caused by bad information or assumptions), conflicting data (facts that don't make sense together), dead ends (you can't seem to locate your great-grandmother's maiden name), or a trail left by your ancestors going cold.

Don't despair. This happens to all researchers, and it doesn't mean you've reached a dead end. Rather than giving up, you may just need to try a new approach.

Many brick walls can be chiseled away with information you already have buried in files or records you forgot about. If you're just starting out and are already stumped, you may need to try some alternative sources and methods to track down what you want to know. This chapter highlights seven methods that can help you overcome your research roadblocks.

TRACE THE WHOLE FAMILY

Remember the concept of whole-family genealogy introduced in chapter 2? This involves researching not only your ancestors, but all of their siblings—because the parents of those siblings are also your ancestors. This approach has the benefit of making your research more thorough and accurate, and it might be the only way to obtain one of those two critical pieces of information: the immigrant's original name and hometown. Maybe your immigrant great-grandfather wasn't naturalized, but his brother was—and that brother's declaration of intention lists the village where they both were born. By researching the brother, you open up new research avenues for your own ancestor. Likewise, you can research those siblings' families forward to identify living cousins who could have documentation of the immigrant family that wasn't passed down in your branch of the family.

JOIN THE FAN CLUB

More likely than not, your Polish, Czech, or Slovak ancestors settled in "cluster communities" with many of their fellow countrymen. These ethnic clusters offer plenty of friends, associates, and neighbors (or "FANs," as dubbed by genealogical author and scholar Elizabeth Shown Mills). In the cases of truly stubborn ancestors, your research success may depend upon all the people whose lives intersected with theirs. As with whole-family genealogy, those FANs' records may provide the best clues to your ancestor—both before and after his death (think about name-filled wills and estate proceedings). And it's not unusual to discover that your ancestors' "whole family" and "FAN club" overlap: Especially in cluster communities, associates and neighbors often encompassed extended family, whose paper trails might offer up answers about your direct line.

When viewing US census records, be sure to study the page carefully. Locate your ancestor and evaluate each of their answers to the questions. Then note the neighbors. Write down the names and other pertinent details on a census worksheet (downloadable from <www.familytreemagazine.com/freeforms>). You may later see a certain surname showing up as a witness to your ancestor's marriage license or naturalization petition or as a godparent for one of your ancestor's children.

Whatever census you start with, work backward through previous enumerations to evaluate how long a particular group of individuals or their families lived in a city or town. Many cluster communities have a rich history—families may have lived in the same area (and maybe even the same house) for several generations. Take, for example, the 1940 census record for John Alzo (my grandfather) and his family in Duquesne, Pennsylvania. John's wife, Elizabeth, had a sister named Anna Bavolar who is listed three entries above her in a neighboring house. Without looking beyond my blood family's entry, I would have missed her and the insight that Slovak families stayed close even after marriage.

LOCALIZE SURNAMES

We've talked about the importance of researching all available records from your ancestors' time and place: This not only ensures you don't miss your forebear in a seemingly unlikely source, it also helps you "localize" your family's surnames—that is, identify the places with the highest concentrations of those surnames—in America and the old country.

Remember, immigrants tended to gravitate toward their own ethnic enclaves in America. So if you're stuck identifying your ancestors' specific place of origin, study US records for the places of origin of others with the same surname. For example, if you search a naturalization database and discover that many of the immigrants with your surname were coming from the same city, that gives you a potential lead to check. While not always foolproof, it's at least a theory to test. Also try searching surname lists and forums such as these to see where others with your surnames came from:

- Ancestry.com message boards **<boards.ancestry.com>** (look for the ethnic-specific boards for Polish, Czech, and Slovak researchers)
- Czech and Slovak Republic Genealogy Yahoo! group **<groups.yahoo.com/neo/ groups/SLOVAK-ROOTS/info>**
- MyCzechRepublic **<www.myczechrepublic.com/boards>**
- Polish Genius Yahoo! group **<groups.yahoo.com/neo/groups/polish_genius/info>**
- PolandGenWeb **<www.rootsweb.ancestry.com/~polwgw/rafal/surname.html>**

Localizing can work across the pond, too. As discussed in chapter 7, surname distribution maps such as Moikrewni **<www.moikrewni.pl/mapa>** can give a breakdown of your name in all the districts in Poland. Similarly, the KdeJsme site **<www.kdejsme. cz>** helps you find the frequency of the surname or names within the Czech Republic, and Slovniky **<www.slovniky.korpus.sk>** allows you to see where a surname appears in Slovakia. Another tactic is to search Polish, Czech, or Slovak data sets on FamilySearch. org **<www.familysearch.org>** and Ancestry.com **<www.ancestry.com>** to see which villages have clusters of your ancestor's surname during the right time period. You still will have to pinpoint exact locations, but it's a start. When you identify these villages, you can then scour their church and civil records to see if your ancestors appear.

If those searches come up empty, try what James M. Beidler calls the "concentric circles" strategy in his *Family Tree German Genealogy Guide* (Family Tree Books, 2014):

> *Increase your search radius to include villages that surround the first you tried. If nothing turns up in those, move the radius out again to include villages surrounding your second set. Don't stop "one village too soon" and find out*

years later that the family you sought was one village farther out from your search radius.

GO FOR GENETICS

DNA testing has become both more affordable and useful for genealogical research in the past few years—and its popularity has exploded. Millions of people have now taken genetic genealogy tests. That's great news for Polish, Czech, and Slovak descendants hoping to bust through brick walls: Your chances of finding cousin "matches" through it is better than ever, and will keep growing as more people get tested.

The three main types of genetic genealogy tests are Y-DNA, which examines only the paternal ancestral line, mitochondrial DNA (mtDNA), which looks at just the maternal line, and autosomal DNA (atDNA), which analyzes all your DNA. Since atDNA covers your entire family tree—not just the outer male and female branches of your pedigree chart—it's the most popular test today, and the best place to begin. Your atDNA results will include cousin matches with an estimated degree of relationship (second cousins, fourth cousins, etc.). By comparing research with your cousin matches, you can try to determine which ancestors you share. AncestryDNA **<dna.ancestry.com>** makes this easier by linking DNA results to online family trees so you can look for surnames and locations in common with your matches.

Of course, you'll need to search for matches across all three major testing companies—AncestryDNA, 23andme **<www.23andme.com>**, and Family Tree DNA **<www.familytreedna.com>**—because you don't want to miss matches who tested with a different service. Since each company's test is a little different, third-party tools such as GEDMatch **<www.gedmatch.com>** have cropped up to help genealogists with this.

Once you've tested, be sure to enable permissions for those who match you to contact you. Having a family tree posted online helps, too (even if it's just a bare-bones tree created just for genetic genealogy purposes).

Joining a DNA surname or locality study can help you connect specifically with Polish, Czech, and Slovak researchers who have done testing on your surname or whose ancestors were from the same town, village, or region. For example, Karen Melis runs a study for the Zamgurie region of Slovakia through Family Tree DNA. To find such projects, search Family Tree DNA's website and consult the International Society of Genetic Genealogists' wiki **<www.isogg.org/wiki/Wiki_Welcome_Page>**.

If your Polish, Czech, or Slovak ancestry is specifically through your direct paternal line (your father, his father, his father's father, etc.), Y-DNA testing might help you identify an unknown village of origin. Because Y-DNA passes relatively unchanged in the same way male surnames did in Eastern Europe, a Y-DNA test can show that cousins come from a common ancestor, usually within the last five hundred years.

Here's how this would work: If you are male, you'd have yourself (or your father/brother if you're a woman) tested, then test a close cousin or two to be sure the Y-DNA is the same (thereby assuring that no one was the result of a "non-paternity event"). Next, find more male cousins descended from the same immigrant and have them tested to firmly establish the immigrant's Y-DNA profile.

Then you would need to convince Polish, Czech, or Slovak men of the same surname (making sure that you have the most authentic Polish, Czech, or Slovak spelling) to take the test, perhaps limited to specific regions if you have clues or a hypothesis about the part of Poland, the Czech Republic, or Slovakia your ancestor came from. If you get any Y-DNA matches in this process, you'd then need to trace those men's genealogies to find where their ancestors lived when your own ancestor immigrated to America. Very likely, you'd find your ancestor nearby.

The field of genetic genealogy is rapidly changing and advancing, and the science can be hard for some people to get their heads around, so read up to ensure you make the most of your investment. Family Tree University's Genetic Genealogy 101 online course <www.familytreeuniversity.com/courses/genetic-genealogy-101> will help you determine which test is right for you, with an instructor who can answer questions.

COLLABORATE ONLINE

Working with other researchers is a great way to jump-start your research when you get stuck. For instance, you could look for someone else researching the same ancestral village; by swapping information, you might spot clues or patterns that solve research problems for both of you. That person might have access to resources you don't, and her familiarity with local records would come in handy when you need a second set of eyes on a document.

Thanks to technology, you have more and more ways to connect with cousins and share information with fellow researchers. Probably the most obvious avenue is online

RESEARCH TIP

Make Connections via Societies

Remember that exchanging information is a key part of a genealogical society's mission. The Polish, Czech, and Slovak societies discussed in this book all have kept surname lists and published queries in their journals to help members connect. Check their websites for details.

HOW FAMILY HISTORY ANSWERS FOUND ME

Sometimes the answers you're searching for can fall out of cyberspace. After more than a decade of researching my Alzo ancestors, I had only connected with two other genealogists interested in researching that surname—and they were related only by marriage.

But from family information, I knew my grandfather Ján (John) Alzo was one of five children. Besides my grandfather, only his sister Mary settled in the United States. One sister (Anna) and two brothers (Michal and Andrej) remained in Slovakia. Except for a few photographs, I had little information on them. Then in December 2008, the following e-mail appeared in my inbox:

> *Dear Lisa,*
>
> *My name is Renata and I live in London. I came across your article today while browsing the Internet and was absolutely astonished by reading it. I read about you some time ago and even though I knew my family had some relatives in America ... well, they were many people who left Monarchy and then Slovakia and settled in USA ...*
>
> *First of all I would like to mention that Kučín is my home place, and if facts are right — IF!! — then your grandfather Ján Alžo would be my father's uncle, and the house my parents built and I grew up in is basically standing on the very land where your grandfather was born and was living there too ... I called my parents this evening to confirm some facts, but would like to discuss them further more in my next e-mail—and if you are interested, of course ...*

If I was interested? You bet I was! Andrej's granddaughter, Renata, had found me. In June 2010, after more than a year of sharing e-mails, photographs, and family tree information, Renata and I finally met in person in Slovakia. Renata showed me around Kučín: the home where my grandfather lived as a boy, the church where he was baptized, and the cemetery with the graves of my great-grandparents.

I also learned more about Andrej. He was born in 1914, nearly four years after my grandfather left for America and almost twenty years to the day my grandfather was born. The two never met, but the family story was that my great-grandmother missed her eldest son so much that she prayed for another baby.

I met Andrej's son (Renata's father), Ján, who agreed to take a Y-DNA test so I could compare the results with my father's. Not surprisingly, he was a twelve-for-twelve match, indicating a recent common ancestor. Having another Alzo take the test also gives me another point of reference in the DNA database, with the potential to connect with other matches.

Thanks to my online presence, Renata—and new family discoveries—found me. Now we visit regularly on Skype and continue to put our heads together to solve other family mysteries.

family trees. All the big genealogy websites, including Ancestry.com **<www.ancestry.com>**, FamilySearch.org **<www.familysearch.org>**, and MyHeritage **<www.myheritage.com>**, host databases of users' family trees. Once you identify a tree that includes one or more of your ancestors (or even just a common ancestral village), you can contact the submitter to compare notes. Just keep in mind that these family trees aren't necessarily accurate—in fact, false information tends to spread rapidly through people who copy and paste entire trees without verifying any of the information. Be sure to evaluate the information in the tree: Do the dates make sense? Did the person cite sources? While data in online trees must be taken with a grain of salt, they can provide the connections, clues, and research theories you need to overcome a brick wall.

RootsWeb **<rootsweb.ancestry.com>**, Yahoo! **<www.yahoo.com>**, and other websites have discussion forums and groups dedicated to Eastern European genealogy. You can join in to ask questions, as well as search the archives to see if someone has already posted the information you seek. Also look for Polish-, Czech-, or Slovak-themed blogs to follow; you can find these by searching Google **<www.google.com>** or GeneaBloggers' Genealogy Blog Roll **<www.geneabloggers.com/genealogy-blogs>**.

Facebook **<www.facebook.com>** users have formed collaborative groups on Polish, Czech, Slovak, and Rusyn genealogy, which you can find by searching Facebook or consulting genealogist Katherine Willson's list of genealogy Facebook groups **<socialmediagenealogy.com/genealogy-on-facebook-list>**. Also search Facebook to see if a group or page exists for your ancestral village. Use Twitter **<www.twitter.com>** to broadcast surnames or villages you're researching or to ask research questions. Check out YouTube **<www.youtube.com>** for anyone posting tours of a particular town or village.

"Pinning" is an increasingly popular form of genealogical collaboration. Genealogists are using Pinterest **<www.pinterest.com>** to create boards for surnames, ancestral towns, recipes, family photos and documents, old letters, favorite genealogy books and resources, and more. Historypin **<www.historypin.com>** lets you pin images related to your own ancestral locations to your own "channel" or view those pinned by others. To find pinned places in Eastern Europe, go to the Maps section and enter the name of the city or town in the search box. For example, *Krakow, Poland* turns up several interesting pins. Since new pins are added all the time, you should check back frequently.

FIND AREA EXPERTS

In my more than two decades of doing family research, I have regularly relied on the expertise of other researchers in the United States and in Europe. How can you find such experts? First, connect with local genealogical or historical societies in the area where your ancestor lived, as well as ethnic societies such as the Polish Genealogical Society of

America or the Czechoslovak Genealogical Society International, who have members living all around the globe.

Next, become well-acquainted with your ancestors' homeland and what's been written about it. Whether it's in a particular township in an American state, a far-flung locality in Poland, or a small, single village nestled in the Carpathian mountains of Eastern Slovakia, someone with encyclopedic knowledge of that area exists. Even if the expert in question is not computer savvy or lives far away, he or she likely will have written something (an article, history, etc.) about the area, and at least the title of this work will turn up in an online search. Perhaps the expert has a website or is on social media.

HIRE A PROFESSIONAL

In challenging research situations, it's often more practical to hire a professional researcher who's familiar with the area's geography, history, and languages—and who can access records in person. This is far less expensive than traveling across the United States or going abroad yourself. A researcher can act as an agent on your behalf to help you obtain post-1900 baptismal, marriage, or death certificates in the old country, and perhaps other records such as court, military, and other administrative documents not yet available on FamilySearch microfilm. Professional researchers may be willing to travel to ancestral villages to take photographs or research in town offices or churches.

You can find qualified professionals through the member directories of the Association of Professional Genealogists <www.apgen.org>, the Board for Certification of Genealogists <www.bcgcertification.org>, and the International Commission for the Accreditation of Professional Genealogists <www.icapgen.org>. The Polish, Czech, and Slovak genealogical societies mentioned throughout this book and in appendix H can also provide referrals.

When hiring a professional, remember these guidelines and expectations: The researcher should provide you with a plan of action of how your research payment will be spent. You should provide the professional with a clear summary of what research you've already done and what specific questions you want answered in the research.

This helps prevent you from getting a report in which you've paid for information that you already knew or sources you already ruled out. Always ask about complete fees for services upfront.

It used to be that genealogical research in Poland, the Czech Republic, or Slovakia was a pursuit entered into only by those who could travel to the homeland or afford to hire someone to do extensive research on their behalf. But thanks to greater access to records, the Internet, and social networking, anyone with knowledge of where to look, a solid research strategy, and plenty of patience and persistence can do it. And that includes you. Good luck with your Polish, Czech, or Slovak genealogical journey.

KEYS TO SUCCESS

✳ Extend your research to your problem ancestor's siblings, friends, and neighbors. Their records may contain the answers you need.

✳ Identify places with high incidences of your Polish, Czech, or Slovak surnames. When you're struggling to locate your ancestors, these places provide theories to try.

✳ Search online family trees and social media to find cousins and others researching your ancestral village. Don't forget to leave your own virtual breadcrumb trail so others can find you.

✳ Use DNA testing to turn up genetic cousins in your Polish, Czech, or Slovak lines.

✳ Tap into local experts and professional researchers to access records and resources you can't.

A

Understanding Polish

Polish is a Western Slavic language related to Russian, Czech, and Slovak. Its native names are *polski* (Polish), *język polski* (the Polish language), or more formally, *polszczyzna* (Polish). Before 1918, Polish-speaking territories were divided between Russia, Germany, and Austria. You'll encounter the Polish language in key genealogical sources throughout Poland and also for records kept in some Polish communities in the United States. Because of the period of Poland's three partitions (Prussia, Russia, Austria), records written before 1918 may be in German, Russian, Latin, or Polish. In Russian Poland, Polish was the official language for vital records from 1808 to 1868. From 1868 to 1917, Russian was the official language. In German Poland, most records were kept in German or Latin, though some were kept in Polish. In Austrian Poland, most records were kept in Latin. Some records were kept in German and some in Polish.

Special thanks to Jonathan D. Shea for providing information in this section.

THE POLISH ALPHABET

This chart shows Polish letters in alphabetical order. The letters *q*, *v* and *x* are used only for foreign names or words.

Capital	Lowercase
A	a
Ą	ą
B	b
C	c
Ć	ć
D	d
E	e
Ę	ę
F	f
G	g
H	h
I	i

Capital	Lowercase
J	j
K	k
L	l
Ł	ł
M	m
N	n
Ń	ń
O	o
Ó	ó
P	p
(Q)	(q)
R	r

Capital	Lowercase
S	s
Ś	ś
T	t
U	u
(V)	(v)
W	w
(X)	(x)
Y	y
Z	z
Ź	ź
Ż	ż

Spelling

Note that the letter *ą* is a separate letter from *a*. Therefore, in proper Polish, *ą* follows *a* in alphabetical listings. This is most important when reading gazetteers—for example, *Baz* comes before *Bąk*. The *s* is sometimes written like an *f* in the old cursive style found in church records, as in *Morofki* for *Moroski*, or *Sasfów* instead of *Sassów*.

When looking at English or other non-Polish documents, watch for certain changes in translation. The Polish letter *ł* (which sounds like the English *w*) is transcribed into English like an *l* or like a *w*. You may find it as a *t* because a non-Polish speaking clerk misread it. The Polish nasal vowels *ą* and *ę* sometimes get transcribed into English simply as *a* and *e*. Or because of the sound heard by a non-Polish speaker, *ą* may be transcribed as *an*, *on*, *am*, or *om*. Likewise, *ę* may appear as *en* or *em*.

Pronunciation Guide

Polish pronunciation is not always intuitive for non-Polish speakers. For example, former Polish president Lech Wałęsa's surname is pronounced *Va-wen-sa*. Keep this fact in mind when looking at records, as those creating official documents likely did not understand Polish pronunciation and so may have created spelling variations.

For additional help with Polish words and grammar, see the Polish Word List at <**www. familysearch.org/learn/wiki/en/Poland_Language_and_Languages#Word_List**>.

Letters	Sound	Example
ą	om, on	h<u>ome</u>
c	ts	ra<u>ts</u>
ch, h	kh	ba<u>k</u>e
ć, cz, ci	ch	<u>ch</u>erry
dz	j	<u>j</u>ury
ę	em, en	s<u>e</u>nse
j	y	<u>y</u>es
ł	w	<u>w</u>alk
ś, sz, si	sh	<u>sh</u>ow
ż, zi	zh	plea<u>s</u>ure

KEY POLISH TERMS

While it might help you in conducting Polish ancestor research, being fluent in Polish is certainly not necessary. Here are some terms you're likely to encounter.

Months

Both nominative (standard) and genitive (possessive) forms of the words are listed. Polish vital records frequently contain the latter.

English	Nominative	Genitive
January	styczeń	stycznia
February	luty	lutego
March	marzec	marca
April	kwiecień	kwietnia
May	maj	maja
June	czerwiec	czerwca
July	lipiec	lipca
August	sierpień	sierpnia
September	wrzesień	września
October	październik	października
November	listopad	listopada
December	grudzień	grudnia

Days of the Week

English	Polish
Sunday	niedziela
Monday	poniedziałek
Tuesday	wtorek
Wednesday	środa
Thursday	czwartek
Friday	piątek
Saturday	sobota

Numbers

In many genealogical records, numbers—especially in dates—are spelled out. The following list gives the cardinal (1, 2, 3) and ordinal (first, second, third) numbers. Dates are written in ordinal form. In dates, ordinal numbers usually end with –*ego*; for example: *pierwszy* means "the first" and *pierwszego* means "on the first" (of the month).

Numeral	Cardinal	Ordinal	Numeral	Cardinal	Ordinal
1	jeden, jedna	pierwszy	11	jedenaście	jedenasty
2	dwa, dwie	drugi	12	dwanaście	dwunasty
3	trzy	trzeci	13	trzynaście	trzynasty
4	cztery	czwarty	14	czternaście	czternasty
5	pięć	piąty	15	piętnaście	piętnasty
6	sześć	szósty	16	szesnaście	szesnasty
7	siedem	siódmy	17	siedemnaście	siedemnasty
8	osiem	ósmy	18	osiemnaście	osiemnasty
9	dziewięć	dziewiąty	19	dziewiętnaście	dziewiętnasty
10	dziesięć	dziesiąty	20	dwadzieścia	dwudziesty

Numeral	Cardinal	Ordinal	Numeral	Cardinal	Ordinal
21	dwadzieścia jeden	dwudziesty pierwszy	70	siedemdziesiąt	siedemdziesiąty
22	dwadzieścia dwa	dwudziesty drugi	80	osiemdziesiąt	osiemdziesiąty
23	dwadzieścia trzy	dwudziesty trzeci	90	dziewiecdziesiąt	dziewięćdziesiąty
24	dwadzieścia cztery	dwudziesty czwarty	100	sto	setny
25	dwadzieścia pięć	dwudziesty piąty	200	dwieście	dwóchsetny
26	dwadzieścia sześć	dwudziesty szósty	300	trzysta	trzysetny, trzechsetny
27	dwadzieścia siedem	dwudziesty siódmy	400	czterysta	czterysetny, czterechsetny
28	dwadzieścia osiem	dwudziesty ósmy	500	pięćset	pięćsetny
29	dwadzieścia dziewięć	dwudziesty dziewiąty	600	sześćset	sześćsetny
30	trzydzieści	trzydziesty	700	siedemset	siedemsetny
31	trzydzieści jeden	trzydziesty pierwszy	800	osiemset	osiemsetny
40	czterdzieści	czterdziesty	900	dziewięćset	dziewięćsetny
50	pięćdziesiąt	pięćdziesiąty	1000	tysiąc	tysięczny
60	sześć dziesiąt	sześćdziesiąty			

Genealogical Words

English	Polish
baptism	chrzest
baptized	ochrzony (m), ochrzona (f)
birth	urodzin, urodzony
birthplace	miejsce urodzenia
burial	pochowanie, pogrzeb
certificate	świadectwo/akt
child	dziecię, dziecko
daughter	córka
death	zgon/śmierć
died	umarł/umarła
father	ojciec
first name	imię, imion
husband	mąż, małżonek
Jewish	żydowski, starozakonny, izraelici, mojżeszowy
marriage	małżeństwo
married	żonaty (m)/mężatka (f)

English	Polish
marriage banns	zapowiedzi
married couple	małżonkowie
mother	matka
occupation/social class	stan/zawód
parents	rodzice
parish	parafia
Protestant	ewangelicki, reformowany, protestancki, luterański
Roman Catholic	rzymsko-katolicki
religion	wyznanie
son	syn
surname	nazwisko
village	wieś
wife	Żona, małżonka, zamena, kobieżta
year	rok, lat

B

Understanding Czech

C zech is a Western Slavic language, related to Slovak, Polish, and Russian. Czech was not recognized as an official language until 1877 in Bohemia and 1905 in Moravia. It was seldom used as a written language until the late 1800s. Except for modern records of the 1900s, records in the Czech Republic were written mostly in Latin and German. You may come across other languages such as Old Church Slavonic, Polish, Hebrew, and Yiddish in certain Czech records. Most of the people in the Czech Republic speak the Czech language.

Special thanks to Jan Ebert for providing information in this section.

THE CZECH ALPHABET

The Czech alphabet uses several letters in addition to the twenty-six letters used in the English alphabet: *á, č, ď, é, ě, í, ň, ó, ř, š, ť, ú, ů, ý, ž*. The letter combination *ch* is also considered a single letter and is alphabetized after *h*. Letters *q, w,* and *x* are used only in words of foreign origin. The Czech alphabet is listed below in the alphabetical order in which it would appear in Czech dictionaries and indexes.

Capital	Lowercase	Capital	Lowercase	Capital	Lowercase
A	a	I	i	S	s
Á	á	Í	í	Š	š
B	b	J	j	T	t
C	c	K	k	Ť	ť
Č	č	L	l	U	u
D	d	M	m	Ú	ú
Ď	ď	N	n	Ů	ů
E	e	Ň	ň	V	v
É	é	O	o	(W)	(w)
Ě	ě	Ó	ó	(X)	(x)
F	f	P	p	Y	y
G	g	(Q)	(q)	Ý	ý
H	h	R	r	Z	z
Ch	ch	Ř	ř	Ž	ž

Spelling

Czech language is highly inflective. Words may have different endings depending on usage. For example, *Josef, syn Antonína Ryby a Anny roz. Novákové* translates to "Josef, son of Antonín Ryba and Anna Novaková." Likewise, *Manželství mezi Michalem Dostalíkem a Anežkou Marii Seidlerovou* refers to a marriage between Michal Dostalík and Anežka Marie Seidlerová. For additional help with Czech grammar, see the Czech Word List at <www.familysearch.org/learn/wiki/en/Czech_Republic_Genealogical_Word_List>.

Pronunciation Guide

With its many additional letters and sounds, the Czech language can be intimidating to pronounce. Below are each of the letters of the Czech language, its equivalent English sound, and an example of the sound as used in an English word.

Letter	Sound	Example
a	uh	f<u>u</u>n
á	a	f<u>a</u>ther
b	b	<u>b</u>ack
c	ts	bi<u>ts</u>
č	ch	<u>ch</u>at
d	d	<u>d</u>og
ď	dih	<u>d</u>o
e	e	l<u>e</u>d
é	ea	w<u>ea</u>r
ě	ye	<u>ye</u>s
f	f	<u>f</u>ast
g	g	gas
h	h	<u>h</u>elp
ch	k	lo<u>ch</u> (aspirated)
i	i	s<u>i</u>t
í	ee	b<u>ee</u>
j	j	<u>y</u>outh
k	k	<u>k</u>iss
l	l	<u>l</u>and
m	m	<u>m</u>an

Letter	Sound	Example
n	n	<u>n</u>ow
ň	y	can<u>y</u>on
o	o	<u>o</u>
ó	oa	b<u>oa</u>t
p	p	<u>p</u>eak
r	r	<u>r</u>an (often rolled)
ř	rsh	ma<u>rsh</u>
s	s	<u>s</u>un
š	sh	<u>sh</u>oe
t	t	<u>t</u>op
ť	ty	<u>t</u>une
u	u	p<u>u</u>t
ú	oo	p<u>oo</u>l
ů	oo	p<u>oo</u>l
v	v	<u>v</u>an
y	i	b<u>i</u>t
ý	ee	b<u>ee</u>
z	z	<u>z</u>oo
ž	zh	mea<u>s</u>ure

Letter Combinations When Reading Old Text

Due to changing writing and spelling conventions, Czech words appearing in older documents may be spelled differently than they are in modern Czech. Use this table to help decipher old Czech manuscripts and records.

Spelling in old text	Modern spelling
cz	c or č
cž/čz	č
rz/rž	ř
ss	š
g	j
y	y or j
j	í
v (at the beginning of words)	u
ie	ě
au	ou
w	v

KEY CZECH TERMS

While it might help you in conducting Czech ancestor research, being fluent in Czech is certainly not necessary. Here are some terms you're likely to encounter.

Months

Months typically have two forms in Czech: the nominative (or standard) form and the genitive form that is used in dates. Czech dates are always given in day-month-year order. Months are often abbreviated using a Roman numeral. For example, *25 February 1848* could be written as *25. února 1848*; *25. 2. 1848*; or *25. II. 1848*.

English	Nominative	Genitive	English	Nominative	Genitive
January	leden	ledna	July	červenec	července
February	únor	února	August	srpen	srpna
March	březen	března	September	září	září
April	duben	dubna	October	říjen	října
May	květen	května	November	listopad	listopadu
June	červen	června	December	prosinec	prosince

Days of the Week

English	Czech
Sunday	neděle
Monday	pondělí
Tuesday	úterý
Wednesday	středa
Thursday	čtvrtek
Friday	pátek
Saturday	sobota

Numbers

In some genealogical records, numbers are spelled out. This is especially true with dates. The following list gives the cardinal (1, 2, 3) and the ordinal (first, second, third) versions of each number. In actual usage, days of the month are written in ordinal form with a genitive grammatical ending. In the following list, the ordinal number in its standard form is given first, followed by the genitive form: *pátý*—the fifth, *pátého*—on the fifth (of the month).

Numeral	Cardinal	Ordinal
1	jeden, jedna, jedno	první, prvního
2	dva, dvě	druhý, druhého
3	tři	třetí, třetího
4	čtyři	čtvrtý, čtvrtého
5	pět	pátý, pátého
6	šest	šestý, šestého
7	sedm	sedmý, sedmého
8	osm	osmý, osmého
9	devět	devátý, devátého
10	deset	desátý, desátého
11	jedenáct	jedenáctý, -ého
12	dvanáct	dvanáctý, -ého
13	třináct	třináctý, -ého
14	čtrnáct	čtrnáctý, -ého

Numeral	Cardinal	Ordinal
15	patnáct	patnáctý, -ého
16	šestnáct	šestnáctý, -ého
17	sedmnáct	sedmnáctý, -ého
18	osmnáct	osmnáctý, -ého
19	devatenáct	devatenáctý, -ého
20	dvacet	dvacátý, -ého
21	dvacet jeden, -jedna, -jedno	dvacátý první, dvacátého prvního
22	dvacet dva	dvacátý druhý, dvacátého druhého
23	dvacet tři	dvacátý třetí, dvacátého třetího
24	dvacet čtyři	dvacátý čtvrtý, dvacátého čtvrtého
25	dvacet pět	dvacátý pátý, dvacátého pátého

Numeral	Cardinal	Ordinal
26	dvacet šest	dvacátý šestý, dvacátého šestého
27	dvacet sedm	dvacátý sedmý, dvacátého sedmého
28	dvacet osm	dvacátý osmý, dvacátého osmého
29	dvacet devět	dvacátý devátý, dvacátého devátého
30	třicet	třicátý, třicátého
31	třicet jedna, or jedenatřicet	třicátáprvního
40	čtyřicet	čtyřicátý, -ého
50	padesát	padesátý, -ého
60	šedesát	šedesátý, -ého
70	sedmdesát	sedmdesátý, -ého

Numeral	Cardinal	Ordinal
80	osmdesát	osmdesátý, -ého
90	devadesát	devadesátý, -ého
100	sto	stý, -ého
200	dvě stě	dvoustý, -ého
300	tři sta	třístý, -ého
400	čtyři sta	čtyřistý, -ého
500	pět set	pětistý, -ého
600	šest set	šestistý, -ého
700	sedm set	sedmistý, -ého
800	osm set	osmistý, -ého
900	devět set	devítistý, -ého
1000	tisíc	tisící, -ího

Genealogical Words

English	Czech
baptism	křest, křestni
birth(s)	narození, rodný
burial	pohřeb
Catholic	katolíký
child	dítě, děcko, děťátko
church	církev
county	okres
daughter	dcera
death	úmrtí, smrt
farmer	hospodář, chlap
father	otec, táta
female	žena
first name	křestni jméno
godparent(s)	kmotři

English	Czech
husband	manžel, choť, muž
Jewish	židovský
male	mužský
marriage	sňatek, sňatky
mother	matka, matky, máma
parents	rodič, rodiče
registry/record	matrika
servant	sluha/služka
son	syn
surname	príjmení
town	město
village	ves, vesnice
wife	manželka, choť, žena

C

Understanding Slovak

Slovak is the official language of the Slovak Republic. The official Slovak written language was adopted in 1843 by Ludovit Stur and is based on the dialect spoken in central Slovakia. The Slovak language holds a central position among Slavic languages. While a West Slavic language, Slovak retains some features of Eastern Slavic languages and is related to Czech and Polish. Slovak-speakers intermingled with Ukrainian and Ruthenian speakers in the east and, before the arrival of Magyars (Hungarians) in the Danube basin, with speakers of the south Slavic languages (especially Slovene). Slovakia's central geographic location and other factors have made it easy for other Slavs to understand Slovak. Slovak is written using an alphabet of Latin origin, with one letter usually indicating one sound. In addition, Slovak is a phonetic language, which means words are pronounced as they are written.

Special thanks to Michal Razus for providing information in this section.

THE SLOVAK ALPHABET

Written Slovak uses several letters in addition to the twenty-six letters used in the English alphabet. These are *á, ä, č, ď, é, í, ľ, ľ, ň, ó, ô, ŕ, š, ť, ú, ý, ž*. The letter combinations *dz*, *dž*, and *ch* are also considered as single letters. Dz and dž are alphabetized after d, and ch is alphabetized after h. Letters q, w, and x are used only in words of foreign origin. The table below lists the capital and lowercase letters for the Slovak alphabet in the order they would appear in Slovak dictionaries and indexes.

Capital	Lowercase	Capital	Lowercase	Capital	Lowercase
A	a	I	i	R	r
Á	á	Í	í	Ŕ	ŕ
Ä	ä	J	j	S	s
B	b	K	k	Š	š
C	c	L	l	T	t
Ć	č	Ĺ	ĺ	Ť	ť
D	d	Ľ	ľ	U	u
Ď	ď	M	m	Ú	ú
DZ	dz	N	n	V	v
DŽ	dž	Ň	ň	(W)	(w)
E	e	O	o	(X)	(x)
É	é	Ó	ó	Y	y
F	f	Ô	ô	Ý	ý
G	g	P	p	Z	z
H	h	(Q)	(q)	Ž	ž
CH	ch				

Spelling

Spelling rules were not standardized in earlier centuries. In Slovak, the following spelling variations are common:

- *i, y,* and *j* used interchangeably
- *s* and *z* used interchangeably
- *w* used for *v*
- *rz* used for *r*
- *sz* used for *š*
- *cz* used for *č*

There are also rules for plural forms of words and for grammatical use. For additional help with Slovak grammar and vocabulary, see the Slovak Word List at **<www.familysearch. org/learn/wiki/en/images/3/34/Slovakwordlist.pdf>**.

Pronunciation Guide

With its many additional letters and sounds, the Slovak language can be intimidating to pronounce. Below are each of the letters of the Slovak language, its equivalent English sound, and an example of the sound as used in an English word. Note that *ĺ* and accented vowels (*á, é, í, ó, ú, and ý*) are pronounced longer than their unaccented counterparts.

Letter	Sound	Example
a, á	ah	mama
ä	eh	aerial
b	b	book
c	ts	cats, pizza
č	ch	cherry
d	d	dog
ď	dj	dew
dz	ds	dads
dž	dj	judge
e, é	eh	bet
f	f	fail
g	g	good
h	h	hand
ch	k	Bach
i, í	ih, ee	sit, beep
j	yih	yes
k	k	kiss

Letter	Sound	Example
l	l	land
ľ	yuh	yes
m	m	map
n	n	neighbor
o, ó	aw	lost
p	p	place
r	r	round (often rolled)
s	s	same
t	t	tape
ť	tch	hatch
u, ú	oo	boot
v	v	vegan
y, ý	ee	sleep
z	z	zoo
ž	dj	gauge

KEY SLOVAK TERMS

While it might help you in conducting Slovak ancestor research, being fluent in Slovak is certainly not necessary. Here are some terms you're likely to encounter.

Months

Unlike the languages of the other two ethnic groups covered in this book, the name of the months in Slovak come from Latin, meaning that they're similar to the English names. The Slovak language doesn't use nominative or genitive forms for months. Rather, Slovaks use the possessive form when writing dates.

English	Possessive
January	Január
February	Február
March	Marec
April	April
May	Máj
June	Jún

English	Possessive
July	Júl
August	August
September	September
October	Október
November	November
December	December

Days of the Week

English	Slovak
Sunday	nedeľa
Monday	pondelok
Tuesday	utorok
Wednesday	streda
Thursday	štvrtok
Friday	piatok
Saturday	sobota

Numbers

In some genealogical records, numbers are written out. This is especially true with dates. The following list gives the cardinal (1, 2, 3) and the ordinal (first, second, third) versions of each number. In actual usage, days of the month are written in ordinal form with a possessive grammatical ending. In the following list, the ordinal number in its standard form is given first, followed by the possessive form (in some cases only the possessive ending is listed), for example: *piaty*—"the fifth"; *na piaty*—"on the fifth (of the month)".

Numeral	Cardinal	Ordinal
1	jeden, jedna, jedno	prvý
2	dva, dve	druhý
3	tri	tretía
4	štyri	štvrtý
5	päť	piaty
6	šesť	šiestý
7	sedem	siedmý
8	osem	ôsmy
9	devät	deviaty
10	desať	desiaty
11	jedenásť	jedenásty
12	dvanásť	dvanásty
13	trinásť	trinásty
14	štrnácť	štrnásty
15	pätnásť	pätnásty
16	šestnásť	šestnásty
17	sedemnásť	sedemnásty
18	osemnásť	osemnásty
19	devätenásť	devätenáaty
20	dvadsať	dvadsiaty

Numeral	Cardinal	Ordinal
21	dvadsaťjeden	dvadsiatym
22	dvadsaťdva	dvadsaťsekunda
23	dvadsaťtri	dvadsiatomtreťom
24	dvadsaťštyri	dvadsiataštvrtá
25	dvadsaťpät	dvadsiateho piateho
26	dvadsaťšesť	dvacátášesté
27	dvadsaťsedem	dvacátésedmá
28	dvadsaťosem	dvacátéosmá
29	dvadsaťdeväť	dvacátédeváty
30	tridsať	tridsiaty
31	tridsaťjeden	tridsiatym
40	štyridsať	štyridsiate
50	päťdesiat	pätdesiaty
60	šesťdesiat	šesťdesiatym
70	sedemdesiat	sedemdesiateho
80	osemdesiat	osemdesiaty
90	deväťdesiat	deväťdesiaty
100	jednosto	stoina
200	dvesto	dvasty
300	tristo	trojstým

Numeral	Cardinal	Ordinal
400	štyristo	štyrib
500	päťsto	päťsto
600	šesťsto	šesťstoprvom
700	sedemsto	sedmis
800	osemsto	osmistý, -ého
900	deväťsto	devítistý, -ého
1000	jedentisíc	tisíc

Genealogical Words

English	Slovak
baptism	krstiť
birth(s)	narodenie(y)
burial	pohreb
Catholic	katolík
child	dieťa
church	kostol, cirkev(ny)
county	zupa
daughter	dcéra
death	smrť
farmer	sedliak/roľník
father	otec
female	žena
first name	krstné meno
godparent(s	kmotri

English	Slovak
husband	manzel
Jew(ish)	žid
male	muz, samec
marriage	manželstvo, sobás
mother	matka
parents	rodiča
registry/record	záznam
servant	sluha
son	syn
surname	priezvisko
town	město
village	dedina
wife	manželka

US Genealogy Archives and Libraries

ALLEN COUNTY PUBLIC LIBRARY
900 Library Plaza
Fort Wayne, IN 46802
<www.acpl.lib.in.us>

Holdings: second only to the Church of Jesus Christ of Latter-day Saints' Family History Library for the extent of its genealogical holdings

**ARCHIVES OF THE CZECHS
AND SLOVAKS ABROAD**
University of Chicago Library
1100 E. 57th St.
Chicago, IL 60637
<www.lib.uchicago.edu/e/su/slavic/acasa.html>

CENTER FOR AUSTRIAN STUDIES
University of Minnesota
314 Social Sciences, 267 Nineteenth Ave. S
Minneapolis, MN 55455
<www.cas.umn.edu>

Holdings: home to one of the largest collections of books on the Habsburg Empire in the United States

**CONNECTICUT POLISH AMERICAN
ARCHIVES AT CENTRAL CONNECTICUT
STATE UNIVERSITY**
Elihu Burritt Library
1615 Stanley St.
New Britain, CT 06053
<library.ccsu.edu/help/spcoll/cpaa/index.php>

FAMILY HISTORY LIBRARY

35 NW Temple St.

Salt Lake City, UT 84150

<www.familysearch.org>

Holdings: more than two hundred local branches in the United States, plus branches in Canada and Europe

GERMANS FROM RUSSIA HERITAGE COLLECTION

North Dakota State University Libraries

NDSU Dept. #2080

PO Box 6050

Fargo, ND 58108

<library.ndsu.edu/grhc/>

Holdings: the largest historical collection on Germans from Russia in the United States

IMMIGRATION HISTORY RESEARCH CENTER

University of Minnesota, College of Liberal Arts

311 Andersen Library

222 Twenty-First Ave. S

Minneapolis, MN 55455

<www.ihrc.umn.edu>

Holdings: large library of materials documenting immigrant experiences in the United States post-1848, with the bulk of the holdings pertaining to immigrants and refugees arriving between 1880 and 1980

INDIANA UNIVERSITY POLISH STUDIES CENTER

1217 E. Atwater Ave.

Bloomington, IN 47401

<www.indiana.edu/~polishst/home>

LIBRARY OF CONGRESS

101 Independence Ave. SE

Washington, DC 20540

<www.loc.gov>

Holdings: the nation's oldest federal cultural institution and the largest library in the world

MORAVIAN CHURCH ARCHIVES— NORTHERN PROVINCE

41 W. Locust St.

Bethlehem, PA 18018

<www.moravianchurcharchives.org>

MORAVIAN CHURCH ARCHIVES— SOUTHERN PROVINCE

457 S. Church St.

Winston-Salem, NC 27101

<moravianarchives.org>

NATIONAL ARCHIVES AND RECORDS ADMINISTRATION

700 Pennsylvania Ave. NW

Washington, DC 20408

<www.archives.gov>

Holdings: central repository for US federal records

NATIONAL CZECH AND SLOVAK MUSEUM AND LIBRARY

1400 Inspiration Place SW

Cedar Rapids, IA 52404

<www.ncsml.org>

NEWBERRY LIBRARY

60 West Walton St.

Chicago, IL 60610

<www.newberry.org/
genealogy-and-local-history>

Holdings: famous for the Genealogical Index of the Newberry Library, a surname index to most personal names found in the Newberry Library's local history and genealogy collection prior to 1917

POLONICA AMERICANA RESEARCH INSTITUTE (PARI)

3535 Indian Trail

Orchard Lake, MI 48324

<www.polishmission.com/genealogy/
polonica-americana-research-institute>

Holdings: this department of the Polish Mission, which has many parish jubilee books, indexes to burials at Holy Cross Cemetery, and references books for Polish research

SLOVAK INSTITUTE

10510 Buckeye Rd.

Cleveland, OH 44104

<www.slovakinstitute.com>

UNIVERSITY OF BUFFALO LIBRARIES POLISH ROOM

517 Lockwood Library

433 Capen Hall

Buffalo, NY 14260

<library.buffalo.edu/polish-room>

Holdings: houses a collection of more than twelve thousand volumes of Polish literature and history, including genealogical literature and the language materials

UNIVERSITY OF PITTSBURGH SLAVIC LANGUAGES AND LITERATURES

1417 Cathedral of Learning

4200 Fifth Ave.

Pittsburgh, PA 15260

<www.slavic.pitt.edu>

Holdings: one of twenty doctoral programs in Slavic Studies in the United States, with courses in Russian, Polish, B/C/S (Bosnian, Croatian, Serbian), Slovak, and Ukrainian

UNIVERSITY OF UTAH SPECIAL COLLECTIONS AND ARCHIVES

Special Collections & Archives, Merrill Library

Utah State University Libraries

Logan, Utah 84322-3000

<library.usu.edu>

Holdings: more than a thousand books, manuscripts, newspapers, periodicals and other research materials from the Tomáš G. Masaryk Collection

Civil Record Archives in Europe

Whether your ancestors came from Poland, the Czech Republic, or Slovakia, it's likely that their records (if extant) have found their way into the government's archive system. While administrative divisions may differ by country (see chapter 6), governments have been taking a larger role in the record-keeping process since the beginning of the twentieth century. This lists the addresses and websites of each country's main regional archives. These resources will likely have any surviving vital, census, and other governmental records. See appendix G for more on writing letters to these institutions.

In addition to national and regional archives, the Polish, Czech, and Slovak governments have smaller, subsidiary branches of their archive systems that may be worth searching for documents including census extracts, passport applications, town and village histories, and other miscellaneous material. You can download a list of these branch or district archives for each country by visiting <**ftu.familytreemagazine.com/ polish-czech-slovak-genealogy-guide**>.

POLAND

The national archives system contains a host of information for genealogists, from Roman Catholic vital records not held by local parishes or vital registry offices to business and judicial records. Regional archives will also have information on individual cities. The government maintains twenty-eight regional archives (each with their own branches) in addition to the main archives in Warsaw.

NATIONAL ARCHIVES

Naczelna Dyrekcja Archiwów
Państwowowych
2D Rakowiecka Street
02-517 Warszawa
POLAND
<www.archiwa.gov.pl>

Regional Archives

BIAŁYSTOK

Archiwum Państwowe w Białymstoku
ul. Kosciuszko Square 4
15-426 Białystok
POLAND
<www.bialystok.ap.gov.pl>

BYDGOSZCZ

Archiwum Państwowe w Bydgoszczy
ul. Dworcowa 65
85-009 Bydgoszcz
POLAND
<www.bydgoszcz.ap.gov.pl>

CZĘSTOCHOWA

Archiwum Państwowe w Częstochowie
ul. Tadeusza Rejtana 13
42-200 Częstochowa
POLAND
<www.archiwum.czestochowa.um.gov.pl>

ELBLĄG

Archiwum Państwowe w Elblągu
(z siedzibą w Malborku)
ul. Starościńska 1
82-200 MALBORK
POLAND

GDAŃSK

Archiwum Panstwowe w Gdańsku
ul. Waly Piastowskie 5
80-958 Gdansk
POLAND
<www.gdansk.ap.gov.pl>

GORZÓW WIELKOPOLSKI

Archiwum Państwowe w Gorzowie
Wielkopolskim
ul. Grottgera 24/25 66-400 Gorzów
Wielkopolski
POLAND
<www.gorzow.ap.gov.pl>

KALISZ

Archiwum Państwowe w Kaliszu
ul. Poznańska 207 62-800 Kalisz
POLAND

KIELCE

Archiwum Państwowe w Kielcach
ul. Warszawska 17
25-512 Kielce
POLAND
<www.kielce.ap.gov.pl>

KOSZALIN

Archiwum Państwowe w Koszalinie
ul. Skłodowskiej-Curie 2
skr. poczt. 149
75-950 Koszalin
POLAND
<www.koszalin.ap.gov.pl>

KRAKÓW

Archiwum Państwowe w Krakowie
ul. Sienna 16
30-960 Kraków
POLAND
<www.archiwum.krakow.pl>

LESZNO

Archiwum Państwowe w Lesznie
ul. Solskiego 71
64-100 Leszno
POLAND
<www.archiwum.leszno.pl/new>

ŁÓDŹ

Archiwum Państwowe w Łodzi
pl. Wolności 1
skr. poczt. 36
90-950 Łódź
POLAND
<www.lodz.ap.gov.pl>

LUBLIN

Archiwum Państwowe w Lublinie
ul. Jezuicka 13
skr. poczt. 113
20-950 Lublin
POLAND
<www.lublin.ap.gov.pl>

OLSZTYN

Archiwum Państwowe w Olsztynie
ul. Partyzantów 18
10-521 Olsztyn
skr. poczt. 412
POLAND
<www.olsztyn.ap.gov.pl>

OPOLE

Archiwum Państwowe w Opolu
45-016 Opole
ul. Zamkowa 2
POLAND
<www.archiwum.opole.pl>

PIOTRKÓW TRYBUNALSKI

Archiwum Państwowe w Piotrkowie
Trybunalskim
ul. Toruńska 4
97-300 Piotrków Trybunalski
POLAND
<www.piotrkow-tryb.ap.gov.pl>

PŁOCK

Archiwum Państwowe w Płocku
ul. Kazimierza Wielkiego 9B
09-400 Płock
POLAND

POZNAŃ

Archiwum Państwowe w Poznaniu
ul. 23 Lutego 41/43
60-967 Poznań
skr. poczt. 546
POLAND
<www.poznan.ap.gov.pl>

PRZEMYŚL

Archiwum Państwowe w Przemyślu
ul. Lelewela 4
37-700 Przemyśl
POLAND
<www.przemysl.ap.gov.pl>

RADOM

Archiwum Państwowe w Radomiu
ul. Rynek 1
26-610 Radom
POLAND
<www.radom.ap.gov.pl>

RZESZÓW

Archiwum Państwowe w Rzeszowie
ul. Bożnicza 2
35-064 Rzeszów
POLAND
<www.rzeszow.ap.gov.pl>

SIEDLCE

Archiwum Państwowe w Siedlcach
ul. Kościuszki 7
08-110 Siedlce
POLAND
<www.siedlce.ap.gov.pl>

SUWAŁKI

Archiwum Państwowe w Suwałkach
ul. Kościuszki 69
16-400 Suwałki
POLAND
<www.suwalki.ap.gov.pl>

SZCZECIN

Archiwum Państwowe w Szczecinie
ul. Św. Wojciecha 13
70-410 Szczecin
POLAND
<www.szczecin.ap.gov.pl>

TORUŃ

<www.torun.ap.gov.pl>

Branch I, archival materials created before the end of the nineteenth century
Archiwum Państwowe w Toruniu
Oddział I
pl. Rapackiego 4
87-100 Toruń
POLAND

Branch II, archival materials from the nineteenth to twenty-first centuries
Archiwum Państwowe w Toruniu
Oddział II
ul. Idzikowskiego 6
87-100 Toruń
POLAND

Branch III, archival materials for the company archives
Archiwum Państwowe w Toruniu
Oddział III
ul. Idzikowskiego 6
87-100 Toruń
POLAND

WARSZAWA

Archiwum Państwowe m. st. Warszawy
ul. Krzywe Koło 7
00-270 Warszawa
POLAND
<www.warszawa.ap.gov.pl>

WROCŁAW

Archiwum Państwowe we Wrocławiu
ul. Pomorska 2
50-215 Wrocław
POLAND
<www.ap.wroc.pl>

ZAMOŚĆ

Archiwum Państwowe w Zamościu
ul. Hrubieszowska 69A
22-400 Zamość
POLAND
<www.zamosc.ap.gov.pl/>

ZIELONA GÓRA

Archiwum Państwowe w Zielonej Górze z
siedzibą w Starym Kisielinie
ul. Pionierów Lubuskich 53
66-002 Stary Kisielin
POLAND
<www.archiwum.zgora.pl>

Other Archives

ARCHIVE, MAJDANEK CONCENTRATION CAMP

Państwowe Muzeum Na Majdanku
ul. The road Martyrs
Majdanek 67
20-325 Lublin
POLAND
<www.majdanek.eu>

AUSCHWITZ-BIRKENAU STATE MUSEUM

ul. Więźniów Oświęcimia 20
32-603 Oświęcim
POLAND

THE CZECH REPUBLIC

In 1960, the Czechoslovak government established seven regional archives in addition to the main archives building in Prague. Regional archives contain vital information through 1900, plus tax records and deeds.

NATIONAL ARCHIVES

Archivní 4/2257
149 00 Prague 4
Chodovec
CZECH REPUBLIC
<www.nacr.cz>

Regional Archives

BRNO

Moravský zemský archiv v Brno
Palachovo náměstí 1
625 00 Brno
CZECH REPUBLIC
<www.mza.cz>

LITOMĚŘICE

ČR–Státní oblástní archiv v Litoměřicích
Krajská 48/1
412 01 Litoměřice
CZECH REPUBLIC

OPAVA (LAND ARCHIVE)

Zemský archiv v Opavě

Sněmovní 1

746 22 Opava

CZECH REPUBLIC

<www.archives.cz/zao>

PILSEN (PLZEŇ)

ČR–Státní oblastní archiv v Plzni

Sedláčkova 44

306 12 Plzeň

CZECH REPUBLIC

<www.soaplzen.cz>

PRAGUE (PRAHA)

ČR–Státní oblastní archiv v Praze

Státní okresní archiv Praha-východ se sídlem v Přemyšlení

Přemyšlení 220

250 66 Zdiby

CZECH REPUBLIC

<www.soapraha.cz>

TŘEBOŇ

ČR–Státní oblastní archiv v Třeboni

Husova 143

379 11 Třeboň

CZECH REPUBLIC

<www.ceskearchivy.cz>

ZÁMRSK

ČR–Státní oblastní archiv v Zámrsku

Zámrsk 1

565 43 Zámrsk

CZECH REPUBLIC

<www.vychodoceskearchivy.cz/zamrsk>

SLOVAKIA

The seven state archives are repositories for most pre-1900 parish books, plus early cadastral records, maps, architectural plans, historical documents, court records, administrative papers, and more.

NATIONAL ARCHIVES

Ministerstvo vnútra SR

Adresa Pribinova 2

812 72 Bratislava

SLOVAK REPUBLIC

<www.minv.sk/?slovensky-narodny-archiv>

Regional Archives

BANSKÁ BYSTRICA

Ministerstvo vnutra SR

Statny Archiv Banska Bystrica

Komenskeho 26

974 00 Banska Bystrica

SLOVAK REPUBLIC

BRATISLAVA

Ministerstvo vnutra SR

Statny Archiv Bratislava

Krizkova 7

811 04 Bratislava

SLOVAK REPUBLIC

BYTČA

Ministerstvo vnutra SR

Statny Archiv Bytča

S.Sakalovej 106/3

014 01 Bytča

SLOVAK REPUBLIC

KOŠICE

Ministerstvo vnutra SR
Statny Archiv Kosice
Bacikova 1
041 56 Kosice
SLOVAK REPUBLIC

LEVOCA

Ministerstvo vnutra SR
Statny Archiv Levoca
054 80 Levoca
SLOVAK REPUBLIC

NITRA

Ministerstvo vnutra SR
Statny Archiv Nitra
Novozamocka 273
951 12 Ivanka pri Nitre
SLOVAK REPUBLIC

PREŠOV

Ministerstvo vnutra SR
Statny Archiv Presov
Slanska 31
080 06 Presov - Nizna Sebastova
SLOVAK REPUBLIC

Church Record Archives in Europe

Local churches shaped your Eastern European ancestors' lives. Whether they were Catholic, Greek Orthodox, Protestant, or Jewish, your ancestors left behind a selection of religious records that can provide valueable information about their lives. While many of these records have been collected into civil archives (see chapter 8), some unique records survive in individual parish, diocese, and synagogue archives. This section lists the addresses for religious archives in Poland, the Czech Republic, and Slovakia; specifically, the Roman Catholic dioceses and archdioceses in Poland and the Czech Republic as well as a selection of Catholic, Greek Catholic, and Evangelical resources in Slovakia. See appendix G for templates to use when requesting religious records from church archives.

While there isn't a central location for Jewish records (and they can be difficult to find), you can find more information about locating Jewish records at the Miriam Weiner Routes to Roots Foundation (Poland) <www.rtrfoundation.org/archdta7.shtml>, the Gundacker List (Czech Republic) <www.jewishgen.org/austriaczech/TOWNS/gundframe1.html>, and "Jewish Family Research in Slovakia" from JewishGen (Slovakia) <www.jewishgen.org/hungary/slovak%20resources%20guide%20rev.pdf>.

POLAND

BIAŁYSTOK
Archiwum Archidiecezjalne w
Białymstoku
ul. Warszawska 46
15-077 Białystok
POLAND
<www.archibial.pl>

BIELSKO-ŻYWIECKA
Kuria diecezjalna
ul. Żeromskiego 5-7
43-300 Bielsko-Biała
POLAND
<www.diecezja.bielsko.pl>

BYDGOSZCZ
Diecezja Bydgoska
ul. Fr.. T. Malczewski 1
85-104 Bydgoszcz
POLAND
<www.diecezja.bydgoszcz.pl>

CZĘSTOCHOWA
Archiwum Archidiecezji
Częstochowskiej
Kuria Metropolitalna Al. NMP 54
42-200 Częstochowa
POLAND
<www.kuriaczestochowa.pl>

DROHICZYN
Archiwum Diecezjalne w Drohiczynie
ul. Kościelna 10
17-312 Drohiczyn n. Bugiem
POLAND
<www.drohiczynska.pl>

ELBLĄG
Archiwum Diecezjalne w Elblągu
ul. Św. Ducha 11
82-300 Elbląg
POLAND
<www.diecezja.elblag.opoka.org.pl>

EŁK
Archiwum Ełckiej Kurii Diecezjalnej
Plac Katedralny 1
19-300 Ełk
POLAND
<diecezjaelk.pl>

GDAŃSK
Archiwum Archidiecezjalne w Gdańsku
ul. The Bishop Edmund Nowicki 1,
80-330 Gdańsk Oliwa
POLAND
<diecezja.gdansk.pl/

GLIWICE
Archiwum Kurii Diecezjalnej w Gliwicach
ul. Łużycka 1
44-100 Gliwice
POLAND
<www.kuria.gliwice.pl>

GNIEZNO
Archiwum Archidiecezjalne w Gnieźnie
ul. Kolegiaty 2
62-200 Gniezno
POLAND

KALISZ

Kuria Diecezjalna w Kaliszu
ul. View 80-82
62-800 Kalisz
POLAND
<www.diecezja.kalisz.pl>

KATOWICE

Archiwum Archidiecezjalne w
Katowicach
ul. Jordana 39
40-043 Katowice
POLAND
<www.archiwum.archidiecezja.katowice.pl>

KIELCE

Archiwum Diecezjalne Kieleckie
ul. Jana Pawła II 3
25-013 Kielce
POLAND
<www.diecezja.kielce.pl>

KOSZALIN-KOŁOBRZEG

Archiwum Diecezji
Koszalińsko-Kołobrzeskiej
ul. Seminaryjna 2
75-817 Koszalin
POLAND
<www.archiwum.koszalin.opoka.org.pl>

KRAKÓW

Archiwum Kurii Metropolitalnej w
Krakowie
ul. Franciszkańska 3
31-004 Kraków
POLAND
<www.diecezja.pl/kuria/archiwum.html>

LEGNICA

Diecezja Legnicka
Kuria Diecezjalna
ul. Jana Pawla II 2
59-220 Legnica
POLAND
<www.diecezja.legnica.pl>

LUBLIN

Archiwum Archidiecezjalne Lubelskie
ul. Prymasa Stefana Wyszyńskiego 2
skr. poczt. 198
20-950 Lublin
<archidiecezjalubelska.pl>

ŁÓDŹ

Archiwum Archidiecezjalne w Łodzi
ul. Fr.. I. Skorupki 3
90-458 Łódź,
POLAND
<archidiecezja.lodz.pl/archiwum>

ŁOMŻA

Archiwum Diecezjalne w Łomży
ul. Sadowa 3
18-400 Łomża
POLAND
<www.kuria.lomza.pl>

ŁOWICZ

Archiwum Diecezji w Łowiczu
Stary Rynek 20
99-400 Łowicz
POLAND

OPOLE

ul. kard. Kominka 1a
45-032 Opole
POLAND
<www.diecezja.opole.pl>

PELPLIN

Archiwum Diecezjalne w Pelplinie
ul. Biskupa Dominika 11
83-130 Pelplin
POLAND
<www.diecezja-pelplin.pl>

PŁOCK

Archiwum Diecezjalne Płocku
ul. Abpa A. Nowowiejskiego 2
09-400 Płock
POLAND
<diecezjaplocka.pl>

POZNAŃ

Archidiecezja Poznańska
Kuria Metropolitalna w Poznaniu
ul. Ostrów Tumski 2
61-109 Poznań
POLAND
<www.archpoznan.pl>

PRZEMYŚL

Archiwum Archidiecezjalne w Przemyślu
37-700 Przemyśl
pl. Katedralny 4A
POLAND
<przemyska.pl>

PRZEMYŚL-WARSAW ARCHDIOCESE, GREEK CATHOLIC CHURCH

Archidiecezji Przemysko-Warszawskiej
Kościoła Greckokatolickiego
ul. bpa Jozafata Kocyłowskiego 4
37-700 Przemyśl
POLAND
<cerkiew.org>

RADOM

Archiwum Diecezjalne
ul. Malczewski 1
26-600 Radom
POLAND
<www.diecezja.radom.pl>

RZESZÓW

Archiwum Diecezjalne
ul. Zamkowa 4
35-032 Rzeszów
POLAND
<www.diecezja.rzeszow.pl>

SANDOMIERZ

Archiwum Diecezjalne w Sandomierzu
ul. Katedralna 1
27-600 Sandomierz
POLAND
<www.diecezjasandomierska.pl>

SIEDLCE

Archiwum Diecezjalne Siedleckie
ul. Piłsudskiego 64
08-110 Siedlce
POLAND

SOSNOWIEC

Kuria Diecezjalna w Sosnowcu
ul. Wawel 19
41-200 Sosnowiec
POLAND
<www.kuria.sosnowiec.pl>

SZCZECIN

Archiwum Archidiecezjalne w
Szczecinie/ Archiwum Archidiecezji
Szczecińsko-Kamieńskiej
ul. Papieża Pawła VI nr 4
71-459 Szczecin
POLAND
<www.archiwum.szczecin.pl>

ŚWIDNICKA

Archiwum Diecezjalne
Świdnicka Kuria Biskupia
pl. Jana Pawła II 1
58-100 Świdnica
POLAND
<www.diecezja.swidnica.pl>

TARNÓW

ul. Katedralna 3
33-100 Tarnów
POLAND
<www.archiwum.diecezja.tarnow.pl/>

TORUŃ

Archiwum Akt Dawnych Diecezji
Toruńskiej
Plac Ks. Frelichowskiego 1,
87-100 Toruń
POLAND
<www.archiwum.diecezja.torun.pl>

WARMIA KURIA METROPOLITALNA ARCHI-DIECEZJI WARMIŃSKIEJ

ul. Pieniężnego 22
10-006 Olsztyn
POLAND
<archwarmia.pl>

WARSZAWA

Archiwum Archidiecezjalne Warszawskie
ul. Dewajtis 3
01-815 Warszawa
POLAND
<archiwum.mkw.pl>

WARSZAWA-PRAGA

Archiwum Diecezjalne
ul. Floriańska 2A
03-707 Warszawa
POLAND
<www.diecezja.waw.pl>

ARCHIWUM KURII METROPOLITALNEJ W WARSZAWIE

ul. Midowa 17/19
00-246 Warszawa
POLAND
<www.archidiecezja.warszawa.pl>

WŁOCŁAWEK

Archiwum Diecezjalne w Włocławku
ul. Gdańska 2/4
87-800 Włocławek
POLAND
<www.diecezja.wloclawek.pl/pl/221/
archiwum-diecezjalne>

WROCŁAW

Archiwum Archidiecezjalne we
Wrocławiu
ul. Kanonia 12
50-329 Wrocław
POLAND
<www.archidiecezja.wroc.pl>

ZAMOŚĆ

Archiwum Diecezjalne w Zamościu
ul. Zamoyskiego 1
22-400 Zamość
POLAND
<www.zamosc.opoka.org.pl/muzeum>

ZIELONA GÓRA -GORZOW

65-075 Zielona Góra
pl. Powstańców Wielkopolskich 2A
skr. poczt. 178
POLAND
<www.archiwum.kuria.zg.pl>

THE CZECH REPUBLIC

APOSTOLIC EXARCHATE

Haštalské nám. 4
CZ-11000 Praha 1
CZECH REPUBLIC
<www.exarchat.cz>

ARCHDIOCESE OF OLOMOUC

Wurmova 9
CZ-77101 Olomouc
CZECH REPUBLIC
<www.ado.cz>

ARCHDIOCESE OF PRAGUE

Hradčanské nám
56/16
CZ-11902 Praha
CZECH REPUBLIC
<www.apha.cz>

DIOCESE OF BRNO

Petrov 8
CZ-60143 Brno
CZECH REPUBLIC
<www.biskupstvi.cz>

DIOCESE OF ČESKÉ BUDĚJOVICE

Biskupská 4, p.schr. 14
CZ-37021 České Budějovice
CZECH REPUBLIC
<www.bcb.cz>

DIOCESE OF HRADEC KRÁLOVÉ

Velké nám. 35
CZ-50001 Hradec Králové
CZECH REPUBLIC
<www.diecezehk.cz>

DIOCESE OF LITOMĚŘICE

Dómské nám. 1
CZ-41288 Litoměřice
CZECH REPUBLIC
<www.dltm.cz>

DIOCESE OF OSTRAVA-OPAVA

Kostelní nám. 1
CZ-72802 Ostrava 1
CZECH REPUBLIC

DIOCESE OF PLZEŇ

Nám. Republiky 35

CZ-30114 Plzeň

CZECH REPUBLIC

<www.bip.cz>

PRAŽSKÁ EPARCHIE

Resslova 9a

CZ 12000 Praha

CZECH REPUBLIC

<pravoslavnacirkev.cz>

KATOLÍCKA CIRKEV NA SLOVENSKU

Konferencia biskupov Slovenska

Kapitulská 11

P.O. Box 113

814 99 Bratislava

SLOVAK REPUBLIC

<www.kbs.sk>

SLOVAKIA

EVANJELICKÉ CIRKEV AUGSBURSKÉHO VYZ-NANIA NA SLOVENSKU

P.O. Box 289

810 00 Bratislava

SLOVAK REPUBLIC

<www.ecav.sk>

GRÉCKOKATOLÍCKA EPARCHIA KOŠICE

P.O. Box G-13

043 43 Košice

SLOVAK REPUBLIC

<www.exarchat.rcc.sk>

GRÉCKOKATOLÍCKE ARCIBISKUPSTVO PREŠOV

Hlavná 1, P.O. Box 135

081 35 Prešov

SLOVAK REPUBLIC

<www.grkatpo.sk>

Sample Letters to Request Records

I f you suspect an archive has records that might include traces of your ancestor—and you've exhausted all online options for finding those records—you'll likely need to contact the archive directly to receive more information. This section features sample letters that you can personalize and use when contacting archives, priests, and officials in Poland, the Czech Republic, and Slovakia. Each letter has an English translation on the opposite page for your reference. You can also download editable versions of these sample letters at **<ftu.familytreemagazine.com/polish-czech-slovak-genealogy-guide>**.

The section for each country also contains notes about how to adapt the sample letters for your own use. Generally speaking, it's more polite to write in the country's native language, but be sure not to use Google Translate **<translate.google.com>** or other online translation tools. While these can be helpful for translating specific words or short phrases, they lack cultural context and can provide translations that are confusing and unintelligible for native speakers.

POLAND

Follow these steps to make a personalized request using this form letter.

1. Fill in the date at the top and your name and address in the upper left-hand corner.

2. Appropriately address the letter (*Panie* for sir, *Pani* for madam) and select the pronoun that best represents your own gender (*wdzięczny* for male, *wdzięczna* for female) in the last paragraph.

3. Fill in information about your ancestors in the appropriate fields and exclude the rest. For example, if you know your ancestor's name, date of birth, place of birth, and date of death (but not his date of marriage, parents' names, or religion), include only those four fields.

SAMPLE LETTER

Szanowny Panie/Pani !

Piszę do Pana z nadzieją,że Pan zechce mi pomóc w odnalezieniu informacji o historii mojej rodziny.

Interesuję się następującą osobą. Podaję wszystkie dane jakie posiadam.

Imię i nazwisko _____

Data urodzenia _____

Miejsce urodzenia _____

Imię ojca _____

Imię matki _____

Data ślubu _____

Data zgonu _____

Wyznanie _____

Proszę o przesłanie odpisu świadectwa urodzenia/ świadectwa chrztu/świadectwa zgonu/świadectwa slubu.

Proszę o poinformowanie mnie jakie będą koszta związane z otrzymaniem tej informacji i w jaki sposób mogę to uregulować. Za wszelką pomoc będę bardzo wdzięczny/wdzięczna.

Z poważaniem,
(your complete name and address)

4. Identify and select which kind of record you're requesting: baptismal, birth, marriage, or death.

5. If you'll be contacting a parish priest rather than a government archive, you'll need to make a few changes. Instead of addressing the letter *Szanowny Panie/Pani* as indicated in the sample letter, begin with *Przewielebny Księże!* (Dear Father) and replace *Pana* and *Pan* in the second paragraph with *Księdza* and *Ksiądz*, respectively.

6. Address the envelope to the appropriate archive. Once you receive a response, include the appropriate fee in euros.

Letter and translation provided by Jonathan D. Shea <**www.pgsctne.org**>.

TRANSLATION

Dear Sir/Madam,

I am writing to you in the hope that you can assist me in gathering information on the history of my family.

I am interested in the following person. I have listed all the information that I possess.

Name and surname ⎯⎯⎯⎯⎯⎯⎯⎯⎯⎯⎯⎯⎯⎯⎯⎯⎯⎯⎯⎯⎯
Date of birth ⎯⎯⎯⎯⎯⎯⎯⎯⎯⎯⎯⎯⎯⎯⎯⎯⎯⎯⎯⎯⎯⎯⎯
Place of birth ⎯⎯⎯⎯⎯⎯⎯⎯⎯⎯⎯⎯⎯⎯⎯⎯⎯⎯⎯⎯⎯⎯
Name of father ⎯⎯⎯⎯⎯⎯⎯⎯⎯⎯⎯⎯⎯⎯⎯⎯⎯⎯⎯⎯⎯
Name of mother ⎯⎯⎯⎯⎯⎯⎯⎯⎯⎯⎯⎯⎯⎯⎯⎯⎯⎯⎯⎯
Date of marriage ⎯⎯⎯⎯⎯⎯⎯⎯⎯⎯⎯⎯⎯⎯⎯⎯⎯⎯⎯⎯
Date of death ⎯⎯⎯⎯⎯⎯⎯⎯⎯⎯⎯⎯⎯⎯⎯⎯⎯⎯⎯⎯⎯
Religion ⎯⎯⎯⎯⎯⎯⎯⎯⎯⎯⎯⎯⎯⎯⎯⎯⎯⎯⎯⎯⎯⎯⎯⎯

Please send me a copy of the baptismal record/birth record, death record, marriage record.

Please inform me of the charges to obtain the information that I am seeking and how this payment may be sent to you. I will be very grateful for any assistance you give me.

Sincerely yours,
(your complete name and address)

THE CZECH REPUBLIC

Follow these steps to make a personalized request using this form letter.

1. Fill in the date at the top and your name and address in the upper left-hand corner.

2. Appropriately address the letter (*Vážená paní* for sir, *Vážený pane* for madam).

3. Identify and select which type of record (birth, marriage, death) and from what religion (Roman Catholic, Evangelic, Greek Catholic, Orthodox, Lutheran, Jewish) you would like to receive.

4. Fill in information about your ancestors in the appropriate fields and exclude the rest. For example, if you know your ancestor's name, date of birth, place of birth, and date

---

SAMPLE LETTER

Vážená paní/Vážený pane matrikářko/matrikáři,

Dovoluji si požádat o doslovný výpis matričních údajů pro následující osobu :

Kniha:
Křtů   Sňatků   Úmrtí
Víra:
Římsko-katolická Evangelická Řecko-katolick Pravoslavná Protestantská Židovská

Jméno: _____

Příjmení: _____

Datum narození: _____

Místo narození: _____

Otec: _____

Matka: _____

Jméno ženicha: _____

Jméno nevěsty: _____

Datum svatby: _____

Místo svatby: _____

Datum úmrtí: _____

Místo úmrtí: _____

Předem děkuji za poskytnutí hledaných údajů.

S pozdravem,
(your complete name and address)

---

of death (but not his date of marriage, parents' names, or religion; include only those four fields).

5. Address the envelope to the appropriate archive.

6. The archive will contact you about a retrieval fee, which will usually be between 50 and 80 Czech korunas/CZK (two to four US dollars).

   *Letter and translation provided by Jan Ebert <**www.czechancestors.com**>.*

TRANSLATION

Dear Mrs./Mr. Registrar,

I would like to ask you to do a copy of parish record for following person:

Book of:
Births   Marriages   Deaths
Religion:
Roman Catholic   Evangelical   Greek Catholic   Orthodox   Protestant   Jewish

Name: _____

Surname: _____

Date of birth: _____

Place of birth: _____

Father: _____

Mother: _____

Name of spouse: _____

Name of bride: _____

Date of marriage: _____

Place of marriage: _____

Date of death: _____

Place of death: _____

Thank you in advance for providing inquired data.

With best wishes,
(your complete name and address)

SLOVAKIA

Follow these steps to make a personalized request using this form letter.

1. Fill in the date at the top and your name and address in the upper left-hand corner.

2. Appropriately address the letter (*Vážený pán* for sir, *Vážená pani* for madam). If you'll be contacting a parish priest rather than a government archive, you'll need to begin the letter with *Vážený pán farár* (Dear Father) rather than *Vážený pán/Vážená pani*.

3. In the first paragraph, fill in the name of your ancestor and the place and date (day, month, year) of his birth. If the ancestor you're looking for was a woman, include her maiden name whenever possible.

SAMPLE LETTER

Vážený pán/Vážená pani:

Za účelom zistenia informácií o minulosti mojej rodiny Vás týmto chcem požiadať o informácie o mojom predkovi: _____ ,
narodený_____ v_____ .

Môžem Vás poprosiť o zaslanie kompletného výpisu z matriky krstených / narodených týkajúce sa hore uvedeného predka.

Ak by to bolo možné chcem Vás poprosiť aj o zaslanie rodných, sobášnych a úmrtných záznamov týkajúcich sa jeho rodičov, ktorí žili v rovnakej obci. Za Vašu pomoc Vám budem veľmi vďačný.

Na pokrytie Vašich nákladov zasielam _____ dolárov ako aj dva kupóny , ktoré je možné vymeniť za letecké poštovné.

Za Vašu pomoc vopred ďakujem.

S pozdravom,
(your complete name and address)

4. Enclose the appropriate fee in bank draft or money order (such as American Express) and two International Reply Coupons (IRC), which are available at your local post office.

5. Address the envelope to the appropriate archive or church.

*Letter and translation provided by Michal Razus <**www.slovak-ancestry.com**>.*

TRANSLATION

Dear Sir/Madam,

To complete my family history I would like to have information about my ancestor
_____ , born _____
in _____.

May I please ask that you send me a complete extract from the birth record for the above named?

Should it be possible to send me extracts of the birth, marriage, or death records for his parents, who lived in the same town, I would be very thankful for this aid.

To cover your fees I am enclosing _____ dollars as well as two coupons that you can exchange for airmail postage.

Thank you in advance for your aid.

Respectfully,
(your complete name and address)

H

Polish, Czech, and Slovak Historical and Genealogical Societies

SOCIETIES IN NORTH AMERICA

General

American Catholic Historical Society
<www.amchs.org>

American Jewish Archives
<americanjewisharchives.org>

American Jewish Historical Society
<www.ajhs.org>

Austrian Cultural Forum New York
<www.acfny.org>

East European Genealogical Society
<www.eegsociety.org>

Foundation for East European Family History Studies
<feefhs.org>

Galizien German Descendants
<www.galiziengermandescendants.org>

German-Bohemian Heritage Society
<www.germanbohemianheritagesociety.com>

Historical Society of Pennsylvania (Balch Institute for Ethnic Studies)
<www.hsp.org>

The Immigrant Genealogical Society
<www.immigrantgensoc.org>

International Association of Jewish
Genealogical Societies
<www.iajgs.org>

The Kosciuszko Foundation
<www.thekf.org>

Minnesota Genealogical Society
<www.mngs.org>

Minnesota Historical Society
Minnesota History Center
<www.mnhs.org>

National Genealogical Society
<www.ngsgenealogy.org>

New England Historic
Genealogical Society
<www.americanancestors.org>

Wisconsin Historical Society
<www.wisconsinhistory.org>

Polish

Jewish Virtual Library—Poland
<www.jewishvirtuallibrary.org/jsource/vjw/
Poland.html>

Polish American Association
<www.polish.org>

Polish Embassy in Washington, DC
<washington.mfa.gov.pl/en>

Polish Genealogical Society of America
<www.pgsa.org>

Polish Genealogical Society of California
<www.pgsca.org>

Polish Genealogical Society of
Connecticut and the Northeast
<www.pgsctne.org>

Polish Genealogical Society
of Greater Cleveland
<www.rootsweb.ancestry.com/~ohpgsgc>

Polish Genealogical Society
of Massachusetts
<www.pgsma.org>

Polish Genealogical Society of Michigan
<www.pgsm.org>

Polish Genealogical Society of Minnesota
<pgsmn.org>

Polish Genealogical Society
of New York State
<pgsnys.org>

Polish Genealogical Society of Texas
<www.pgst.org>

Polish National Tourist Office
<www.poland.travel>

Pope John Paul II Polish Center
<www.polishcenter.org>

Toledo Polish Genealogy Society
<tpgs02.org>

Czech, Slovak, and Rusyn

American Czech-Slovak Cultural Club
<www.acscc.org>

American Friends of the Czech Republic
<www.afocr.org>

American Sokol—Los Angeles
<www.sokolla.org>

Carpatho-Rusyn Society
<www.carpathorusynsociety.org>

Czech & Slovak Cultural Center of
Minnesota
<cs-center.org>

Czech and Slovak Heritage Association—
Baltimore, MD
<www.panix.com/~czslha>

Czech and Slovak Sokol Minnesota
<sokolmn.org>

Czech Center Museum Houston
<www.czechcenter.org>

Czech Embassy in Washington, D.C.
<www.mzv.cz/washington>

Czech Heritage Club
<www.czechheritageclub.com>

The Czech Heritage Society of Texas
<www.czechheritage.org>

Czechoslovak Genealogical Society
International
<www.cgsi.org>

Czechoslovak Society of Arts
& Sciences (SVU)
<www.svu2000.org>

The Moravian Heritage Society
<www.czechusa.com/index.html>

Nebraska Czechs, Inc.
<www.nebraskaczechs.org/contact.html>

Nebraska Czechs of Lincoln
<www.lincolnczechs.org>

Nebraska Czechs of Wilber
<www.nebraskaczechsofwilber.com>

Omaha Czech Cultural Club
<omahaczechclub.com/index.html>

Slovak Catholic Sokol
<www.slovakcatholicsokol.org>

Slovak Embassy in Washington, DC
<www.mzv.sk/App/WCM/ZU/
WashingtonZU/main.nsf/vw_ByID/
index_EN>

Slovak Heritage & Folklore Society
International
<our-slovakia.com/genealogy.html>

Western Pennsylvania Slovak Cultural Association
<wpsca.org>

Wisconsin Czechs
<www.wiczechs.com/index.html>

Wisconsin Slovak Historical Society
<www.wisconsinslovakhistoricalsociety.org>

SOCIETIES IN EUROPE

AUSTRIAN GENEALOGICAL AND HERALDRY SOCIETY

Heraldisch-Genealogische Gesellschaft ("ADLER")
Universitäts Strasse 6/9b
A-1069 Wien
AUSTRIA
<www.adler-wien.at>

CATHOLIC FAMILY HISTORY SOCIETY

c/o Mrs KM Black
14 Sydney Road
Ilford
Essex
IG6 2ED
UNITED KINGDOM
<www.catholic-history.org.uk/cfhs>

CZECH REPUBLIC FOLKLORE ASSOCIATION

Zdeněk Pšenica
předseda
Senovážné nám. 24
116 47 Prague 1
CZECH REPUBLIC
<www.folklornisdruzeni.cz/en>

EKOMUSEUM RUZE

<ruze.ekomuzeum.cz/en>

THE EMANUEL RINGELBLUM JEWISH HISTORICAL INSTITUTE

ul. Tłomackie 3/5
00-090 Warsaw
POLAND
<www.jhi.pl/en>

POLISH GENEALOGICAL SOCIETY (WARSAW)

ul. Broniewskiego 47 m. 8
01-716 Warszawa
POLAND
<genealodzy.pl>

SUDETENLAND GENEALOGICAL SOCIETY

Vereinigung Sudetendeutscher Familien-forscher e.V.
Landshuter Strasse 4
93047 Regensburg
GERMANY
<www.sudetendeutsche-familienforscher.de>

I

Websites and Publications

WEBSITES

General Resources

Ancestry.com Message Boards: Central Europe
<boards.ancestry.com/mbexec/board/an/localities.ceeurope>

Austrian Family History
<www.austrianfamilyhistory.org>

Behind the Name
<www.behindthename.com>

Complete List of Fraternal Organizations
<www.exonumia.com/art/society.htm>

Cyndi's List: Eastern Europe
<www.cyndislist.com/eastern-europe>

Radix: Genealogical Research in Hungary
<www.bogardi.com/gen/index.shtml>

US Citizenship and Immigration Services
<www.uscis.gov/portal/site/uscis>

Poland

About.com: Polish Genealogy & Family History
<genealogy.about.com/od/poland>

AGAD Polish State Archives Online
<www.agad.gov.pl/inwentarze/testy.html>

BASIA
<basia.famula.pl>

Central Region/Łódź
<tgcp.pl>

Civil Registration Offices: Poland
<www.usc.pl/zasieg>

Cyndi's List: Poland
<www.cyndislist.com/poland.htm>

FORGEN Genealogical Forum
<www.forgen.pl>

Galicia Mailing List
<lists.rootsweb.ancestry.com/index/
intl/POL/GALICIA.html>

Galician Town Locator
<www.polishroots.org>

Genealogy and Poland: A Guide
<donhoward.net/genpoland>

Geneteka
<geneteka.genealodzy.pl/index.
php?op=se>

GenForum: Message boards for your
ancestral country
<www.genforum.genealogy.com/
regional/countries>

GenPol
<www.genpol.com>

HalGal (Genealogy of Halychyna/Eastern
Galicia
<www.halgal.com>

Ksiegi-parafialne
<ksiegi-parafialne.pl>

Lesser Poland Society
<www.mtg-malopolska.org.pl>

Lublin Genealogical Society
<ltg.pl/>

MasterPage (Facts About Poland)
<www.masterpage.com.pl/imieniny.html>

Moikrewni genealogy
<www.moikrewni.pl/mapa>

National Digital Library
<www.nac.gov.pl>

Parishes and Dioceses
<www.opoka.org.pl/struktury_kosciola/
diecezje>

Poland GenWeb
<www.rootsweb.ancestry.com/~polwgw/
index.html>

PolishOrigins
<polishorigins.com>

Polish Roots
<www.polishroots.com>

Poznan Marriage Project
<www.poznan-project.psnc.pl>

PTG Pomorskie Towarzystwo Genealogiczne (Pomeranian Genealogical Society)
<www.ptg.gda.pl>

RootsWeb: Poland
<rootsweb.ancestry.com/~polwgw/maillists.html>

RootsWeb's Guide to Tracing Family Trees: Polish Ancestors
<rwguide.rootsweb.ancestry.com/lesson27.htm#Polish>

Wielkopolskie Towarzystwo Genealogiczne "Gniazdo" Main Site
<wtg-gniazdo.org>

Ziemia Dobrzyńska (historical area near Dobrzyń nad Wisłą)
<www.szpejankowski.eu/index.php/metryki-wykazy-osob/102.html>

Czech Republic

About.com: Czech Republic
<goeasteurope.about.com/od/czechrepublic/p/profileczech.htm>

Cyndi's List: Czech Republic and Slovakia
<www.cyndislist.com/czech>

Czech and Slovak Heritage
<www.czechheritage.net/interest.html>

Czech Census Searchers
<www.czechfamilytree.com/distarchives.htm>

Czech Everything
<www.czecheverything.com>

Czech Genealogy for Beginners
<czechgenealogy.nase-koreny.cz>

Czech Research Outline by Shon R. Edwards
<www.shon.150m.com/czechhtm.htm>

Czech Telephone Directory
<www.infobel.com/en/world/WorldTeldir.aspx?page=/eng/euro/cz&qSelLang=EN>

Czechoslovak Americana on the Net
<www.svu2000.org/cs_america/americana.htm>

Delphi Forums Genealogy: Czech and Slovak Republic
<forums.delphiforums.com/n/main.asp?webtag=iarelative&nav=start&prettyurl=%2Fiarelative>

The East Europe GenWeb (Czech Republic)
<www.rootsweb.ancestry.com/~czewgw>

Researching Czech Church Records on the Internet
<www.wwjohnston.net/famhist/czech-research.htm>

RootsWeb's Guide to Tracing Family Trees: Czechs and Slovaks
<rwguide.rootsweb.ancestry.com/lesson27.htm#Czechs>

Slovakia

About.com: Slovakia
<goeasteurope.about.com/od/othercountries/p/slovakiaprofile.htm>

Cyndi's List: Czech Republic and Slovakia
<www.cyndislist.com/czech>

Czech and Slovak Heritage
<www.czechheritage.net/interest.html>

Czechoslovak Americana on the Net
<www.svu2000.org/cs_america/americana.
htm>

Delphi Forums Genealogy: Czech and
Slovak Republic
<forums.delphiforums.com/n/main.
asp?webtag=iarelative&nav=start&prettyurl
=%2Fiarelative>

The EastEurope GenWeb (Slovak
Republic)
<www.rootsweb.ancestry.com/~svkwgw>

Heart of Europe
<www.heartofeurope.co.uk>

It's All Relative
<www.slovakia.org>

Our Slovakia (Slovak Pride Database)
<www.our-slovakia.com>

Slovak Links
<www.slovakia.org/links.htm>

Slovakia & Environs Genealogy Research
Strategies
<www.iabsi.com/gen/public>

Slovakia.org
<www.slovakia.org>

Slovak Telephone Directory (Telefónny
Zoznam SR)
<www.infobel.com/en/world/WorldTeldir.
aspx?page=/eng/euro/sk&qSelLang=EN>

Virtual Cemeteries of Slovakia
<www.cemetery.sk/english>

Translation

Babel Fish Text Translation
<www.babelfish.com>

Cyrillic Alphabet
<www.volgawriter.com/VW%20Cyrillic.
htm>

Czech Letter Writing Guide
<familysearch.org/learn/wiki/en/
Czech_Republic_Letter_Writing_Guide>

English-Czech/Czech-English Online
Dictionary
<www.wordbook.cz/slovnik.php?fjazyk=en>

FamilySearch Word Lists
<familysearch.org/learn/wiki/en/
Category:Word_List>

Google Translate
<translate.google.com>

Learn Slovak 101
<learn101.org/slovak.php>

Lexilogos Polish Dictionary
<www.lexilogos.com/english/polish_
dictionary.htm>

Local Lingo
<www.locallingo.com>

Polish Grammar in a Nutshell
<polish.slavic.pitt.edu/firstyear/nutshell.pdf>

Polish Letter Writing Guide
<familysearch.org/learn/wiki/en/Poland_Letter_Writing_Guide>

Polish Translation Aids
<www.sggee.org/research/translation_aids>

Script Tutorials (Brigham Young University)
<script.byu.edu>

Slovak Letter Writing Guide
<familysearch.org/learn/wiki/en/Slovakia_Letter_Writing_Guide>

Sound System/Phonetics
<www.mowicpopolsku.com>

Geography Tools

1882 Gazetteer of Hungary (Radix)
<www.bogardi.com/gen/g104.shtml>

1913 gazetteer of Hungary (Radix)
<www.bogardi.com/gen/g168.shtml>

Atlas geograficzny illustrowany królestwa polskiego
<pgsa.org/polish-geographic-atlas>

Atlas of Austria-Hungary
<commons.wikimedia.org/wiki/Atlas_of_Austria-Hungary>

Atlas of Czechoslovakia
<commons.wikimedia.org/wiki/Atlas_of_Czechoslovakia>

Dvorzsák Gazetteer (1877)
<kt.lib.pte.hu/cgi-bin/kt.cgi?konyvtar/kt03110501/tartalom.html>

Eastern Borderlands Gazetteers and Maps
<www.kami.net.pl/kresy>

FEEFHS Map Library
<feefhs.org/maplibrary.html>

Fuzzy Gazetteer
<dma.jrc.it/services/fuzzyg/>

Gazetteer of Slovakia
<www.iarelative.com/gazateer.htm>

Google Maps of Slovak State Archives
<google.com/maps/d/viewer?mid=zhdjRcR_t4jl.kFjuOrPk6HQk&msa=0>

Historical Atlas of the Twentieth Century
<users.erols.com/mwhite28/20centry.htm>

Index of Hungarian Maps (1910)
<lazarus.elte.hu/hun/maps/1910>

Index to Place Names in the Republic of Poland, 1934
<www.wbc.poznan.pl/dlibra/docmetadata?id=12786>

JewishGen Gazetteer
<www.jewishgen.org/shtetlseeker>

Kartenmeister
<www.kartenmeister.com>

Mapy.cz
<mapy.cz/zakladni?x=15.6252330&y=49.80
22514&z=8>

Mapy.pl
<mapy.pl>

Mapy.sk
<mapy.atlas.sk/?whatdisp=search&phrase=
aquariusnet+frm_uvod.asp>

Osztrák-Magyar Monarchia vármegyéi
(1910 County Maps)
<lazarus.elte.hu/hun/maps/1910/vmlista.
htm>

Ravenstein Atlas des Deutschen Reichs
<www.library.wisc.edu/etext/ravenstein/
home.html>

Wojskowy Instytut Wojskowy Maps
(1918–1939) Military Institute Maps
<www.mapywig.org>

WorldAtlas.com: Poland
<www.worldatlas.com/webimage/countrys/
europe/pl.htm>

Wykaz urzędowych nazw miejscowości i
ich części (List of official names of places
and their parts)
<ksng.gugik.gov.pl/urzedowe_nazwy_
miejscowosci.php>

Professional Researchers

CentroConsult
<www.centroconsult.sk/genealogy/
resources.html>

Cisarik Genealogy
<www.cisarik.com>

Cyndi's List: Professional Researchers,
Volunteers & Other Research Services
<www.cyndislist.com/profess.htm>

Czech Ancestors
<www.czechancestors.com>

Genoroots
<www.genoroots.com>

Slovak Ancestry
<www.slovak-ancestry.com>

Tadeusz Pilat
<www.icapgen.org/find-an-ag-professional/
tadeusz-pilat>

PUBLICATIONS

General Resources

Advanced Genealogy Research Techniques
by George G. Morgan and Drew Smith
(McGraw-Hill Education, 2013)

*Evidence Explained: Citing History
Sources from Artifacts to Cyberspace*, third
edition by Elizabeth Shown Mills (Genealogical Publishing Co., 2015)

The Family Tree Sourcebook: The Essential Guide to American County and Town Sources (Family Tree Books, 2010)

Genealogical Proof Standard, third edition by Christine Rose (CR Publications, 2009)

Google Earth for Genealogy, Vols. I and II by Lisa Louise Cooke (DVDs, Genealogy Gems)

A History of the Habsburg Empire 1790–1918 by Jean Bérenger, translated by C.A. Simpson (Addison Wesley Longman, 1997)

Hungarian Village Finder, Atlas, and Gazetteer for the Kingdom of Hungary (CD) **<www.hungarianvillagefinder.com/cdrom/CD.html>**

They Came in Ships: Finding Your Immigrant Ancestor's Arrival Record, third edition by John Philip Colletta (Ancestry, 2002)

Unofficial Guide to Ancestry.com by Nancy Hendrickson (Family Tree Books, 2014)

Unofficial Guide to FamilySearch.org by Dana McCullough (Family Tree Books, 2015)

Uprooted from Prussia, Transplanted in America by Eugene W. Camann (Gilcraft Print Co., 1991)

Where Once We Walked: A Guide to the Jewish Communities Destroyed in the Holocaust, revised edition by Gary Mokotoff and SallyAnn Amdur Sack with Alexander Sharon (Avotaynu, 1991)

Where She Came From by Helen Epstein (Holmes & Meier Publishers, 2005)

Poland

Dictionary of Surnames in Current Use in Poland at the Beginning of the 21st Century, compiled by Kazimierz Rymut (CD, Polish Genealogical Society of America, 2002)

First Names of the Polish Commonwealth: Origins and Meanings by William F. Hoffman and George W. Helon (Polish Genealogical Society of America, 1998)

God's Playground: A History of Poland, Vol. I: The Origins to 1795, revised edition by Norman Davies (Columbia University Press, 2005)

God's Playground: A History of Poland, Vol. II: 1795 to Present, revised second edition by Norman Davies (Columbia University Press, 2005)

Going Home: A Guide to Polish-American Genealogical Research by Jonathan D. Shea (Language & Lineage Press, 2008)

Polish Roots, second edition by Rosemary A. Chorzempa (Genealogical Publishing Company, 2014)

Polish Surnames: Origins and Meanings, second edition by William F. Hoffman (Polish Genealogical Society of America, 2001)

Sto Lat: A Modern Approach to Polish Genealogy by Ceil Wendt Jensen (2009)

Czech Republic

Cleveland Czechs by John T. Sabol and Lisa A. Alzo (Arcadia Publishing, 2009)

History of Czechs in America by Jan Habenicht (Czechoslovak Genealogical Society International)

Slovakia

Cleveland Slovaks by John T. Sabol and Lisa A. Alzo (Arcadia Publishing, 2009)

Finding Your Slovak Ancestors by Lisa A. Alzo (Heritage Productions, 2005)

Handbook of Czechoslovak Genealogical Research by Daniel M. Schlyter (Genealogy Unlimited, 1985)

A History of Slovakia: The Struggle for Survival, second edition by Stanislav Kirschbaum (Palgrave Macmillan Trade, 2005)

History of Slovaks in America by Konstantin Culen (Czechoslovak Genealogical Society International, 1942)

History of the Slovaks of Cleveland and Lakewood by Jan Pankuch (The Czechoslovak Genealogical Society International

and The Western Reserve Historical Society, 2001)

Názvy Obcí Slovenskej Republiky (Names of Villages, Slovak Republic) by Milan Majtan (VEDA (1998)

Out of This Furnace by Thomas Bell (University of Pittsburgh Press, 1976)

Slovak Pittsburgh by Lisa A. Alzo (Arcadia Publishing, 2006)

Three Slovak Women by Lisa A. Alzo (CreateSpace, 2011)

Translation

Concise Czech-English/English-Czech Dictionary by Nina Trnka (Hippocrene Books, 1990)

Following the Paper Trail: A Multilingual Translation Guide by Jonathan D. Shea and William F. Hoffman (Avotaynu, 1994)

Harrap's Czech Phrasebook (McGraw-Hill Education, 2006)

In Their Words: A Genealogist's Translation Guide to Polish, German, Latin, and Russian Documents: Volume I: Polish edited by Jonathan D. Shea and William F. Hoffman (Language & Lineage Press, 2000)

In Their Words: A Genealogist's Translation Guide to Polish, German, Latin, and Russian Documents: Volume II: Russian compiled by Jonathan D. Shea and William F. Hoffman (Language & Lineage Press, 2003)

In Their Words: A Genealogist's Translation Guide to Polish, German, Latin, and Russian Documents: Volume III: Latin compiled by Jonathan D. Shea and William F. Hoffman (Language & Lineage Press, 2013)

Slovak/English & English/Slovak Dictionary by Nina Trnka (Hippocrene Books, 1992)

A Translation Guide to 19th Century Polish-Language Civil Registration Documents, second edition by Judith Frazin (Jewish Genealogical Society of Illinois, 2009)

Geography Tools

Administratives Gemeindelexikon der Čechoslovakischen Republik (Statistischen Staatsamte Praha, 1927–1928)

Alphabetisches Ortsnamenverzeichnis der Deutschen Ostgebiete unter fremder Verwaltung, Band II (Selbstverlag der Bundesanstalt für Landeskunde, 1955)

Autoatlas Česká republika 1:100 000 (Geodézie ČS, 2006)

Euro-Reiseatlas Polen (RV Verlag, 2006)

Euro-Reiseatlas Tschechische Republik, Slowakische Republik (RV Verlag, 1991)

The Family Tree Historical Maps Book: Europe by Allison Dolan (Family Tree Books, 2015) <www.shopfamilytree.com/family-tree-historical-maps-book-europe>

Gemeindelexikon der im Reichsrate vertretenen Königreiche und Länder (K.K. Hof- und Staatsdruckereri, 1905–1908)

Gemeindelexikon für das Königreich Preußen. Königlichen Statistischen Landesamts (Verlag des königlichen Statistischen landesamts, 1907)

Genealogical Gazetteer of Galicia, third and Expanded Data Edition by Brian J. Lenius (1999)

Hammond Concise Atlas of World History, sixth edition by Geoffery Barraclough (Hammond World Atlas Corporation, 2001)

Hammond Historical Atlas (Hammond World Atlas Corporation, 2000)

Historical Atlas of East Central Europe by Paul Robert Magocsi (University of Washington Press, 2002)

Jewish Roots in Poland by Miriam Weiner, (1997)

Magyarország Atlasza és Adattára 1914 (Talma, 2001)

Magyarország helységnévtára tekintettel a közigazgatási, népességi és hitfelekezeti viszonyokra by János Dvorzsák (1877)

Magyar helységnév-azonosító szótár by György Lelkes (Talma, 1998)

Meyers Orts-und Verkehrslexikon (Genealogical Publishing Co., 2000)

Militär-Landesaufnahme und Spezialkarte der österreichisch-ungarischen Monarchie (The Genealogical Society of Utah, 1977)

Oficjalny Spis Pocztowych Numerów Adresowych (Andrzej Bonarski, 1993)

The Palgrave Concise Historical Atlas of Eastern Europe: Revised and Updated by Dennis P. Hupchick and Harold E. Cox (Palgrave Macmillan, 2001)

Po mieczu i po kądzieli (Towarzystwo Autorów i Wydawców Prac Naukowych Universitas, 2011)

Podrobný autoatlas Slovenská Republika: 1:100 000 (Harmanec, 1995)

Polska Atlas Drogowy: 1:200,000 (Geo-Center, 1996)

Polska atlas samochodowy (Polskie Przedsiębiorstwo Wydawnictw Karto-graficznych, 1992)

Posen Place Name Indexes: Identifying place names using alphabetical and reverse alphabetical indexes (GRT Publications, 2004)

Roman Catholic parishes in the Polish People's Republic in 1984 by Lidia Műllerowa (Polish Genealogical Society of America, 1995)

Skorowidz miejscowości rzeczypospolitej polskiej (Wydawnictwo Książnicy Nau-kowej, 1934)

Słownik geograficzny królestwa polskiego i innych krajów słowiańskich (Wydawnic-twa Artystyczne i Filmowe, 1986)

Słownik nazw geograficznych Polski zach-ódniej i północnej (1951)

Spis miejscowości Polskiej Rzeczypospo-litej Ludowej (Warszawa Wydawnictwa komunikacji i Łączności, 1967)

Velký Autoatlas Československa 1:200 000 (Kartografie Praha, 1990)

ARTICLES

General Resources

"American Names: Declaring Indepen-dence" by Marian L. Smith (Immigration Daily, 2005)
<www.ilw.com/articles/2005,0808-smith.shtm>

"Central and Eastern European Magnates and Their Archives" compiled by Edward David Luft (Avotaynu)
<www.avotaynu.com/magnates.htm>

"Ellis Island.org Web Guide" by *Family Tree Magazine*
<www.shopfamilytree.com/ellis-island-web-guide>

FEEFHS Journal back order of articles
<feefhs.org/journal.html>
(For articles of special interest to Polish, Czech, and Slovak researchers, see <ftu.familytreemagazine.com/polish-czech-slovak-genealogy-guide>)

"A Guide for Locating Military Records for the various Regions of the Austro-Hungarian Empire" by Carl Kotlarchik (Slovak Genealogy Research Strategies, 2012–13)
<www.iabsi.com/gen/public/ahm.html>

"A Guide to Interpreting Passenger List Annotations," by Marian L. Smith (JewishGen, 2002)
<www.jewishgen.org/InfoFiles/Manifests>

"Jewish Names and Genealogies" by Jeff Malka
<www.jewishgen.org/sephardic/yohasin.htm>

"Jewish Onomastics" by Edwin D. Lawson
<www.jewish-languages.org/onomastics.html>

"Mutilation: the Fate of Eastern European Names in America," by William F. Hoffman (Polish Genealogical Society of America, 2002)
<pgsa.org/wp-content/uploads/2015/09/Mutilation.pdf>

"Research in the Former Austro-Hungarian Empire," five-part series by Feliz Gundacker (Heritage Quest, 1996)

"Road Map to Your Roots" by Lisa A. Alzo (*Family Tree Magazine*, January 2011)
<www.familytreemagazine.com/article/genealogy-research-plan>

"Skillbuilding: Guidelines for Evaluating Genealogical Evidence," by Linda Woodward Geiger (*On-Board Newsletter for the Board for Certification of Genealogists*, 2008)
<www.bcgcertification.org>

"Victory in Europe," by Lisa A. Alzo (*Family Tree Magazine*, January 2010)
<www.familytreemagazine.com/article/Victory-in-Europe>

Poland

"A Guide to Researching Indices to Jewish Records of Poland" compiled by Stanley Diamond (JRI-Poland, 2012) <jri-poland.org/brochure/jri_guide_2012en.pdf>

"The Keeping of Vital Records in the Austrian Partition" by Jonathan D. Shea (*Pathways and Passages*, Vol. 9, Winter 1992) <www.halgal.com/vitalrecordsaustria.html>

"Pole Vault" by Lisa A. Alzo, (*Family Tree Magazine*, May 2007)
<www.familytreemagazine.com/article/pole-vault>

"Polish Genealogy Guide Digital Download" by *Family Tree Magazine*
<www.shopfamilytree.com/family-tree-magazine-polish-genealogy-guide-digital-download>

Polski Krok po Kroku by Stempek, et al.
<polskikrokpokroku.pl>

"Vital Records in Poland" by Warren Blatt
(JewishGen, 2013)
<www.jewishgen.org/infofiles/polandv.html>

Czech Republic and Slovakia

"Center of Attention" by Lisa A. Alzo
(*Family Tree Magazine*, August 2005)
<www.familytreemagazine.com/article/center-of-attention>

"Finding My Ancestral Village in Bohemia, Without a Clue! (How I Got to Milevsko)" by Scott W. Phillips, (*Slovo*, Summer 2010)
<onwardtoourpast.com/genealogy_blog/finding-my-ancestral-village-in-bohemia-without-a-clue.html>

"Getting Started With Czech-Jewish Genealogy" by E. Randol Schoenberg and Julius Mueller
<www.jewishgen.org/austriaczech/czechguide.html>

Naše Rodina: Newsletter of the Czecho-slovak Genealogical Society International back order of articles
<www.cgsi.org/publications/article-index>
(*For articles of special interest to Polish, Czech, and Slovak researchers, see* <ftu.familytreemagazine.com/polish-czech-slovak-genealogy-guide>)

INDEX

CREDITS

Thank you to the following individuals or organizations for giving permission to use images in this book. The following images are published in this book with permission as indicated.

Chapter 2

Page 26: Image C, Timeline for Elizabeth Fenscak Alzo. Timelines courtesy of **<www.ourtimelines.com>**. Timeline formatting and technology copyright © 2000-2003 Charles B. Blish, ALL RIGHTS RESERVED under the Pan-American Conventions.

Chapter 3

Page 35: Image A, 1930 census image for John Figlar. Retrieved from Ancestry.com.

Page 39: Image B, Declaration of intent for John Piontkowski. Courtesy of Donna Pointkouski.

Page 40: Image C, Petition of naturalization for John Piontkowski. Courtesy of Donna Pointkouski.

Page 42: Image D, sample passenger list. Retrieved from Ancestry.com.

Chapter 4

Page 49: Image A, Map of Polish-Lithuanian Commonwealth at its maximum extent from Wikimedia Commons, created by user Samotny Wędrowiec and reproduced under the GNU Free Documentation License.

Page 53: Image B, Map of the three Partitions of Poland from Wikimedia Commons, created by user Halibutt and reproduced under the GNU Free Documentation License.

Chapter 6

Page 71, Image A, Austro-Hungarian Monarchy. (inset) Continuation of Dalmatia &c from *Cram's Standard American Railway System Atlas Of The World* by George Franklin Cram

(1901). Retrieved from the David Rumsey Map Collection.

Chapter 8

Page 98: Image B, Polish civil marriage record. Courtesy of Donna Pointkouski.

Page 99: Image C, Czech marriage record. Courtesy of Jan Ebert.

Page 100: Image D, Church death record. Courtesy of Jan Ebert.

Polish 102: Image F, Polish birth record. Courtesy of Jonathan D. Shea.

Chapter 11

Page 135: Image A, Polish Parish Census. Courtesy of Jonathan D. Shea.

Page 137: Image B, The Practical English Slovak Dictionary. Retrieved from Internet Archive.

Chapter 13

Page 151: Tombstone for James Pointkouski. Courtesy of Donna Pointkouski.

Page 155: *Reisepass* (passport) for Tomáš Kohout. Courtesy of Lee James.

Page 155: US citizenship papers for Thomas Kohout. Courtesy of Lee James.

Page 156: Declaration of Intent for Thomas Kohout. Courtesy of Lee James.

Page 158: Certificate of Arrival application for Andrew Matviya. Courtesy of John Matviya.

Page 160: Greek Catholic birth register entry for Andrew Matviya. Courtesy of John Matviya.

ACKNOWLEDGEMENTS

This guide is the result of a collaborative effort. I would like to thank the following individuals for their time and willingness to contribute advice, photographs, stories, translations, and text for this book: Erik Dirbák, Jan Ebert, Lee James, Paul Makousky, John Matviya, Donna Pointkouski, anfed Michal Razus. In particular, I would like to thank Professor Jonathan D. Shea, whom I consider the preeminent Polish genealogist, for sharing his knowledge and expertise by providing text and select images for the sections on Polish history, migration, language, and records.

In addition, over the past twenty-five years, I have had the good fortune of learning from many skilled research colleagues who were instrumental in helping me navigate the complexities of Eastern European genealogy. While there is not enough space in this book to include everyone by name, I would like to specifically thank Matthew Bielawa, Rich Custer, Thomas K. Edlund, Duncan Gardiner, William "Fred" Hoffman, Kahlile B. Mehr, Dave Obee, John Righetti, and Professor Martin Votruba (University of Pittsburgh), as well as members of the Czechoslovak Genealogical Society International, the Carpatho-Rusyn Society, the Foundation for East European Family History Studies, and anyone else I have worked with along the way whom I may have inadvertently overlooked.

Finally, I would like to thank Allison Dolan, Andrew Koch, and the staff of *Family Tree Magazine* for their help and guidance throughout the editorial process.

LISA A. ALZO

ABOUT THE AUTHOR

Lisa A. Alzo, MFA, is a freelance writer, instructor, and internationally recognized lecturer specializing in Slovak/Eastern European genealogical research, writing family history, and using the Internet to trace female and immigrant ancestors. She has written hundreds of magazine articles and ten books, including the award-winning *Three Slovak Women*. She is a contributing editor for *Family Tree Magazine* and teaches online courses for Family Tree University and the National Institute for Genealogical Studies. As a lecturer, she's been a frequently invited speaker for all of the largest US genealogical conferences, as well as genealogical and historical societies across the nation and in Canada. An avid genealogist for more than twenty-five years, Lisa also chronicles her family history adventures on her blog, *The Accidental Genealogist* <www.theaccidentalgenealogist.com>, and her website <www.lisaalzo.com>.

Lisa grew up in Duquesne, Pennsylvania. She graduated *magna cum laude* with a Bachelor of Science degree in Nutrition in 1987 from West Virginia Wesleyan College in Buckhannon, West Virginia, and earned a Master of Fine Arts in Nonfiction Writing from the University of Pittsburgh in 1997. She and her husband, Michael, currently live in New York, but she is proud of her Pittsburgh roots and hopes to move back there someday.

DEDICATION

This book is dedicated to the memory of my grandparents and the countless other Slavic immigrants who had the courage to get on those boats. May the research we do continue to honor you and inspire future generations to understand their past.

ISBN: 978-1-4403-4327-8

Other Family Tree Books are available from your local bookstore and online suppliers.
For more genealogy resources, visit **<shopfamilytree.com>**.

20 19 18 17   5 4 3 2

DISTRIBUTED IN CANADA BY FRASER DIRECT
100 Armstrong Avenue
Georgetown, Ontario, Canada L7G 5S4
Tel: (905) 877-4411

DISTRIBUTED IN THE U.K. AND EUROPE BY
F&W Media International, LTD
Brunel House, Forde Close,
Newton Abbot, TQ12 4PU, UK
Tel: (+44) 1626 323200,
Fax (+44) 1626 323319
E-mail: enquiries@fwmedia.com

DISTRIBUTED IN AUSTRALIA BY CAPRICORN LINK
P.O. Box 704, Windsor, NSW 2756 Australia
Tel: (02) 4577-3555

fw
a content + ecommerce company

PUBLISHER/COMMUNITY LEADER: Allison Dolan

EDITOR: Andrew Koch

DESIGNER: Julie Barnett

PRODUCTION COORDINATOR: Debbie Thomas

4 FREE
FAMILY TREE TEMPLATES

- decorative family tree posters

- five-generation ancestor chart

- family group sheet

- bonus relationship chart

- type and save, or print and fill out

Download at <ftu.familytreemagazine.com/free-family-tree-templates>

More Great Genealogy Resources

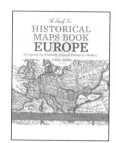
 Join our community! <facebook.com/familytreemagazine>